GO
for the
GREEN

JEFF HOPPER

FOREWORD BY
BEN CRANE

COUNTRYMAN

A Division of Thomas Nelson Publishers

THOMAS NELSON
Since 1798

NASHVILLE DALLAS MEXICO CITY RIO DE JANEIRO

Published in Nashville, Tennessee, by Thomas Nelson. Thomas Nelson is a registered trademark of Thomas Nelson, Inc.

PGA professional Doug Scrivner contributed to the daily golf tips.

Photos on pages 12–13 and 140–141 by Mike Houska, Bend, Oregon.

Thomas Nelson, Inc., titles may be purchased in bulk for educational, business, fund-raising, or sales promotional use. For information, please e-mail SpecialMarkets@ThomasNelson.com.

Unless otherwise indicated, all Scripture quotations are from The New King James Version®. Copyright © 1982 by Thomas Nelson, Inc. Used by permission. All rights reserved. Scriptures marked KJV are taken from the King James Version of the Bible. Scriptures marked NASB are taken from the NEW AMERICAN STANDARD BIBLE®, copyright © The Lockman Foundation 1960, 1962, 1963, 1968, 1971, 1972, 1973, 1975, 1977, 1995. Used by permission. Scriptures marked NIV are taken from THE HOLY BIBLE: NEW INTERNATIONAL VERSION®. Copyright © 1973, 1978, 1984 by International Bible Society. Used by permission of Zondervan Publishing House. All rights reserved. Scriptures marked NLT are taken from the *Holy Bible*, New Living Translation. Copyright © 1996. Used by permission of Tyndale House Foundation, Inc., Wheaton, Illinois 60189. All rights reserved.

ISBN 978-1-4003-1965-7

Printed in China

12 13 14 15 WAI 6 5 4 3 2 1

www.thomasnelson.com

To
KATHLEEN AND DOUG,
who know well
how rewarding and how challenging
the game can be.

FOREWORD

I began playing the game of golf as a young boy with my grandpa in Oregon. It wasn't long before it became the focus of my life. As I grew up and pursued it more seriously in high school and college, it became apparent to me that golf, although a wonderful game, did not deserve to hold a position higher than that of God. As I relentlessly pursued the game, I realized that my relationship with Christ gave me much more purpose and direction, and I needed to be diligent about how I lived out my priorities and where I placed my hope and my trust.

I have had the privilege of playing on the PGA Tour for several years now. It is a dream come true, and God has done amazing things to allow me to compete at such a high level. At the beginning of last year, I set out to pursue my life on tour with my number one goal being to glorify God. I have realized that when living and playing for Christ, the rest takes care of itself. I live this out by starting my day with a daily devotional that I read and talk about with my caddie before each round, then praying before we go to competition. Throughout the day, I often find that the thoughts and verses read in the morning calm my nerves and refocus my perspective as I go through the challenges and victories on the course. My hope is that this devotional will give you the same sense of guidance and inspiration as it relates to the great game of golf.

—*Ben Crane*

For God is working in you,
giving you the desire and the power
to do what pleases Him.

—PHILIPPIANS 2:13 NLT

INTRODUCTION

ON THE TEE

Each round of golf begins the same. You pull a ball from the bag, place a tee in the ground, balance that ball, swing loosely a few times, and step up to hit away. In the next few moments, we will find out a lot about you.

Do you hit far? Do you hit it straight? Do you only talk as if you know what you're doing, or do you really know golf?

With so much on the line, that first shot can demand more from you than makes you comfortable. Which means, of course, that golf is much like life.

If we live a life of real activity, each day we are challenged by situations and circumstances that require us to step out in ways that may seem uncomfortable. How we respond in moments like these can reveal who we really are.

Do we act with courage or do we shrink timidly? Are we in the know or in the dark? What are the chances we will succeed, and how are afraid are we that we will fail?

This book encourages you to spend a few minutes each day examining your life through the lens of golf. Since a 4-iron in the backyard literally split my chin before I'd even started my first day of kindergarten, I have been marked by this game. It has taught me many lessons, some of them harshly and some of them with great favor.

But most of all golf has taught me that God doesn't show up only at church. He can meet us wherever we are. Often for me that has been on the golf course.

—*Jeff Hopper*

THE OFF-SEASON

In the dead of winter, golf is often the thing furthest from your mind. You might watch some of those sunny tournaments from some warm course in the desert, but your own clubs are stored away in the closet with your sandals and your swimsuit.

Nothing is innately harmful about walking away from the game. One of America's finest amateurs in years past, Jay Sigel, lived in the Northeast, and like many of us, he put his clubs away for much of the winter and went about his other business. It never seemed to hurt his game. He was three times U.S. Amateur champion.

Jesus was master of many things. One of them was getting away from the routine to a quiet place where He could put things back into perspective, beginning first with God. We can accomplish much when we are busy. But sometimes we can gain more by stepping back, taking a break, and reordering our lives.

JANUARY

TRUE DESIRE

For a day in Your courts is better than a thousand. I would rather be a doorkeeper in the house of my God than dwell in the tents of wickedness.

PSALM 84:10

Just because you have the time to play golf doesn't mean you have no time left to dream—time to dream of a lower handicap, a better driver, a house on the fairway.

Though we know by experience that the world is full of traps, we still are coaxed by the lust of the eyes. We see something we do not have and assume that it will replace the missing pieces in our lives.

The psalmist saw something so different—so permanent—in the courts of heaven. To spend a day in God's presence is to fulfill the longing of a thousand days. More complete, though, is the new covenant, when Christ's work has restored our relationship with God! For now our body is the temple of the Holy Spirit. We can dwell with God, and God with us, wherever we go. Every day is that spectacular one day.

TIP

CONCENTRATE ON A ONE-PIECE TAKEAWAY—WRISTS AND ARMS TOGETHER.

CAN'T GET AWAY?

*You comprehend my path and my lying down, and
are acquainted with all my ways.*

PSALM 139:3

Time to get away from it all? That makes sense in the thick of winter, with no sun in sight. And likely, the golf course is on your mind when it comes time to escape.

As far as we want to get away from our world sometimes, let's look for something else in our relationship with God—let's look to get closer to Him. For God's nearness is so good.

God's nearness brings confidence. How grand to be loved by the Author of the universe, to be part of His story!

God's nearness brings forgiveness. How wonderful to be granted grace we do not deserve, only because we are willing to be called by His name!

God's nearness brings rich gifts that empower us to do His very bidding. How awesome to gain strength from the ultimate Source of all that is strong, and to use that strength for all the right reasons!

TIP

THE CLUB'S DESCENT DICTATES THE BALL'S ASCENT. HIT DOWN ON THE BALL TO WATCH IT FLY UP.

FOLLOW THE CROWD

Many nations shall come and say, "Come, and let us go up to the mountain of the LORD, to the house of the God of Jacob; He will teach us His ways, and we shall walk in His paths." For out of Zion the law shall go forth, and the word of the LORD from Jerusalem.

MICAH 4:2

Have you ever tried to invite a friend to Sunday services? It's not so easy when the competition is NFL pregame shows or morning foursomes. You can predict the apologies. Sure, they're cordial, but they all have to do with time. Time to relax, time to be with family, time to get away—"our only chance."

Whatever happened to time for God? No worry: God has always made time for Himself. Since the line of sin was opened, people have been preoccupied with the attractions of this world. None of this has concerned God. He just keeps repeating His promise: the Day is coming. Despite sin, God would forgive. Despite Satan, God would rule. Despite death, the Redeemer would live—and give life to us.

Remember, the temple of the Lord is the ultimate edifice for our Ultimate Attraction. People will yet stream to Him.

TIP

AS YOU IMPROVE WITH YOUR WEDGES, YOU'LL WANT TO KEEP THOSE GROOVES CLEAN FOR MORE SPIN.

SUFFERING

*And not only that, but we also glory in tribulations,
knowing that tribulation produces perseverance; and
perseverance, character; and character, hope.*

ROMANS 5:3–4

Golfers must suffer. Of the many truths about
the game, this may be the greatest. If you have
played enough golf in your life—that is, more
than two or three holes—you know much about
suffering.

Life is full of suffering too. In fact, suffering
is one of the great issues for the nonbeliever. But
the biblical writers did not shrink from the matter.
They met it head-on, and they saw it as a positive
experience.

In all aspects of life, suffering can produce one
of two responses: retreat or advance.

When the suffering goes beyond all human
capacity, it is then that we find we can persevere only
by keeping our Goal in sight.
For as believers our Goal and
our Source of strength are the
same: Jesus Christ. In Him, we
can advance in spite of suffering.

TIP

WHEN READING
PUTTS, PAY
CLOSEST
ATTENTION TO THE
LAST FIVE FEET.

STAYING SHARP

He who is slothful in his work is a brother to him who is a great destroyer.

PROVERBS 18:9

We all have seen what happens when we cannot pay attention to our golf game because of other commitments or interests in our lives. "The short game is the first to go," people say. But truthfully, it is consistency that first abandons us when we do not practice. Practice is vital because discipline maintains quality.

The Bible is unafraid of discipline. Even though our work is not what saves us (Ephesians 2:8–9), work does improve us. Here's how:

—*Work provides for our earthly needs.* Work is often how God makes provision for us.

—*Work proves our commitment.* We are willing to give our time and energy to what we love.

—*Work produces character.* When we work, we often must set aside what is easy for what simply must be done. Each time we do this, we are putting our desires in their proper place: subject to our faith.

TIP

NO TIME TO WARM UP? MAKE "SLOW AND EASY" YOUR EARLY SWING THOUGHT.

MEETING THE MAKER

Our help is in the name of the LORD,
who made heaven and earth.

PSALM 124:8

Many golfers, if asked to name one reason they love the game, would choose the beauty of the places they play. Thus, we should know God in a way that other athletes do not. Our eyes are regularly filled with the land formed by His own hand.

For too many of our golfing friends, however, this is where the communion with heaven ends. They defer to a Creator when it comes to the majesty of earth, but when they look at their own lives, they see no such presence. God made the worlds, set them in motion, and ever since has taken one long "seventh-day retreat." But the joy of knowing Christ is that we also know the Father Himself, not just His creation. What good news for us—and what good news for our friends who think that God is awesome yet distant!

> **TIP**
>
> TEE IT UP ON THE SAME SIDE AS THE TROUBLE, SO YOU'LL BE ANGLED AWAY FROM IT.

ARRESTING THE SLIDE

The steps of a good man are ordered by the LORD,
and He delights in his way. Though he fall,
he shall not be utterly cast down;
for the LORD upholds him with His hand.

PSALM 37:23–24

Is it time to change your spikes? A big swing can produce a big embarrassment if your feet aren't firmly planted!

Firm footing was one of King David's chief metaphors for his place with God. Warrior that he was, knowledgeable in wilderness craft, he was adamant that the footing of his life was not secured by his own strength or intellect—both of which he had in kingly abundance. When it came to security, David was clear that this was a gift from God.

Our own lives are full of slippery circumstances too. At such times, our focus may be heightened—looking for that one safe step—or our focus may be lost. In either case, God is there to help us. We catch our step and go on with Him. Or we fall into His rescuing arms. We are clearly not in control of our circumstances. But focusing on Christ will relieve us of the fear of falling.

> **TIP**
>
> HELP YOUR PARTNERS KEEP AN EYE ON THEIR BALLS. YOU'LL HELP SPEED PLAY.

BACK IT UP

Most men will proclaim each his own goodness,
but who can find a faithful man?

PROVERBS 20:6

Plenty of advertisers have the answer for you—for your driving game, your iron game, your short game, your putting. And they have much to say about why their answer is better than another.

Long ago Solomon exposed the chasm of difference between "a man of many words" and "a man of his word."

The airy man announces who he is and who he thinks he can become. He sets himself up for failure. And if his failure touches others, he sets them up as victims of his unfaithfulness.

But the godly man admits who he is, rather than announcing it. He lays his life before God and says without reservation, "My future is Yours, Lord. Make me what You will." He places his trust exclusively in the heavenly Father. Full of faith, he takes the key step to becoming faithful.

TIP

BE SURE YOUR GOLF BUDGET INCLUDES A REGULAR LESSON. YOU'LL LOVE THE RESULTS.

ETERNITY'S TREASURES

"Do not lay up for yourselves treasures on earth, where moth and rust destroy and where thieves break in and steal; but lay up for yourselves treasures in heaven, where neither moth nor rust destroys and where thieves do not break in and steal."

MATTHEW 6:19–20

Scorecards from special courses. Hole-in-one balls. Club championship trophies. A beautifully crafted persimmon driver. These are the keepsakes of an avid golfer, one who has spent a significant portion of his or her life playing the game. These are a golfer's "treasures on earth."

We all recognize a treasure on earth. It is a temporal item that you can't take out of this life. But what about treasures in heaven? We know we are to build our portfolios for eternity—but how?

Here's a key start: prayer, praise, and obedience. This powerful trio helps us establish and sustain our relationship with our heavenly Father. Well rehearsed, these disciplines will condition us for the activity of heaven, where we will find ourselves in the direct presence of God.

TIP

THE AVERAGE PLAYER IS WISER TO BUY BALLS THAT LAST LONG THAN BALLS THAT GO LONG.

GLORY DAYS

"Look among the nations and watch—be utterly astounded! For I will work a work in your days which you would not believe, though it were told you."

HABAKKUK 1:5

What would you give to see Nancy Lopez or Arnold Palmer at the top of the leaderboard again? Your favorite wedge, perhaps? Even when we love where we are now, we all reflect on glory days.

Habakkuk did. Faced with destruction, Habakkuk longed for help, wanting to see God work as his ancestors had seen. He needed a miracle, and he was convinced God was the only source for one.

Habakkuk got more than he imagined, however. He got an out-loud answer and a promise. God was going to come through in a remarkable way.

You may feel like Habakkuk yourself—surrounded by forces that have you flustered, fearful, or downright angry. Perhaps you need to claim the prayer of Habakkuk for your own: "LORD, I have heard of your fame; I stand in awe of Your deeds, O LORD. Renew them in our day" (3:2 NIV).

TIP

DON'T FORGET THE SUNSCREEN. IT MAY EARN YOU YEARS MORE GOLF ENJOYMENT.

SALVATION'S STAMP
OF AUTHENTICITY

How shall we escape if we neglect so great a salvation,
which at the first began to be spoken by the Lord, and
was confirmed to us by those who heard Him, God
also bearing witness both with signs and wonders, with
various miracles, and gifts of the Holy Spirit, according
to His own will?

HEBREWS 2:3–4

For all the choices golfers face in each round, it is a bigger choice that can make the difference—which driver, which irons, which putter? But how do you know? You try them out, of course. No amount of advertising stands up like a slew of test shots on the range.

Christ's deity was authenticated in the same way. First, His words were heard, and those who heard Him repeated them. And beyond the words were actions—His signs, wonders, and miracles. And from the Holy Spirit, the gifts given to each who follows Him. God, through us, still provides His own testimonial as He reveals Himself in our lives. All who seek Him will find Him, and all who honestly pursue Him will have His salvation confirmed.

TIP

IF YOU KNOW THE RULES, YOU'LL FIND THEY HELP YOU AS OFTEN AS THEY HARM YOU.

DO THE DO

For the commandments, "You shall not commit adultery," "You shall not murder," "You shall not steal," "You shall not bear false witness," "You shall not covet," and if there is any other commandment, are all summed up in this saying, namely, "You shall love your neighbor as yourself."

ROMANS 13:9

To succeed in golf, accomplished players select a positive target and hone in on it. Then, instead of negative *don'ts*, they feed themselves positive mental morsels—take it back slow; swing through to the target.

Our walk with Christ also can be crippled by concentrating on the *don'ts*. When we grow attached to restrictions, we can eliminate unrighteous behavior, but we also can grow robotic or prideful.

God offers a more complete righteousness in two essential *dos*. These two envelop all other commands of Scripture: "Love the LORD your God with all your heart, with all your soul, with all your mind, and with all your strength" and "Love your neighbor as yourself" (Mark 12:30–31). Begin there and focus exclusively on those two *dos*. You'll be amazed to see how all the *don'ts* fall into place.

> **TIP**
>
> BE CERTAIN YOU'RE TEEING FROM LEVEL GROUND—IT'S THE ONLY PLACE YOU CHOOSE YOUR LIE.

IN OUR RIGHT MINDS

We know that we are of God, and the whole world lies under the sway of the wicked one.

1 JOHN 5:19

Who is your opponent in golf? Survey your golfing friends, and you'll likely get three answers: other players, the golf course, and ourselves. In truth, the "enemy" in golf may be all of these.

In the spiritual world, we have a more defined enemy, but the way he works can leave us guessing as well. Satan is real, and he will seek to influence us. But in encountering him, we must not overestimate his power. For our Savior is greater still, having defeated Satan at the cross.

We cannot forget the devil. But neither can we surrender to him, throwing up our arms in despair for the evil he has wrought. If there is any arm-raising to be done, it is to be done in praise of the One who is Faithful and True. At the sound of His name—King of kings and Lord of lords—the devil will flee.

TIP

IF YOU KEEP YOUR GRIP RELAXED, THE REST OF YOUR SWING WILL USUALLY PLAY ALONG.

TAKE IT OR LEAVE IT

"When you reap the harvest of your land, you shall not wholly reap the corners of your field when you reap, nor shall you gather any gleaning from your harvest. You shall leave them for the poor and for the stranger: I am the LORD your God."

LEVITICUS 23:22

Avid golfers are experts at gleaning. We constantly look for magic little clues to improve our game. We search the many golf magazines, watch the tips during the weekend telecasts, and eavesdrop on lessons being given to the neighboring player on the range.

The nice thing is, gleaning is okay. But the origin of gleaning did not put the emphasis on the gatherer. Instead, when God directed His Hebrew people to leave behind the extra crops for those who had less, the law was aimed at the giver. In God's design, those who had plenty shared with those who did not.

The grace of God is like the abundant fruit at the edge of the orchard, the wheat left lying in the field. It is rich with nourishment, even unto salvation, and it is there for all who need it. We must continue to offer it just this freely.

TIP

IF YOU'RE PRONE TO WEDGE MISTAKES, USE YOUR PUTTER MORE OFTEN FROM AROUND THE GREEN.

THE RANGE OF GOD

Therefore consider the goodness and severity of God.

ROMANS 11:22

Finding a partner for the next big tourney is never an easy task. Each candidate has strengths and weaknesses the others do not. And how can you predict which come most ready to play? It's such an uncomfortable decision!

God is something like these partners. He doesn't come with one flat character trait. He is deep in every way, beyond our ability to know Him completely. We cannot relax around Him.

We'd prefer a predictable God who does everything as we think He should. But it is God's kindness that leads to repentance; it is His sternness that brings finality for those who refuse to repent. And then there is His mercy and His justice, His tenderness and His strength, His peace and His conviction.

We must let God be all that He is. We may not always be comfortable with Him, but we will marvel at Him from beginning to end.

CAN'T WAIT

*For the earnest expectation of the creation eagerly
waits for the revealing of the sons of God.*

ROMANS 8:19

Ah, how easy it is to enjoy even the anticipation
of that next great golf outing! Maybe you're
making plans for a golf trip right now. Hard not to
daydream, isn't it? Lush fairways, pure shots, joyous
camaraderie.

Yet how much greater the expectation of creation when it looks forward to our revelation as
the sons of God! In His death, Christ negated the
curse of sin; in His resurrection, He ended the grip
of death. The hard work, like the threshing of the
wheat, has been done. Now creation waits for the
return of the Master to gather up the grain and blow
the chaff away. What will be left is freshness and
life, unabated. There is just one name for such a
state: glory. That is the place we will be. Oh, that
we would anticipate the moment
with the eager expectation of the
rest of creation!

TIP

"NOT TENSE
BUT FIRM" IS A
GOOD THOUGHT
FOR ANY SHOT.

GOD'S TIMING

These words Jesus spoke in the treasury,
as He taught in the temple; and no one laid
hands on Him, for His hour had not yet come.

JOHN 8:20

Second-guessing is a popular pastime among sports fans. Golfers are no exception. When a player goes for the green and the outcome is costly, it is easy to question the player's decision.

But dare we second-guess the plans and timing of God? Jesus didn't—although He was surely tempted. In the Garden of Gethsemane, we see a strong Savior reduced to tearful plaints: "O My Father, if it is possible, let this cup pass from Me." But Christ never let His own desires, His own feelings, overrule His submission to the purposes of God: "Nevertheless, not as I will, but as You will" (Matthew 26:39).

God will indeed work out His purpose for us. And the path toward that purpose is walked by our obedience. Do not question what God is having you do today. Simply do it. Then you will arrive at what He has in store for you tomorrow.

TIP

ON AVERAGE, EVERY 1,000 FEET IN ELEVATION ADDS ABOUT 5 PERCENT TO YOUR DISTANCE.

LET IT RAIN

Then Elijah said to Ahab, "Go up, eat and drink; for
there is the sound of abundance of rain."

1 KINGS 18:41

Rain sure can undo the best plans of golfers. Especially heavy rain. But rain also can remind us of God's great history.

When Elijah originally reported to King Ahab, the prophet announced that there would be no dew or rain in the next few years except at his word. It was a bold statement, what we would expect of a true messenger of the God of heaven. But Ahab hated Elijah, so he kept Elijah on the run.

Until God gave Elijah more to do. Three years later, Elijah's passion put him in the proper place: on his knees. Then upon God's promise, Elijah told Ahab that he heard the sound of heavy rain. Elijah, "a man just like us" (James 5:17 NIV), saw God's answer to his powerful and effective prayer.

And when that answer came, God's power came with it. Elijah tucked his cloak into his belt and outran Ahab's chariot all the way to Jezreel!

TIP

MOST FOLKS
DON'T CARE WHAT
YOU SHOOT AS
LONG AS YOU
KNOW HOW TO
KEEP MOVING.

TALKING A GOOD GAME

"Although my house is not so with God, yet He has made with me an everlasting covenant, ordered in all things and secure. For this is all my salvation and all my desire; will He not make it increase?"

2 SAMUEL 23:5

What confident questions these are! Certainly they must be the words of a man going from victory unto victory. In truth, they are David's last words, spoken as he approached death. Mightiest of Judah's kings, the prolific voice of praise, David had much to be confident in as he surrendered his earthly existence for the promise of eternity. But his boast, as always, was in the Lord.

What words are we preparing for the day we die? We place a lot of importance on sports talk these days. We don't just want our favorite players to win; we want them to speak eloquently of winning. But in the final hours of his life, David didn't list his earthly accomplishments or even speak long about the children who would follow him. Rather, he gave himself over one last time to his heavenly Father. And then he received all that God had for him.

TIP

PRACTICE MOST WITH YOUR MOST-USED CLUB. (HINT: IT'S NOT YOUR DRIVER.)

THE LOUD CROWD

*Pilate said to them, "What then shall
I do with Jesus who is called Christ?"
They all said to him, "Let Him be crucified!"*

MATTHEW 27:22

No place in golf is like the PGA Tour stop in Phoenix. Lining the sixteenth hole from tee to green are literally thousands of raucous golf fans. Sixteen is the golf's Roman Colosseum. These people want blood. More than once, they have called for it just as a player made his move at the ball.

Perhaps you have acted out in just such a crowd. Certain that others' actions were wrong, you went along with them anyway. And now you are not sure how to undo the damage.

Begin with repentance. No matter how long it has been, go to God and say that you are sorry for what you did. Then prepare to face the crowd again. If the enemy has captured you with one form of temptation before, he will return with that same weapon. This time say, "That is not the way I choose to go. Even alone, I must go God's way."

TIP

IF YOU'VE CHOSEN A "DISTANCE BALL," DON'T EXPECT WONDERS AROUND THE GREENS.

DIGNITY

So David said to Michal, . . . "I will play music before the LORD. And I will be even more undignified than this, and will be humble in my own sight."

There's a problem with golf etiquette: it can turn us into sticklers. We even show disdain for those who are not like us. (Remember the last time you found your ball in an unraked footprint?)

Like Michal, those of us who love golf etiquette would have struggled with David's dance through the streets in partial dress. But David dismissed her concern with a strict statement of his strict priorities: "I choose God over all else."

David's choice included reverence and passion, traits admired by those high on tradition. But it also included celebration, which Michal did not appreciate. In her mind, David had lost his good sense. David knew better. "I may be humiliated even in my own eyes," David told her. "But by these slave girls, I will be held in honor." David respected their opinion, because as a man after God's own heart, he was willing to be a slave too.

> **TIP**
>
> ENJOY WORKING OUT? HAVE YOUR TRAINER DESIGN A REGIMEN TO AID YOUR GOLF GAME.

IN THE BAG

Stand therefore, having girded your waist with truth, having put on the breastplate of righteousness, and having shod your feet with the preparation of the gospel of peace; above all, taking the shield of faith with which you will be able to quench all the fiery darts of the wicked one. And take the helmet of salvation, and the sword of the Spirit, which is the word of God.

EPHESIANS 6:14–17

The "in the bag" look at the equipment a player carries has long been a popular feature in golf magazines. We have a fascination with the clubs the professionals choose and how those clubs are specially tweaked according to the professional's wishes.

Well, if many professionals could see your life with spiritual eyes, they would be even more enamored with the tools that you have been given to walk with Christ. Paul calls these tools "the full armor of God" (Ephesians 6:11 NIV), and this armor is fitted for each of us, allowing us to take up the offensive when necessary and to stand in bold defense when challenged.

And the best news about this spiritual equipment? You don't have to be a professional to use it. You just have to belong to Christ.

> **TIP**
>
> BE CAREFUL WHAT YOU PLAY FOR—THE RULES ARE STRICT ABOUT AMATEUR STATUS.

LOVE-HATE RELATIONSHIPS

"Remember the word that I said to you, 'A servant is not greater than his master.' If they persecuted Me, they will also persecute you. If they kept My word, they will keep yours also."

JOHN 15:20

Think of one of your favorite professional golfers. Is it a dominant competitor, like one of the multiple-major winners? Maybe you prefer the easygoing players, or those with the intensity, who play aggressively. Go ahead; take your pick. Then start naming your friends who can't stand that very same player.

It's the way we are as fans. And all too often it is the way we are as people. We build our relationships along lines of love and hate. We admire people or we are maddened by them.

Jesus did not comment on whether such a dichotomous stance toward others is right. He simply noted that it is the way of the world, and something that we, as His followers, will have to live with—in the same way He did. It is all part of being "in the world, though not of it." It is what comes with taking a stand.

TIP

FOR GREATER DISTANCE, BEGIN BY RELAXING.

ABOUT-FACE

"But many who are first will be last, and the last first."

MATTHEW 19:30

If you are geared toward success—and golfers in general tend to be—you likely have spent a significant portion of your life pursuing things that define success in our world: a house of your own, an advanced degree, exclusive memberships, resort vacations, fancy electronics, and more.

But when you come to this passage in Matthew, you may stumble a few rungs on that ladder of pursuit. You are faced with a most difficult question: Yes, I am among those who are first now, but where will I stand in the end?

This teaching takes all our own accomplishments out of the picture. Which leaves us in the only place we can be left. We must follow Him who is first.

There is one formula for success that is biblical: it's not what you do—it's what He's done. Jesus Christ came to unite an unholy people with a holy God.

TIP

HAVING TROUBLE WITH YOUR LONG IRONS? REPLACE THEM WITH FAIRWAY OR UTILITY WOODS.

THE OTHER GODS

"Then they sweep past like the wind and go on—guilty men, whose own strength is their god."

HABAKKUK 1:11 NIV

Golfers ponder endlessly how to improve their game. Maybe a small change in posture, or a long putter, or a harder ball.

What makes it so difficult not to desire to improve in life is that so much of what is sold on the open market is geared in this direction. Get thinner. Grow richer. Build muscle. Save time. Make space. It is easy to get caught up in catching up. You would think it was in our nature to succeed.

The Bible teaches the opposite. As the sons and daughters of Adam, we are born to sin. We pursue the wrong goals. We serve the wrong gods.

The only chance we have is not in fortifying our minds or our bodies. No, the only chance we have is in fortifying our spirits by pursuing Christ. He alone moves us from being "guilty men" to forgiven ones.

TIP

SHORT SHOTS CAUSE THE HIGHEST PRESSURE. THINK "SMOOTH."

IN CONDITION

Then He came to the disciples and found them sleeping, and said to Peter, "What! Could you not watch with Me one hour? Watch and pray, lest you enter into temptation. The spirit indeed is willing, but the flesh is weak."

MATTHEW 26:40–41

If you find yourself with a weakened prayer life, you may be wise to think like a beginning golfer. You cannot build a swing by pounding a million balls your first time out. You must start briefly but purposefully.

Likewise, you build—or rebuild—your prayer life by spending five minutes in focused conversation with God each day for a week. (You can still go ahead and pray those momentary prayers that arise throughout the day!) Next week, increase the time to ten minutes, then fifteen, and so on.

Where will it end? That's between you and God. But you may ask in one of your first requests that He show you what unnecessary activities can be carved from your life so that you can give more of this vital time to Him. It will be the best trade you've ever made!

TIP

AS A BEGINNER, YOU'LL SEE FAST IMPROVEMENT IN YOUR SCORE IF YOU PRACTICE THOSE LONG LAG PUTTS.

TO THE MOUNTAIN

Many people shall come and say, "Come, and let us go up to the mountain of the LORD, to the house of the God of Jacob; He will teach us His ways, and we shall walk in His paths." For out of Zion shall go forth the law, and the word of the LORD from Jerusalem.

ISAIAH 2:3

Take a look at any list of the Top 100 courses, and you're sure to start dreaming—and sure to start changing plans if ever an invitation comes. We'll sacrifice our golf budget for two or three months to get a shot at one of these super spots.

To go to the mountain of the Lord, to a place to worship God, we must also change course. We must leave our regular distractions and disturbances and give our minds to our heavenly Father. The payoff will be more beautiful than any golf course you can imagine.

Are you a recruiter, the one who assembles the foursome? Make a different call this week. Call some men, call some women, and say, "Let us go to the mountain of the Lord to meet with Him!" Then spend eternal minutes together in the presence of the heavenly Father.

TIP

IF YOU TALK TO YOURSELF ON THE GOLF COURSE, BE SURE TO INCLUDE ENCOURAGEMENT.

BOOKISH TYPES

Of making many books there is no end,
and much study is wearisome to the flesh.

ECCLESIASTES 12:12

In a modern bookstore, the golf section alone would leave Solomon, who apparently authored Ecclesiastes, dumbfounded. From short game lessons to golf tales, from mental approaches to famous course pictorials, the selections fill the shelf at your local bookseller.

Interestingly, however, Solomon's caution about the wearying effect of study and the proliferation of books comes on the heels of this observation: "The words of the wise are like goads, and the words of scholars are like well-driven nails, given by one Shepherd" (Ecclesiastes 12:11). Solomon wasn't liquidating his library. He was just reminding himself that answers in life come from more than one direction. Books are important, but we learn, too, from experience, the voices of others, and above all, the wisdom of God as revealed in that most important of books, the Bible.

TIP

ENJOY THE WILDLIFE ON THE COURSES YOU PLAY—IT'S LIKE TWO SPORTS IN ONE!

BLIND FAITH

*Now faith is the substance of things
hoped for, the evidence of things not seen.
For by it the elders obtained a good testimony.*

HEBREWS 11:1–2

Blind greens. You likely hate them, especially if you have never played a course before. You have to select your distance and trust that if you hit your shot well, it will land on the green.

This is faith, the strength of "the ancients," as the author of Hebrews called them (Hebrews 11:2 NIV). With no visible promise, and sometimes no spoken one, these people acted in faith that God had their well-being in mind. They acted with certainty that their obedient actions would be rewarded. They believed that God knew better than they.

We have two choices when we read of faith such as this. We may dismiss it, telling ourselves that these people were exceptional, and their faith was never really meant to be an example. Or we can "throw off everything that hinders and the sin that so easily entangles, and . . . run with perseverance the race marked out for us" (Hebrews 12:1 NIV).

> **TIP**
>
> LOST BALLS CREATE SLOW PLAY. WAVE A GROUP THROUGH IF YOU'RE SEARCHING.

PROMISES, PROMISES

*For whom He foreknew, He also predestined to be
conformed to the image of His Son, that He
might be the firstborn among many brethren.
Moreover whom He predestined, these He also
called; whom He called, these He also justified;
and whom He justified, these He also glorified.*

ROMANS 8:29–30

No honest teaching professional would make promises about how far he or she could take your game. Too much depends on you and your commitment to practice, your mental makeup, and your physical limitations.

But when promises come from God, we can be certain of their hope. Our God is lavish with His love. His promises come multitiered.

So we are not just predestined; we are called. In our hearts or in our ears—or both—we suddenly know God's voice. Then we are justified—made right in the eyes of God. Remarkable! And more, His further work glorifies us before Him. We are not just a people rescued, but a people renewed. Where once we were surrounded by accusation, we are now surrounded by celebration.

TIP

TO LOWER YOUR HANDICAP, USE YOUR PRACTICE TO ELIMINATE YOUR WEAKNESSES.

NEW CLOTHES

*For the wages of sin is death, but the gift
of God is eternal life in Christ Jesus our Lord.*

ROMANS 6:23

Ever walked off the golf course feeling lowly? You take your game to a special course—and that course wallops you. Or you look to strut your stuff in a foursome of low handicappers—and they beat you like an old rug.

Now imagine what it was like for Moses when one by one God etched those stone commandments. Then comes number 6: "You shall not murder" (Exodus 20:13). Talk about exposure! Moses' marquee sin renounced right there in one of God's marquee laws. Naked in sin—what a horrible feeling!

In golf, we know that if we're tough, the putts will fall again someday. In the spiritual realm, however, toughness won't cut it. This is because sin scars. But through Jesus our Savior, our heavenly Father brings us back from the dead and gives us the gift of eternal life. We stand dressed in the Savior's finery before the King of creation—what a wonderful feeling!

TIP

STRONGER PLAYERS USUALLY NEED STRONGER SHAFTS. ASK YOUR PRO WHAT'S BEST FOR YOU.

HEART CHECK

"Do to others as you would have them do to you."

LUKE 6:31 NIV

In golf we call our own fouls—no refs necessary. That is one component that makes golf so very different. And we are proud that it is so.

In life, there is a way to play by the rules as well. Christ might have put it this way: *The rules you want others to play by, these are the rules you must use.* In sports, we would call this fairness.

Would you have someone forgive your silly error? Forgive the errors of others. Would you have someone offer a word of encouragement during times of trouble? Encourage others. Would you have someone listen attentively when you talk your way through a problem? Tune in to the problems of others—yours may be the only ears to do so.

You see, it really is an overarching rule. It doesn't so much govern our actions as it governs our character. It shows you have Christ's heart.

TIP

LIGHTNING COMING? GET OFF THE COURSE NOW—AHEAD OF THE STORM!

FUNDAMENTALS

*Then Shemaiah the prophet came to Rehoboam and
the leaders of Judah, who were gathered together in
Jerusalem because of Shishak, and said to them, "Thus
says the LORD: 'You have forsaken Me, and therefore
I also have left you in the hand of Shishak.'" So the
leaders of Israel and the king humbled themselves; and
they said, "The LORD is righteous."*

2 CHRONICLES 12:5–6

In life, as in golf, it is easy to let fundamentals
slip. We fall into doing what feels right—after
all, it's often easier.

What we need is a prophet to give us what-for.
God sent Shemaiah to Rehoboam, king of Judah,
and warned, "It's now or never." God had poised
an enemy on the doorstep because Rehoboam had
abandoned God. The consequences were clear.
Rehoboam was sinful, not stupid. He set things
right. He humbled himself and admitted that he
deserved God's punishment.

Are you in a position of
neglect today? Perhaps the consequences are piling up. Here is
great news: God still waits for
you. He is just, but He is also
ready to forgive.

> **TIP**
>
> IF YOUR BALL IS
> SITTING UP ON A
> FLUFFY LIE, DON'T
> GROUND YOUR
> CLUB BEHIND IT
> AND RISK
> A PENALTY.

NOT MINE

"But the LORD said to my father David, 'Whereas it was in your heart to build a temple for My name, you did well that it was in your heart. Nevertheless you shall not build the temple, but your son who will come from your body, he shall build the temple for My name.'"

1 KINGS 8:18–19

Oh, the courses you would love to play someday—Augusta National, Pine Valley, Cypress Point! Or do dreams like this just plague you as goals you have not reached?

As a shepherd, David probably never dared to dream too big. But as his life progressed, and his victories accumulated, his dreams grew. Eventually, just one thing was on David's mind—building a temple for the Lord. Yet God told David that the task was for another man. Nearly all of us would have been crushed by such news. But David accepted the Lord's plan.

Like David, you may possess talent or desire to pursue your goals. But are you willing to surrender these dreams to others if God requires that of you? Perhaps today is the day to begin praying that you will be so humble in accepting His will for you.

TIP

OPEN YOUR FEET SLIGHTLY AT ADDRESS TO ALLOW FOR A BIGGER BACKSWING WITH YOUR DRIVER.

SERVICE AND WORSHIP

*I desire therefore that the men pray everywhere,
lifting up holy hands, without wrath and doubting.*

1 TIMOTHY 2:8

Too often, when we warm up for a round, even on a course where we've never putted the greens, we spend fifteen or twenty minutes loosening up and hitting balls and about three minutes stroking putts. This imbalance keeps us from scoring our best.

In your spiritual life, we must watch another critical balance between service and worship. We tend toward work in our relationship with Christ. Yet we must make room for worship. Our work in the Lord is only an outflow of our relationship with Him. And our role in this relationship is the recognition of the amazing things that He has done for us. It is worship.

It is essential, then, that we never separate our service and our worship. In golf, we must have both the short game and the long game. In our walk with Christ, we must serve Him and worship Him. The two are perfect complements.

TIP

AFTER SETTING UP, ALWAYS TURN YOUR HEAD AND TAKE ONE LAST GOOD LOOK AT YOUR TARGET.

SETTING OUR SIGHTS

If then you were raised with Christ,
seek those things which are above, where
Christ is, sitting at the right hand of God.

COLOSSIANS 3:1

If you are familiar with the themes of sports psychology, you will recognize this one instantly: banish the bad, visualize the good. The most successful mental coaches are those who do the best job of enabling their clients to "see what's good."

There is basis for this kind of coaching in Scripture. Of course, rather than making us better athletes, the Bible's teaching is intended to make us more complete followers of our Lord Jesus Christ.

What is required in the spiritual realm, if we are to live our lives for Christ, is to set our sights on Him. Conquering trouble is not done by opposing the trouble but by casting our gaze on the One who has overcome all trouble. It's a positive focus on the perfect Savior.

Our walk with Christ is not about pointing out what lurks ahead. It's about following in His sure steps.

TIP

SOME WEDGES ARE BETTER FOR CERTAIN TYPES OF SAND. ASK YOUR PRO WHAT'S RIGHT FOR YOUR COURSE.

CHANGE OF PLANS

Then the LORD opened Balaam's eyes,
and he saw the Angel of the LORD standing in the
way with His drawn sword in His hand; and he
bowed his head and fell flat on his face.

NUMBERS 22:31

When an unexpected storm opens up on our golf day, it's hard not to grumble. One of maturity's toughest jobs is getting us to deal rightly with things we do not anticipate.

Like Balaam, we persist in governing our own lives. We do not inquire of the Lord. And sometimes, the only way He can get our attention is by bringing about a serious change of plans. For Balaam, this meant new orders, and an obedience he never would have considered before.

Confronted with a change of plans, we can get back on track by employing the perspective of Balaam, who became instantly willing to reverse his set direction. Let us be so willing to follow one priority, as Christ did—doing the will of the Father, no matter how much we think it inconveniences us.

> **TIP**
>
> THE BREAK OF EVERY PUTT IS DICTATED BY SPEED. BE SURE TO CONSIDER HOW HARD YOU'LL HIT IT.

FRIENDS LIKE THESE

*And when the Pharisees saw it, they said
to His disciples, "Why does your Teacher eat
with tax collectors and sinners?"*

MATTHEW 9:11

We all have favorite golf partners. They are
friends who typically share a lot of our same
perspectives and practices in life.

But let's not close the doors of our foursomes.
Like the traditional hostess who prepares a place
setting for the uninvited guest, we might even plan
a spot for a single to join us.

That would be Jesus' way. Our Savior did not
surround Himself with a proven band of "yes-men."
Many were plainly notorious. But Jesus, who one
day literally would hang between sinners, was not
afraid to hang out with them during His life. For
here was the One who "did not come to call the
righteous, but sinners" (Matthew 9:13).

So let us pursue Christ's nature.
We cannot serve only those who
serve us in return. We must serve,
we must entertain, we must love
all people. Even "sinners" like
ourselves.

TIP

SMILING AS
YOU SET UP
CAN PRODUCE
SURPRISINGLY
GOOD RESULTS.

FROM GOD

"Give us this day our daily bread."

MATTHEW 6:11

Ever whisper a prayer before a round of golf? Something this simple perhaps: "Lord, gimme a birdie today." After all, He does give us what we need!

Consider a strange juxtaposition in Jesus' teaching about prayer. First Jesus stated, "Your Father knows what you need before you ask him" (Matthew 6:8 NIV). Then in His prayer, He reminded us to ask God for our daily bread.

Oddly, we are to ask for something God would give us anyway. Here are three possible reasons: First, we need to defer to our heavenly Father as the source of all things, big and small. Second, we need to be reminded that God is the God of our every day. And third, we need to build the habit of conversation with God.

By asking God for something as simple as our daily bread, we are saying plainly that we rely on His presence.

TIP

PLAN TO PLAY EACH HOLE AS IT SETS UP BEST FOR YOU—NOT AS IT SETS UP FOR THE PROS.

CAN'T HELP MYSELF

"For we cannot but speak the things
which we have seen and heard."

ACTS 4:20

If making a hole in one is golf's most enjoyable achievement, witnessing one is pretty close. Either way, we have a story to tell.

Peter and John were firsthand witnesses of the God-man, Jesus Christ. And nothing was going to keep them from reporting what they had seen.

When Jesus had gone to heaven, the apostles weren't sure what to do with this stunning story they had witnessed. While they pondered their strategy, the promise of Jesus, the Holy Spirit of God, fell upon them. And then they knew just what they were to do: start talking!

Ask God to fill you as well with the boldness that comes from the Holy Spirit. Ask Him to give you the eyes to see and the ears to hear what God is still doing in our time through Jesus Christ. And then ask Him to give you the tongue to tell of His remarkable wonders.

TIP

ONE OF GOLF'S GREATEST TRADITIONS IS THE LAST-GREEN HANDSHAKE—BE SURE TO PARTAKE IN IT!

POWER TO DISCERN

"But when the Helper comes, whom I shall send to you from the Father, the Spirit of truth who proceeds from the Father, He will testify of Me."

JOHN 15:26

It's awful to be caught in between clubs. Add a bit of swirling wind and maybe some water, and you have a recipe for resounding confusion. What a dose of discernment would mean at a moment like that!

In life, many of us need help with right and wrong. Indeed, the great error of the Pharisees was that they often could not let go of what was "right" and what was "wrong" and do what was truly right, with love and compassion.

Here's good news: In choosing Christ, you do not have to conduct an in-depth study to find truth. Truth is in you in the person of the Holy Spirit. "The Counselor," Jesus called Him, "the Spirit of truth" (John 15:26 NIV). And what the Spirit does in each of us is testify to Christ's authentic oneness with God, speaking to our hearts about how to live within the will of this marvelous three-in-one Godhead.

TIP

NO TIME FOR A ROUND? "PLAY" A ROUND, CLUB BY CLUB, ON THE DRIVING RANGE.

FIRED UP

And they said to one another, "Did not our heart burn within us while He talked with us on the road, and while He opened the Scriptures to us?"

LUKE 24:32

There is no telling where God will meet you! As golfers, we know the joy of discovery. We anticipate trips to a new course touted among our golfing friends. And we hope—silently, perhaps, but vigorously—that we will not just play such a course, but that we will play well there. After all, we never know just when our A-game will show up.

Such a prodigious moment arose for the two followers of Christ on the road to Emmaus—a moment when time and place and person converged. For in that hour, as these two were met by a stranger, they no longer followed Christ; they walked with Him. And, known in their hearts but not in their eyes, He talked with them, encouraged them, and made them come alive again in this day so soon after tragedy.

God may meet you in just such a moment. Aren't you eager?

TIP

DON'T TOSS YOUR OLD BALLS AND CLUBS. DONATE THEM TO JUNIOR GOLF PROGRAMS.

BACK TO HIM

Draw near to God and He will draw near to you.

JAMES 4:8

No matter which skill abandons you first when you must take a break from golf, certainly the best way to falter in any endeavor is to break the chain of discipline that has placed you at your highest level.

Intimacy with God, too, requires consistent attention to our relationship with Him. We cannot expect to walk consistently in step with His purposes for our lives if we are always trying first to catch up from long hours at the office, late mornings in bed, or "just one more game" in front of the TV.

God never intended His people to stray far from Him. Our strength comes from our proximity to its Source.

TIP

KEEP MORE THAN THE SCORE. TRACK GREENS AND FAIRWAYS HIT, AS WELL AS PUTTS.

THINK ABOUT IT

Finally, brethren, whatever things are true,
whatever things are noble, whatever things are just,
whatever things are pure, whatever things are lovely,
whatever things are of good report, if there
is any virtue and if there is anything
praiseworthy—meditate on these things.

PHILIPPIANS 4:8

Once golf is "in your blood," it's hard not to think about it, even when you know your mind should be on something else.

Paul wrote frequently of thinking rightly. "Renew your minds," he told the Romans. "Take every thought captive," he instructed the Corinthians. And then there is this passage to the Philippians, rich like cheesecake. Was Paul using repetition as a literary device here? Or was his list literal, almost like those frame-by-frame sequences of the perfect swing that occupy your dreamy golf brain? Either way, we are strengthened by considering the list item by item. Truth. Honor. Purity. Loveliness. Good repute. Excellence. Praiseworthiness.

With "life thoughts" as powerful as those, it may be hard to find room for swing thoughts anymore.

TIP

YOU HAVE SEVERAL CHOICES FOR DROPPING A BALL FROM A LATERAL HAZARD. USE THE ONE THAT HELPS YOU MOST.

OPEN HOUSE

And it may be that I will remain,
or even spend the winter with you, that you
may send me on my journey, wherever I go.

1 CORINTHIANS 16:6

Golfers know that hospitality doesn't have to take place in one's home. Guests and strangers can be well entertained in public places too—golf courses and restaurants and ballparks and churches. Abraham sat with his famous guests under a tree (Genesis 18). In fact, we can welcome people into our world by the way we answer the phone!

Godly hospitality is given freely, without any expectation placed on the recipient. The cheerful host enjoys the company so much that the cost of serving—in money and in time—is not even considered. Moreover, biblical hosts feel the same whether or not they have "selected" the guests. In fact, to the Hebrews Paul offered this wonderful possibility: "Do not forget to entertain strangers, for by doing so some people have unwittingly entertained angels" (Hebrews 13:2).

> **TIP**
>
> UNORTHODOX SWINGS RARELY WORK—BETTER TO LEARN TRIED-AND-TRUE ONES.

FULLY FUNCTIONAL

For we are His workmanship, created in
Christ Jesus for good works, which God prepared
beforehand that we should walk in them.

EPHESIANS 2:10

Let's reminisce for a minute. Remember when you would set a persimmon-headed driver down in front of you and wrap your fingers around the grip, almost ready to tee off right there in the pro shop? When you said, "I like the way this looks," you weren't referring only to the size or shape of the head as we do with metal clubs. You were talking of the color and the finish. What workmanship!

Maybe you have heard the claim that "God don't make no junk!" Whoever first spoke those words may need more time in grammar class, but he or she hit on absolute truth. For not only are we God's beautiful workmanship, but we have been designed with great functionality as well. Each of us has a place in God's great design—not a place of chance or accident, but a place of true purpose.

> **TIP**
>
> TO KEEP YOUR CLUB ON PLANE, MAKE SURE THE BUTT OF THE GRIP POINTS AT THE BALL HALFWAY DOWN THE DOWNSWING.

FULL SUPPORT

And so it was, when Moses held up his hand,
that Israel prevailed; and when he let down
his hand, Amalek prevailed. But Moses' hands became
heavy; so they took a stone and put it under him,
and he sat on it. And Aaron and Hur supported
his hands, one on one side, and the other on the other
side; and his hands were steady until the going down of
the sun. So Joshua defeated Amalek and his people with
the edge of the sword.

EXODUS 17:11–13

The rules of golf are clear: in no way can a partner or caddie physically help a player. On the golf course, then, Moses would have received a penalty for the support he was given, but in God's "rule book," this simple but vital support was exactly what was needed. Moses was gifted in miracles, drawing on God's power to meet the needs of God's people. Although Moses grew older and physically frail, his spiritual gifting was not diminished!

Open your eyes. Do you have a friend whose spiritual gift is lying dormant for lack of practical support from a brother or sister in the kingdom? Now you know what you are called to do!

> **TIP**
>
> WHEN CHIPPING, GET THE BALL ON THE GREEN EARLY, ROLLING LIKE A PUTT THE REST OF THE WAY.

HONOR

Honor all people.

1 PETER 2:17

Golf is certainly a game we all start humbly. For this very reason, we are extra patient with earnest novices who pick up the game. No golfer greatly enjoys playing regularly with players severely below his or her own ability, but when given the chance to teach the game to a new player, we honor him or her by doing so with longsuffering eagerness.

And that player honors us. He or she knows that we are not as good as the players on television. Yet beginners treat us like royalty, appreciating the handful of tips we dispense out of rote repetition more than anything else: "Take it away low and slow," "Let the clubhead do the work," that kind of thing.

It's a rare thing, such honor across such disparate stations in life. But it is a beautiful picture of what we are called to do in Christ, honoring those who are not honored by others.

TIP

NEW TO A COURSE? SPEND MOST OF YOUR WARM-UP TIME ON THE PUTTING GREEN.

INSIDERS

Love the brotherhood.

1 PETER 2:17

Like those who huddle in most any group, golfers have their own language, their own experiences, their own pilgrimages. Golfers enjoy each other because they understand each other.

In the body of Christ, understanding one another is a primary way we can love one another. When we recognize that others are as human as we are, we are much quicker to forgive. When we hear how much they want to grow in their relationship with Christ, we can set forth in encouraging them. We can do unto others as we would have them do unto us.

Too often we get hung up on what we cannot do. We think of loving the entire world, knowing full well that we cannot. God alone can love the whole world—that is, touching each one individually. But we can love those right here by serving them, inspiring them, listening to them, and praying with them.

TIP

JUST 5 PERCENT OF GOLFERS PLAY IN THE 70S. DON'T FRET IF YOU DON'T.

HEALTHY INTIMIDATION

Fear God.

1 PETER 2:17

Most of us don't know fear on the golf course. But then, most of us don't tee it up opposite world-class players every week. Absolutely need to win? You'd better go find a lesser opponent!

Fear of God is a common biblical theme. What a daunting perspective! We are to fear the One we love?

Of course, this is not the fear of horror, brought on by our dread that God will do something horrible to us. But it is the understanding that He could.

Our God should not scare us. But He should intimidate us: IN-TIMID-ATE. He should cause us to come before Him with utter humility. Isn't that what we want from the God of the whole universe? Shouldn't He be that big? Only a fool would pretend that he was not intimidated before God—a fool, or one whose God is just too small.

TIP

KNOW YOUR LIMITATIONS. GOOD DECISIONS MAKE FOR GOOD ROUNDS.

ANTIESTABLISHMENT?

Honor the king.

1 PETER 2:17

It's funny what we fight for in life. If the golf course rules say wear a collared shirt, we wear a collared shirt. But if the government demands the collar off our shirt (a portion of what we possess), we hem and haw and haggle.

Earth knows little of singular political leaders today. But although governmental structure has changed, those of us who live under God's instructions are still commanded to honor those in authority over us. Christ said it, Paul wrote it, and Peter cemented it.

We weave a tangled web when we discuss submission to worldly authority, no question. But we must begin and end with what we have been given: honor authority. We will not always agree with authority, and like Daniel, we may even face situations in which we must disobey the laws of authority. But we must honor those in charge.

TIP

WAIT FOR THAT GROUP AHEAD TO CLEAR. WHEN YOU HIT IT WELL, YOU'LL BE DOUBLY GLAD YOU DID.

NOTHING IN THE WAY

Marriage is honorable among all,
and the bed undefiled.

HEBREWS 13:4

Not having to buy their own as the rest of us do, tour professionals do not hesitate to pull out a brand-new ball in the middle of a round. They are not about to let the purity of the equipment they use, including their golf balls, be compromised.

As people serving the great King, we, too, should be careful to guard the purity of our service to Him. Our obedience should be absolute, and our intimate relationships should be undefiled.

In His design, if God intends for you to marry, He has set aside one spouse for you, and once you have married this one, he or she is forever the right one. It is your righteous duty to uphold and honor each other above all other earthly relationships. But it is not just your duty—it is your joy. That is how good God's design is.

TIP

SCHEDULE ROUNDS THAT "DON'T COUNT" TO TRY SHOTS YOU NORMALLY WOULDN'T.

THE GOD WHO'S NOT HIDDEN

> *"And you will seek Me and find Me,*
> *when you search for Me with all your heart.*
> *I will be found by you, says the LORD, and I*
> *will bring you back from your captivity."*
>
> JEREMIAH 29:13–14

We all despise losing a golf ball. Some hate losing the ball itself. Others dread the serious penalty of stroke and distance. So, where is that ball?!

Sadly, we are often more earnest in seeking a lost ball than in seeking our heavenly Father. Yet the refrain of the Old Testament prophets was that although God's people have strayed so very far from Him, He is ever willing to take them back in. He wants to be found.

It is not that our God hides, of course. But if we find God, we must surrender to Him, a notion that deters us. Yet this is the God who has plans for us, offering us a hope and a future (Jeremiah 29:11). What more could we want?

There are but two reasons for finding a golf ball; there are a million reasons to find God.

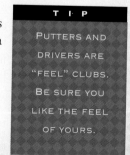

TIP

PUTTERS AND DRIVERS ARE "FEEL" CLUBS. BE SURE YOU LIKE THE FEEL OF YOURS.

DON'T MISS THIS

He said to them, "Did you receive the Holy Spirit when you believed?" So they said to him, "We have not so much as heard whether there is a Holy Spirit."

ACTS 19:2

If you're really into golf, you're going to pay for all the quality you can afford. You won't buy the best driver then tee off with mushy X-out balls.

It's an important lesson for us in our spiritual lives. The last thing we want is an incomplete faith. Especially when we know that our heavenly Father has the best of everything for us.

The problem for those who had received only John's baptism of repentance was not that they looked forward to the coming of Christ. But once the Savior had come and gone, He had sent another to follow—the Holy Spirit. By receiving Christ, the early believers had gained salvation, just as we do today. But by receiving all that God now had for them—Jesus' salvation *and* the Holy Spirit—they were more completely empowered, just as we are when we give our lives to Him.

TIP

PASS GOLF ON TO ANOTHER. IT WILL ENCOURAGE YOU TO KEEP UP YOUR OWN GAME.

FEARLESS

"I will ransom them from the power of the grave; I will redeem them from death. O Death, I will be your plagues! O Grave, I will be your destruction! Pity is hidden from My eyes."

HOSEA 13:14

Like a golf ball launched into the water are sin and death. In their grip, our hopes are sunk.

Likely, you have friends caught in this trap. They know they have missed the mark with their lives. They have driven their ball in the water. But rather than playing the next one clear, they try instead to cut more of the corner, coming up wet again. It's not a pretty picture.

Let's face it. Our earthly selves are headed to the grave. We are like golf balls sinking to the bottom. But we must never call ourselves sunk.

We have a Redeemer who pulls us up from the grave, up from our sin and our death, up from our very destruction, and lays us back on the green grass. Where we rest beside the still waters. Where our soul is restored. Where He guides our paths in righteousness for His name's sake.

> TIP
>
> KNOWING THE RULES WILL SAVE TIME AND STROKES.

BACK TO GOD

"I say to you, though he will not rise and give to him because he is his friend, yet because of his persistence he will rise and give him as many as he needs."

LUKE 11:8

 It is one of those bare-your-soul spiritual questions: Are you consistent—are you persistent—in prayer? In golf, we might ask it like this: Are you putting as well as you'd like?

Although it is unlikely that we would answer either of these questions favorably, we should still be encouraged to move forward in the key endeavors of living before God. Regular prayer is one of these.

We might not understand why we must be persistent with an omniscient God. We may need to swallow our pride to keep going back to Him. But Jesus' parable of the knock-knocking friend spurs us in this direction. Sometimes, perhaps, God wants to know just how committed we are to our request. But always, it appears from Luke 11, He will honor a request He knows is truly and nobly desired.

TIP

UPSET ABOUT THE LAST HOLE? CONTROL AND RELEASE YOUR ANGER ON YOUR NEXT TEE SHOT.

HIGHEST REGARD

While he was still speaking, behold, a bright cloud overshadowed them; and suddenly a voice came out of the cloud, saying, "This is My beloved Son, in whom I am well pleased. Hear Him!"

MATTHEW 17:5

Do you know what your golf friends say about you when you're not there? As followers of Christ, we hope that our lives reflect the heavenly Father. We hope that we are seen as genuine people, not proud and not stuffy. People aren't naive, but they sure wish there were more honest people in the world, so they could be more trusting. If you are a person with your heart (and not just your finger) pointing to God, people will recognize that and be drawn to it.

Many people spend their lives trying to work up this kind of character. But like the golfer who beats hundreds of range balls and never improves, they just come away frustrated. To gain godliness, you must first gain God, through His Son, Jesus Christ. His character comes first. Ours follows.

TIP

IF YOU NEED TO HIT A LOW HOOK, TAKE IT BACK SLOW AND FLAT AND SWING "AROUND" THE BALL.

HOLY CURIOSITY

*Who has believed our report? And to whom
has the arm of the LORD been revealed?*

ISAIAH 53:1

When it comes to sports via computer, we can get up-to-the-minute scores whenever we want. It sure satisfies the curiosity, doesn't it?

Isaiah's call to us, however, is to be curious about the spiritual lives of others. In this introductory verse to the chapter that foretold Christ's sacrifice for us, Isaiah asked the most critical of all questions: Who knows the Lord?

Our Savior came not to reveal another, as prophets do, but to be Himself the revelation of all we need. So among the many things we want to know about those we call our friends, highest on our list should be the answer to this question: Has God revealed Himself to you? It's really not a threatening question, for it allows even the stargazer and the atheist to answer plainly. And it's a question that sure gets the conversation rolling.

TIP

FOR NEARLY EVERY SHOT AROUND THE GREEN, YOU WANT TO KEEP YOUR WRISTS FIRM.

HOOKED

*Then He said to them, "Follow Me, and
I will make you fishers of men." They
immediately left their nets and followed Him.*

MATTHEW 4:19–20

Hooked on golf? Many people who love the
game have described their experience just that
way. In virtually no time, they went from knowing
little about the game to something near addiction.
They've gone bonkers!

It's the nature of any addiction to keep calling
you and calling you.

But first—as with all things created—it was the
nature of God. From the time of man's sin, God has
been calling us (Genesis 3:9). And if our hearts are
right, we come running. Peter and Andrew did.

It wasn't a rash decision, mind you. Peter and
Andrew had heard Jesus often. They had considered
His teachings and made up their minds. No, the
decision wasn't rash, but it
was firm. When the call came,
they were ready. In fact, they
were hooked. They knew that
everything else paled in com-
parison. Even a good day fishing.

TIP

MOST PEOPLE
DON'T THINK
OF ASKING FOR
A PUTTING
LESSON. MAYBE
THEY SHOULD.

GOD'S PRIORITIES

"Why do you spend money for what is not bread, and your wages for what does not satisfy? Listen carefully to Me, and eat what is good, and let your soul delight itself in abundance."

ISAIAH 55:2

In the Sermon on the Mount, Jesus pleaded with His followers not to be hung up on food and clothing. God will provide these, Jesus assured them. Consider instead, Jesus taught, how you stand in your accumulation of the treasures of heaven.

It's a sense that applies even on the golf course.

Although in many sports coaches pay lip service to the ethics of sportsmanship, winning is placed on the center stand. In golf, however, every beginners clinic is fortified with lessons in etiquette and an understanding of golf's self-applied rules. And although anger or frustration gets the better of all of us from time to time, we are reminded that there is an ethic higher than winning in golf. We must honor the very game.

In the spiritual regard, the question is much the same: Are we ready to pursue God above all else?

TIP

THE KISS METHOD—KEEP IT SIMPLE, STUPID—WORKS IN GOLF TOO!

MARCH

TIME WELL SPENT

*Unless the LORD builds the house, they labor
in vain who build it; unless the LORD guards
the city, the watchman stays awake in vain.*

PSALM 127:1

Don't worry. You're not the only golfer around who has ever wondered why you bother to practice. As infrequently as most golfers play, what might be gained in an afternoon hour on the range typically is lost by the time they get to the course several days later.

It is even more frustrating that life is sometimes like this as well. But God gives our work greater purpose. Too often we pursue our dreams, our ideas, our goals—and then we invite God to bless us. By then the house is already built. We're not doing much more than asking Him to be the welcome mat. What we need, however, is structural support.

You don't nail boards together and then see which ones fit the blueprint. You go to God first, asking, "Father, what shall I do next?" He'll lay out the plan. Then it is for you to build on it!

TIP

EVEN WHEN
YOU'RE LAYING
UP, BE SURE TO
COMMIT TO THE
SHOT AND HIT IT
AGGRESSIVELY.

CASE CLOSED

*In You, O LORD, I put my trust; let me never be
ashamed; deliver me in Your righteousness.*

PSALM 31:1

You know your weaknesses. You miss too
many fairways. You don't finish that swing.
Your wedge play is rarely crisp and clean. On the
greens, four-footers might as well be forty. You're
still laughing, though. Surely you don't feel guilty
about your suspect game. This is, after all, just golf.

In life, however—where our impatience leads
to anger, envy to revenge, lust to indiscretion, and
worry to excess—we permit ourselves those guilty
feelings. We fight wanton thoughts, wicked words,
and wayward actions. Sometimes we give in. We
sin. We cover it. We feel guilty.

But we never, never fall from grace.

Are you certain how firm this commitment is
from our heavenly Father? In the same way that
we forgive ourselves for those
golf course errors, God forgives
us when we wander from Him.
His grace is that steady, His
forgiveness that constant.

TIP

REMEMBER, YOUR
ATTITUDE ON THE
GOLF COURSE
MAKES A BIGGER
IMPRESSION THAN
YOUR PLAY.

FULL-SERVICE GOD

Many are they who say of me, "There is no help for him in God." . . . *But You, O LORD, are a shield for me, my glory and the One who lifts up my head.*

PSALM 3:2–3

Too much in our world now is self-serve. Even golfers try to fix their own games by dropping five bucks on the latest golf magazine rather than fifty on a much-needed lesson.

Some people have tried to present God as self-serve, starting with that altogether unbiblical adage "God helps those who help themselves." Surely we need to be disciplined in our walk with God—but if we can do it all by ourselves, why would we need God?

No, our God is full-service. As David proclaimed, He protects us, encourages us, and grants us mercy. He also sustains us, equips us, and saves us. What He does not do is give out piecemeal trinkets of His affection. He only gives all that He is, which you can have by giving Him all that you are—and that's not so much if you were thinking of trying to do it yourself anyway.

TIP

KEEP YOUR GAME IN SHAPE BY SWINGING A TWELVE-INCH PIECE OF PVC IN FRONT OF YOUR MIRROR.

TURNING THE TIDE

And do not be like your fathers and your brethren,
who trespassed against the LORD God of their fathers,
so that He gave them up to desolation, as you see.

2 CHRONICLES 30:7

It does no good to watch a bad swing. In fact, you have probably turned away from some really ugly efforts, hoping your first glance would not bring contagion.

Ugly can beget ugly. That's the message that Hezekiah, king of Judah, sent to his people. That's not a typical way to endear folks to your cause—showing disrespect to their families. But Hezekiah knew from his own ungodly lineage that these were not ancestors who deserved respect. His own father, Ahaz, had sacrificed Hezekiah's brothers to idols.

You, too, can turn the tide of a sinful lineage that has clouded your relationship with God. You do this simply by telling Him daily how much you want to know Him. By His wonderful Holy Spirit, He will respond to this earnest call by drawing you to Him. Really, there is no time like the present to put away the past.

TIP

A BALL THAT HAS HIT A TREE CAN BE KNOCKED OUT OF ROUND. THINK ABOUT RETIRING IT.

WHOLE NEW BALL GAME

*And you, being dead in your trespasses and the
uncircumcision of your flesh, He has made alive together
with Him, having forgiven you all trespasses, having
wiped out the handwriting of requirements that was
against us, which was contrary to us. And He has taken
it out of the way, having nailed it to the cross.*

COLOSSIANS 2:13–14

Although we play golf recreationally, many of us
would walk away from it if no one kept score.
Without competition the game would be no fun.

The minute Satan convinced Adam and Eve
to follow his lead, competition—not the friendly
kind!—entered the world. Until then, Satan had
been shut out, and he gained momentum in a most
subtle way. In our fleshly minds, he changed the
focus of the game so that we became enamored
by who scored last. Like the Hebrews, we grow
impatient with God, seeking lesser gods who appear
more "active" right now.

On the cross, Christ made
a way for us to look past the
moment and "see the final score."
Let's ask Him for the eyes always
to see the glory of that outcome.

TIP

IF THE GOOD
PLAYERS DO IT,
THERE MUST
BE A REASON.
DON'T BE AFRAID
TO COPY THEM.

OPEN THEIR EYES

And Elisha prayed, and said, "LORD,
I pray, open his eyes that he may see."

2 KINGS 6:17

Do you know folks who just don't "get" golf? They simply cannot understand the attraction of the game.

In the same way, you may have a friend who cannot see God. You make an extra effort to render patient, understanding love to this person. You have taken your friend to hear the most respected evangelists or to see those gifted in miracles. But your friend still lives in a fog. Perhaps you have even begged God in prayer for the salvation of this friend, and you can't imagine what else to do.

Now may be the time to step back and be honest with God. Say, "Lord, I don't want this friend for myself. I know that my friend will not come to You through my study or my preaching or my prayer. My friend will only come to You through You." Like Elisha, we can pray, "Lord, let my friend see."

TIP

IN A WASTE AREA, UNLIKE IN A BUNKER, YOU MAY GROUND YOUR CLUB. BE SURE YOU KNOW THE DIFFERENCE.

BETTER

So Samuel said: "Has the LORD as great delight in burnt offerings and sacrifices, as in obeying the voice of the LORD? Behold, to obey is better than sacrifice, and to heed than the fat of rams."

1 SAMUEL 15:22

One of golf's oldest adages says, "Drive for show; putt for dough." But for all the love of power these days, you wonder who is living by that adage anymore. We are so very excited to stretch our bodies and our equipment to their limits. And why not? It is so cool, so enticing, so visible.

The people of Samuel's day were intent on the visible as well, led by a king who had fallen into this trap himself. Saul believed that the details of his obedience were not so important, as long as he glossed over them with an especially visible sacrifice in the end. He brought a cover-up rather than contrition.

But our lives must be lived in spiritual balance. Obedience is our living sacrifice. If we sacrifice in any other way, our giving will be hollow at best and plainly false at worst.

> **TIP**
>
> PLAYING DOWNWIND, TEE THE BALL A LITTLE HIGHER TO GET EXTRA LOFT.

GUESSING GAME

What then? Only that in every way, whether in pretense or in truth, Christ is preached; and in this I rejoice, yes, and will rejoice.

PHILIPPIANS 1:18

Golf commentators sometimes display a disconcerting knack for climbing into a player's head after a wayward shot: "I'm not sure what he was thinking there," or "I wouldn't have played the shot that way."

Second-guessing one's motives or designs in sports may be one thing, but we should not grow comfortable with it in the church. That's where Paul was coming from in his letter to the Philippians. Some will pass on the good news of Christ with placards and pronouncements that may not fit our mold. Others will pass it on quietly, in a coffee shop or locker room. God's evangelists come with many approaches. They come with different programs, plans, and motives. But if they come with one mission—to preach "Christ the power of God and the wisdom of God" (1 Corinthians 1:23–24)—then they come with the same mission we do. Let's not question that!

TIP

PROPER ALIGNMENT BEGINS WITH A SQUARE CLUBFACE.

TRUE BLESSINGS

Blessed be the God and Father of our Lord
Jesus Christ, who has blessed us with every
spiritual blessing in the heavenly places in Christ.

EPHESIANS 1:3

Many an avid golfer has enjoyed a wonderful round of golf only to walk off the eighteenth green with trouble in mind. Troubles at home. Troubles in business. Troubles with friends.

When difficulties mount, either day by day or one upon another, it is not easy to count your blessings, especially blessings "in the heavenly realms" (Ephesians 1:3 NIV).

Today, let's remember these blessings. Foremost is salvation, built on the dual blessings of grace and mercy that enable us to live in spite of our sinful natures. And there is the joy of the Lord, which is our strength; the peace that passes understanding; the love as strong as death; and the friendship of the Creator of the universe.

These blessings matter deeply to our spirits. They are not always blessings we can see, but that may be best, for sometimes what we see will look very, very bad.

TIP

FROM A GREENSIDE BUNKER, "SPLASH" THE SAND UP ONTO THE GREEN AND THE BALL WILL COME OUT WITH IT.

PRESENT AND POWERFUL

> *Then he said to Him, "If Your Presence does*
> *not go with us, do not bring us up from here. For*
> *how then will it be known that Your people and*
> *I have found grace in Your sight, except You go with*
> *us? So we shall be separate, Your people and I, from*
> *all the people who are upon the face of the earth."*
>
> EXODUS 33:15–16

Moses would have known what it was like to be a golfer, playing an individual sport but engaged in four-hour conversations with his partners.

On the one hand, Moses' forty years as a lonely shepherd had left him weak of speech and weak of conviction. Yet God had given Moses this crowd to lead. And knowing the plans of His God, Moses reckoned that he was going to be charged with leading these people against enemies into the promised land. Moses knew he stood a chance only if he had the presence of God. Some biblical lessons are more obvious than others. This is one of them. Without God, without His living presence in our lives, we have no distinction or purpose. But fortified by His presence, we can be victorious people, distinguished on the earth.

TIP

YOU WANT TO BE RELAXED WITH YOUR PUTTER, NOT FLIMSY. COMMIT TO YOUR STROKE.

ARGUING WITH GOD

Then Hezekiah turned his face toward the wall, and prayed to the LORD, and said, "Remember now, O LORD, I pray, how I have walked before You in truth and with a loyal heart, and have done what is good in Your sight." And Hezekiah wept bitterly.

ISAIAH 38:2–3

Golf is a lot more enjoyable when you compete with trustworthy partners. They're not angling the rules to get an advantage. Rather, because they have proven themselves, you're willing to give these people a full, fair hearing when they do ask for relief.

Threatened by a deadly illness, King Hezekiah of Judah received such a hearing from God. Hezekiah reminded the Lord that he had walked in faithful obedience. The king pleaded for his very life. And God, in one of the most direct answers we see in all of Scripture, rewarded Hezekiah with fifteen more years.

Theologically, we cannot carry this story too far. God's greater purposes and our personal desires do not always mesh. But Hezekiah's example is clear: you have a right to argue with God. The question is, will your argument, your reputation, be as strong as Hezekiah's?

> **TIP**
>
> LIMIT YOUR SWING THOUGHTS AND YOU'RE LESS LIKELY TO LIMIT YOUR SWING!

SPANNING IT ALL

He has put eternity in their hearts, except
that no one can find out the work that
God does from beginning to end.

ECCLESIASTES 3:11

Here's a simple truth about golfers: although we play the longest of games, we are always yearning for more. This might be a subject to broach with nonbelieving friends who do not reason with their lives as they reason with their golf. Life, too, is long, yet relatively few people yearn for more. Few pursue eternity.

Are we remembering to live eternally ourselves? People would see what it is that makes us different . . .

. . . if we remembered that only three things go on forever: God, His Word, and people . . .

. . . if we remembered that only three traits remain: faith, hope, and love . . .

. . . if we remembered that life is like the pains of labor, and eternity with Christ is like the overwhelming joy of the newborn child (John 16:21).

If we remembered these things and lived them each day, eternity would be a whole lot more attractive, don't you think?

TIP

IF ONLY ONCE, HIRE A CADDIE. YOU WON'T REGRET THE EXPERIENCE.

SHARE ON

Blessed be the God and Father of our Lord Jesus Christ, the Father of mercies and God of all comfort, who comforts us in all our tribulation, that we may be able to comfort those who are in any trouble, with the comfort with which we ourselves are comforted by God.

2 CORINTHIANS 1:3–4

Ever get a great golf tip? It's pretty hard to keep quiet about it, isn't it? When a tip really works, improving your shot making and lowering your score, you're excited to tell others about that tip.

So it should be with all we receive from God. We are, as Abraham was in the beginning, "blessed to be a blessing." This isn't some quaint suggestion. This is the whole message of the kingdom: we pass on what we have received because it is of infinite and eternal value. After all, you cannot lose love by giving it away!

In fact, this is the general rule of grace—freely we have received, freely we give. We forgive, we encourage, we comfort, we teach, we pray, we show mercy. On and on it goes, for on and on it is given to us by our ever-loving God.

> **TIP**
>
> REPAIRED BALL MARKS AND RAKED SAND TRAPS ARE YOUR GIFT TO THE PLAYERS BEHIND YOU.

VISUALIZING LIFE

A man's heart plans his way,
but the LORD directs his steps.

PROVERBS 16:9

We have all heard the same instruction: Visualize the shot you want to hit. Then swing the club.

And we all know the truth: rarely does our result match our vision.

Solomon noticed a very similar circumstance in life. By nature, we are planners. We are, after all, created by God, and He has made us an intelligent people. We think, we plan, we dream. Yet none of this removes God from His sovereign position. So even Solomon, Scripture's wisest ruler, observed that his plans were not universally successful. For God knew better, and sometimes He changed even the king's finest plans.

When our golf shots do not match what we have visualized, we do not quit the game. More likely, we work harder at it. Let it be so in our relationship with God. Have your life plans collapsed? Don't give up. Just look to increase your fullness in Him.

TIP

WHEN WATCHING A GOOD PLAYER PRACTICE, NOTICE TEMPO ABOVE ALL ELSE.

KNOWING GOD

The fear of the LORD is the beginning of wisdom, and the knowledge of the Holy One is understanding.

PROVERBS 9:10

We all have golf partners who are golf trivia maniacs. They alternately fascinate us with information and bore us with it. For most of us, all that information—about players, courses, swings, clubs, carts, balls—amounts to real overload.

But there is one type of knowledge that should never tire us—the knowledge of the Eternal and Infinite One, the mighty God of heaven. It is a knowledge that results in fear of the Lord, which in turn leads to wisdom.

You see, if we know God and who He is, we will wisely fear Him, and that healthy fear will in turn cause us to act wisely. If we were created by a perfect God and our lives are acted out before Him—and if we remember this day to day—we will watch our every action and every thought. That is real wisdom.

TIP

RUNNING OUT OF BALLS IS A BIG EMBARRASSMENT. BE SURE YOU'RE STOCKED.

BEST WISHES

For this reason we also, since the day we heard it, do not cease to pray for you, and to ask that you may be filled with the knowledge of His will in all wisdom and spiritual understanding.

COLOSSIANS 1:9

As golfers, we are not always trained well to root for others. Of course, that is the nature of competition. It pits one against another. Paul wrote of "winning the race," so competition can provide a positive spark in our lives. But far more frequently, Scripture points to an entirely different approach that should dominate the culture of Christ's body.

At its core, that culture should be one of love. We have a shining example of such love early in Paul's letter to the Colossians.

Paul wrote that he and his partner Timothy began praying for the Colossians not when they had first met them, but even before that—when they had only first heard of them. Now, that's a great way to start a relationship! Start it with prayer, a prayer that God would fill our new friends with the knowledge of His will.

TIP

TO GET TO KNOW A COURSE, WALK. TO GET TO KNOW A PARTNER, RIDE.

SELF-MADE?

For we are the circumcision, who worship
God in the Spirit, rejoice in Christ Jesus,
and have no confidence in the flesh.

PHILIPPIANS 3:3

The physical body is the prize and the curse of any athlete. Each season swimmers swim faster, baseball players hit more home runs, and golfers send drives sailing farther down the fairway. Yet all athletes also face the risk of career-threatening injury.

It makes sense, then, that Paul warned the Philippians not to place confidence in the flesh, neither in the present nor in the past. As much as we'd like the credit, we do not get into heaven because we have "done good" but because good has been done in us. While we are still here on earth, we want that heavenly good to play itself out in the way we serve Christ. For it is His flesh, His body broken on the cross and renewed by resurrection, that makes us forever confident. It is boasting in Him that gives us our greatest joy.

TIP

KEEP A RULE
BOOK IN YOUR
BAG AND USE IT.
YOU'LL BE
A BETTER
PLAYER FOR IT.

WHAT WE REALLY WANT

For in this we groan, earnestly desiring to be clothed with our habitation which is from heaven.

2 CORINTHIANS 5:2

You know what you most hate about golf, don't you? It's the same thing we all hate: we can never play to what we believe is our true potential. We are always a shot or two (or ten) away.

The struggle between our bodies and our souls is much the same. Our bodies are never where our souls want them to be. We think dumb things. We do dumb things. And we are most uncomfortable with this imperfection.

We are wrong to see this dissatisfaction negatively, however. When we were made new in Christ and our lives were given to Him, so, too, were our souls. And they will never be satisfied anywhere aside from their true home, which is in heaven. We will no longer be comfortable with sin. That is a very good thing.

> **TIP**
>
> DISTANCE IS A PRODUCT OF TORQUE, SO DON'T RUSH YOUR DOWNSWING.

NUMBER ONE

But earnestly desire the best gifts. And yet
I show you a more excellent way.

1 CORINTHIANS 12:31

Those who have read the Old Testament law and Paul's New Testament epistles know just how many instructions are laid out there.

That's the trouble. It's easy to fall into a pattern of following instructions for instructions' sake. Like a golfer who has not taken a lesson in a while, we soon become victims of our lifeless habits. That golfer progressively grips the club more weakly or opens the stance a bit more each day to compensate for that ugly slice. Likewise, we can become slaves to comfort in our walk of faith.

But in Scripture there is a tried-and-true way, superior to simply following the instructions. It is the way of love. Christ taught it, and the apostles reiterated it. In fact, James called it "the royal law." Superseding the instructions, love brings life to obeying God. No wonder it is the most excellent way.

TIP

ON AN UNEVEN LIE, SET YOUR SHOULDERS PARALLEL TO THE SLOPE OF THE GROUND.

COMMITMENT

*"I know your works, that you are neither
cold nor hot. I could wish you were cold or hot.
So then, because you are lukewarm, and neither
cold nor hot, I will vomit you out of My mouth."*

REVELATION 3:15–16

If you spend time at the driving range when the
serious players come out, you have seen your share
of disciples—those who follow. Golf's disciples attach
themselves to a teacher who advises and ignites them.
Sometimes these teachers give simple, small counsel.
Other times, they are in the overhaul business.

Many players, however, are unwilling to make
such a full-fledged commitment. And the changes
often bring an undoing rather than a redoing.

Spiritually, there are also those (perhaps all of
us to one degree or another) who never make the
full commitment necessary to see real change in
their lives. Christ wants a commitment that burns
for Him. And He wants us to
use such fervor to disciple others.
Those new to the faith need to be
encouraged: "Stick with it. It will
work." Taking this as your role
will keep your own fire burning!

TIP

ON AN UPHILL
LIE, PLAY THE
BALL A BIT
FORWARD IN
YOUR STANCE.

FREE SLAVES

For he who is called in the Lord while a
slave is the Lord's freedman. Likewise
he who is called while free is Christ's slave.

1 CORINTHIANS 7:22

Golfers should readily understand the complexities of being two people at once. Every time we have followed a perfect drive with a bladed wedge, we remember our childhood readings of Jekyll and Hyde. So we have extra insight into Paul's intriguing statement about the overlap between the slave and the free man that indwells us all.

Paul told literal slaves that, despite their earthly position, no spiritual bonds held them. Although not always free to come and go as they pleased, they were free from the bondage of sin and free to acquire the joy of the Lord and the peace that passes understanding.

Yet those who had freely walked among earth's enticements but now had become followers of Christ were to make themselves slaves to righteousness, choosing the leading of the Holy Spirit in every endeavor.

Free in Christ, then, we choose to enslave ourselves to Him.

TIP

ON A DOWNHILL
LIE, PLAY
THE BALL A BIT
BACK IN
YOUR STANCE.

JUST DESSERTS

For what credit is it if, when you are beaten for your faults, you take it patiently? But when you do good and suffer, if you take it patiently, this is commendable before God. For to this you were called, because Christ also suffered for us, leaving us an example, that you should follow His steps.

1 PETER 2:20–21

Did you deserve your last bad round of golf? If you had been practicing diligently, maybe not. But if you laid off for six months, you surely didn't go out with high expectations.

Peter addressed two sides to suffering—the suffering that is deserved and the suffering that is not. It is easier, he implied, to bear the pain when it comes from our own sin: the long rebuilding of trust after vows have been broken, the contrite restitution when a rumor runs amok, the months behind bars for playing loose with other men's money. More noble it is, Peter wrote, to patiently endure the suffering that comes upon us undeserved, particularly when it comes as a result of our life in Christ. We don't seek suffering unnecessarily but look to endure it righteously, with self-control.

TIP

FOR CHIP SHOTS, FOCUS ON THE LANDING POINT AS YOUR TARGET, NOT ON THE HOLE.

IF YOU SAY SO

*You were enriched in everything by Him
in all utterance and all knowledge.*

1 CORINTHIANS 1:5

Stepping back from the game, we sometimes look at our poor behavior and say to ourselves, "I need to stay in control of my emotions on the golf course. I'm certainly not glorifying God."

Such self-directed sermonettes come from our heavenly Father. Before you knew Christ, you didn't preach to yourself in this way. Even if you knew in your spirit the kind of character traits you should have been displaying, you weren't going to be so bothered with changing your behavior that you would read or talk to someone about how to act. And you surely weren't going to beat yourself up about it!

But just because something is easier said than done, this does not eliminate the value of saying it. In fact, if what we tell ourselves moves us to the next level of commitment to Christ, it is something that needs to be said.

TIP

ELIMINATE MOVING PARTS WITH YOUR PUTTER. LET YOUR SHOULDERS ALONE DO THE WORK.

EARNESTLY SEEKING

*But without faith it is impossible to please Him, for
he who comes to God must believe that He is, and
that He is a rewarder of those who diligently seek Him.*

HEBREWS 11:6

You have heard it, and maybe you have said it.
They are the words of a golfer who just cannot
hit it straight: "I'm searching for a swing, anything
that will work." Oh, we are a desperate people, we
golfers! For all the talk of rhythm and swing plane
and letting the clubhead do the work, when we get
to the course, we'll accept anything that gets the
ball on the green.

When it comes to theology, a lot of us know
plenty of right things to say. But what God is
wondering is how we are doing "out on the course."
Are we chasing after our Savior?

By the Holy Spirit's inspiration the writer of
Hebrews coupled two powerful thoughts: Do you
believe that God exists, and do
you earnestly seek Him? It could
well be that the seeking is what
confirms the belief.

TIP

GOLF IS VERY
TECHNICAL,
BUT YOU
WANT TO
PLAY IT SIMPLY.

NEAR MISSES

*Blessed be the God and Father of our Lord
Jesus Christ, who according to His abundant
mercy has begotten us again to a living hope through
the resurrection of Jesus Christ from the dead, to an
inheritance incorruptible and undefiled and that
does not fade away, reserved in heaven for you.*

1 PETER 1:3–4

A round shows up just to torture you every now
and then. A million little misses, and a score
that adds up to awful. But what gets remembered?
The birdie you made on the course's toughest hole!

Many well-meaning people expect to arrive in
heaven and recount their lives in the same fashion.
Their collection of sins would not mean much to the
tabloids, so find comfort that on Judgment Day, the
balance of their lives will include a few great moments
that they can present during the deliberation. But
they add up, all those little sins. One a day makes
twenty-five thousand in a lifetime.
That's a weighty scale to tip. We're
not getting into an impeccable
heaven on our own. The joy of
eternity is ours only through Jesus.
We must trust Him. In the story
of our lives, He is the birdie on the
toughest hole.

TIP

REMEMBER,
WHEN HITTING
INTO THE WIND,
LEFT AND RIGHT
BALL FLIGHT WILL
BE EXAGGERATED.

OUT OF OUR HANDS

You do not know what will happen tomorrow.

JAMES 4:14

If you have ever stood on the back patio of a home along a fairway, you know the odd sensation of seeing a golfer swing but not being able to see the result. Although you can watch the ball begin its flight, you have no idea where it lands or the outcome of the golfer's play on the hole. A good wedge or a made putt can turn a bad hole into a good one quite quickly.

God can do the same in our lives. He can turn tragedy into triumph. So He says to us, through His Son and through His writers, to live each day as its own, with a common approach. Worry? No! Concern? No! Plotting? No! What we are to do each day, knowing that our God is in full control, is this: trust Him. Tomorrow is in His hands.

> **TIP**
>
> KEEP UP WITH THE GROUP IN FRONT, NOT JUST AHEAD OF THE GROUP BEHIND.

SLOW

So then, my beloved brethren, let every man
be swift to hear, slow to speak, slow to wrath.

JAMES 1:19

In golf, we've been taught never to play slowly. Many courses have target times posted around the course, encouraging you to keep up. With God, however, speed is not always a requirement.

We must be slow to speak, thinking first. We frequently violate that principle with our words. No wonder we have to eat so many of them!

And we must be slow to become angry. Our anger usually exposes the weaknesses in us, not the shortcomings of another. Anger has a nasty tendency to overshadow the original error and turn gape-mouthed faces in our direction.

To help us slow down, God tells us to listen at the outset, which gives us a full understanding of others' circumstances. And when we know what others are facing, we're more likely to respond with compassion—which may mean saying nothing at all.

TIP

"THE MORE
I PRACTICE,
THE LUCKIER
I GET."
—GARY PLAYER

MARCH 27

102

GO FOR THE GREEN

GIVE IT UP

[Cast] all your care upon Him,
for He cares for you.

1 PETER 5:7

How far down would we find golf on God's list of priorities? Although He surely cares for those in the golf business, it is easy to doubt that God really could take an interest in the game of an amateur who plays every now and then.

Yet golf makes all of us anxious at one time or another. And when Peter wrote that we should cast all our anxiety upon God, he meant that very word—"all." There was no picking and choosing, no prioritizing to be done.

Now, it may seem rather silly that as you stand over a knee-knocking, left-to-right breaking four-footer, you stop and cast your anxiety on God. But that just might be the kind of practice your faith needs! If we can give up the games to Him, how much more ready we will be to give up the things of real life!

TIP

PAY TO BUILD
YOUR SWING
FIRST; PAY TO
STOCK YOUR BAG
SECOND.

BEING TRANSFORMED

*But we all, with unveiled face, beholding as
in a mirror the glory of the Lord, are being
transformed into the same image from glory
to glory, just as by the Spirit of the Lord.*

2 CORINTHIANS 3:18

Instruction you receive from a teaching professional will nearly always be better than what you can extract from a magazine. The teacher sees you, gets to know your swing, and then begins the teaching.

Through Christ, Paul saw his protégés as well. He saw that Christ, through the Holy Spirit, had marked each one of us in ways that made the rest of his teaching—what is righteous and what is not—possible for us to follow. One of these marks was revealed to the Corinthians: we are being transformed into Christ's likeness.

This transformation is not something that we can achieve for ourselves through hard work or extended study. We cannot attend lectures to attain it. We can't even attend church to get it! We must simply surrender our lives to Christ, for God transforms those who call on His name.

TIP

LEARN MATCH PLAY. IT WILL MAKE FOR QUICKER GAMES IN YOUR GROUP.

PRIVILEGED PEOPLE

But who am I, and who are my people, that we should be able to offer so willingly as this? For all things come from You, and of Your own we have given You.

1 CHRONICLES 29:14

We are certainly privileged to play golf. To have income and time enough to break away even for just nine holes is something we likely take for granted more than we should.

David never forgot the simplicity of his roots. From the fields he was called, an afterthought on the day that Samuel came to anoint a king. Only after years of difficult and trusting obedience did David receive the fruit of his anointing.

Yet David never saw himself as the source of his own success. When all that luxury had come his way, he still gave credit where it was due: to God, the source of all David possessed.

So we, too, would be wise to give God the hours that we spend on the golf course, to give Him our attitude and our conversation. For it is He who has given us golf in the first place.

TIP

IF YOUR REGULAR GROUP PLAYS LOOSELY, BE SURE TO FRESHEN UP ON THE RULES BEFORE PLAYING A TOURNAMENT.

WHAT COUNTS

And David's heart condemned him after he had numbered the people. So David said to the LORD, "I have sinned greatly in what I have done; but now, I pray, O LORD, take away the iniquity of Your servant, for I have done very foolishly."

2 SAMUEL 24:10

Golfers are counting people. Most everything we do on the golf course relates to a number. Beyond score, we can tell you how many greens we hit, how many putts we had, what our index is.

The trouble with counting in golf is the trouble with counting in every other arena of life. Numbers can become definitions. They can come to say too much about us: our age, our wage, our net worth.

Consider how we use that last number. We do not say, "You have financial holdings worth this much when you subtract the liabilities." Instead we say, "This is your net worth." Aren't you glad that this is only a financial application? For spiritually, we all have the same gross worth. Sinful people, we all are bankrupt. But if we are in Christ, our net worth is something infinitely greater—it is equal to the riches of heaven!

> **TIP**
>
> GOOD RECOVERIES GET YOU OUT OF TROUBLE, BUT STRAIGHT DRIVES KEEP YOU OUT OF IT.

GO FOR THE GREEN

THE MAJORS SEASON

It begins each year in April, with the coming of "the tradition unlike any other." Professional golfers hone their games for the Masters at Augusta National, and in the ensuing months, the level of challenge is raised again and again for golf's most important contests—the majors.

The height of the season comes in June when the PGA, the Senior PGA, and LPGA Tours stage four or five major championships among them, depending on the year's calendar.

In our own lives, we, too, are faced from time to time with circumstances greater than the usual matters of life. For Moses, these moments came in Pharaoh's court, for David in the Valley of Elah, for Daniel in the lions' den. At these times, they had to raise the level of their "game." To do so, they always went one place for strength. They turned to God.

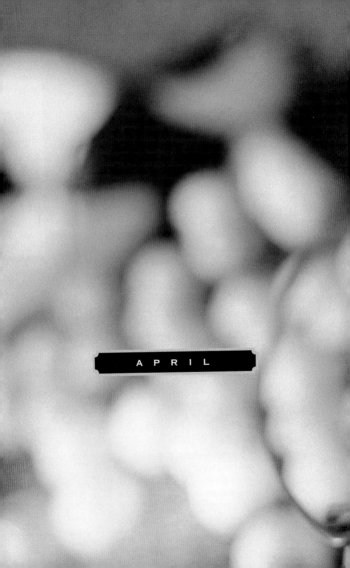

APRIL

FULLY ACCREDITED

"Men of Israel, hear these words: Jesus of Nazareth, a Man attested by God to you by miracles, wonders, and signs which God did through Him in your midst, as you yourselves also know."

ACTS 2:22

It's a lot of fun when the pros come to town. These greats have proven over time that they know how to play marvelous golf. They have credibility above all other golfers—when it comes to golf.

So what makes Jesus credible? Far more than golf—and far more than any one trait. Peter chose three in his message to the Acts crowd: Jesus' miracles, signs, and wonders. These acts were so unique that they established Him as the One we should notice above all others.

When we show Christ to others, we want to present His incomparable fullness. He was miraculous. He was obedient to the Father. He died to cleanse our sin. And He rose to guarantee eternal life. All of these accredit Him to us and to the world.

TIP

IF YOUR BALL LIES ON A SAND-FILLED DIVOT, CONSIDER A BUMP-AND-RUN SHOT.

IN THE NEIGHBORHOOD

So we, being many, are one body in Christ,
and individually members of one another.

ROMANS 12:5

In golf, there may be no one to pass or kick to, but don't fool yourself—professional golf is not an individual sport. In order to be able to concentrate on what they do best—play golf—tour players need a quality caddie and an attentive manager.

Like tour golf, life is not an individual sport. We cannot pretend to live high on a hill with God alone. He has placed us smack in the middle of a great neighborhood of faith called the body of Christ. Each of us, no matter where we work or how large our family is or what we do for leisure, has the common goal of strengthening our relationship with God. And each of us has the responsibility of helping our neighbors along in this regard. To serve God, we, too, must stay right in the thick of the crowd—His crowd.

TIP

YOU CAN KEEP YOUR BODY STEADY WHILE PUTTING BY BRINGING YOUR KNEES TOGETHER.

OUR GUARANTEE

Now He who has prepared us for this very thing is
God, who also has given us the Spirit as a guarantee.

2 CORINTHIANS 5:5

There are no guarantees in golf. One week, a tour favorite breaks the tournament record, and the next week he misses the cut. Oh, what a game!

But with a God who is the same yesterday, today, and forever, there is nothing quite like the hopeful assurance of His everlasting love. In fact, Paul wrote, it is precisely what we are made for. Establishing a stark dichotomy between heaven and earth, the apostle likened our earthly existence to life in a tent—flimsy, cold, and susceptible to every storm.

But for our souls, there is another, more wonderful story. Because we have placed our faith in Christ, we are headed for our eternal house, for which a deposit has already been paid by Jesus Christ. This is a deal that cannot fall through, sealed by God Himself. It is the sweetest guarantee.

TIP

IMMEDIATELY AFTER YOUR ROUND, DECIDE WHICH SWING THOUGHT YOU'LL BRING BACK NEXT TIME.

THE JOY OF THE LORD

*"Do not sorrow, for the joy of
the LORD is your strength."*

NEHEMIAH 8:10

In golf, kissing a trophy often represents the height of celebration. Maybe you harbor a secret hope that these winners get home and go temporarily nuts. A barrage of victory shouts. Some good old-fashioned jumping up and down. Even a cluster of really bad dance steps.

At least this is what the joy of the Lord would look like.

It's true. Through Jeremiah, God foretold the celebration that would take place upon the restoration of His people to Him. There would be tambourines and dancing, the planting of new vineyards and the enjoyment of their fruit, clarion calls to worship, singing for joy and shouting unto the nations. The celebrants would come from everywhere and include people of all kinds. Their mourning would turn to gladness (Jeremiah 31:1–14).

You see, there is really nothing wrong with quiet "maturity." It just might not be very good practice for heaven.

> **TIP**
>
> ALWAYS ASK
> IF A COURSE'S
> DISTANCE
> MARKERS ARE TO
> THE FRONT OR
> THE CENTER OF
> THE GREEN.

ON THE BOARD

God was in Christ reconciling the world to
Himself, not imputing their trespasses to them,
and has committed to us the word of reconciliation.

2 CORINTHIANS 5:19

As a golf fan, do you like watching the leader-board? Do you want to know who is climbing and who is fading? It sure gives you a sense of how fickle the game is, even for the tour players.

A lot of us would feel better if we could see in big numbers just how we're doing in life! The trouble is that we may look at our sin and disqualify ourselves from God's kingdom on the basis of our poor living. In pride, we think that we have "excelled" so greatly at sin that not even God can forgive us. Oh, how we must learn that God is exactly what we are not! God does not watch the scoreboard, ticking off our many sins. Rather, God sees the Jumbotron, where He watches the death and resurrection of Jesus Christ, the stunning act that reconciled us to God.

TIP

SOMETIMES IT'S BETTER NOT TO CALL "FORE" IF YOUR SHOUT WILL CAUSE PLAYERS TO RUN INTO THE BALL.

FITTING REMEMBRANCES

"Then you shall answer them that the waters of the Jordan were cut off before the ark of the covenant of the LORD; when it crossed over the Jordan, the waters of the Jordan were cut off. And these stones shall be for a memorial to the children of Israel forever."

JOSHUA 4:7

Perhaps the most well-known of golf memorials is Augusta National's Sarazan Bridge. What does it commemorate? Ah, that is the question!

In the Bible, memorials were built to remember the works of God. Such memorials were never grandiose, as we might build them today. They typically consisted of stones in a heap—and often a small heap at that. When Joshua heard the word of the Lord regarding a memorial to remember the ceased flow of the Jordan River, the instruction was to use twelve stones only, one gathered by a man from each tribe.

The idea with noting times and places in our spiritual lives is not to build great monuments; it is to remember the One who has given us those moments. For what we want to remember is the work of His hands, not the work of ours.

> **TIP**
>
> GENE SARAZEN WON THE 1935 MASTERS AFTER MAKING DOUBLE EAGLE ON THE PAR-5 FIFTEENTH HOLE, A FEAT COMMEMORATED BY THE SARAZEN BRIDGE.

COMMANDER

But Simon answered and said to Him, "Master,
we have toiled all night and caught nothing;
nevertheless at Your word I will let down the net."

LUKE 5:5

To match all the dreaming we golfers do of the Masters, let's consider for some moments the Master, or "commander," as the title is rightly rendered from the Greek.

At the water's edge, when Simon Peter and his crew had returned from a luckless night, Jesus said in so many words, "Go back out. Do it like this." It is tough enough to be told that our job was not done well, but to be told by one who doesn't even share our profession—ouch!

Yet Peter knew that Jesus' knowledge encompassed every subject. Pride swallowed, Peter obeyed. He did not obey because Jesus was a more experienced fisherman. Rather, Peter obeyed because Jesus was Master. His authority extended even beyond His own experience.

Today, we still hesitate, unsure that Jesus knows best. He does. We should simply be answering Him, "Yes, Master, because you say so."

> **TIP**
>
> ALL PRACTICE REGIMENS MEAN LITTLE IF YOU DON'T PICK A TARGET FOR EACH SHOT.

TRUE HEROES

Receive [Epaphroditus] therefore in the Lord with all gladness, and hold such men in esteem; because for the work of Christ he came close to death, not regarding his life, to supply what was lacking in your service toward me.

PHILIPPIANS 2:29–30

It has always been hard to be a sports fan without selecting heroes. In golf, fans connect with pros not only as golfers but often as people with endearing personalities too.

Surely there are no men or women that God "looks up to." But perhaps there are those whom God would want us to look up to, if not as heroes, then as prime examples. This is what Paul was hinting at when he wrote to the Philippians about Epaphroditus. He gave them a background of this extraordinary man and told them how much he would lift their spirits. And he told them just how to receive them: "Honor men like him" (Philippians 2:29 NIV).

As followers of Christ, we must remember that our heroes will look quite different from those the world would choose. God's heroes are identified by actions produced in faith, not by their earthly accomplishments.

TIP

KEEP A BROKEN TEE IN YOUR POCKET TO USE ON PAR-3S.

GO FOR THE GREEN | 117

HOPE BEATS HYPE

For the Lord Himself will descend from heaven with a shout, with the voice of an archangel, and with the trumpet of God. And the dead in Christ will rise first. Then we who are alive and remain shall be caught up together with them in the clouds to meet the Lord in the air. And thus we shall always be with the Lord. Therefore comfort one another with these words.

1 THESSALONIANS 4:16–18

In sports, half the fun is looking forward. Before the tournament, we are all experts with "sure" ideas about who will win.

When it comes to our future as followers of Christ, we can indeed be experts, just by turning to our Bibles. We can all read the signs: numerous wars, Israel's nationhood, the sinful pursuits of man. Indeed, it appears that Christ's return is imminent.

Take heart! Where hype can fail, the hope of Christ cannot. His coming will far exceed our expectations. This hope is the very thing established to encourage us in Christ. We are literally meant to regale one another with this story as often as we like. It will carry us above the hoopla and the fray.

> **TIP**
>
> RIDING CARTS ARE AN AMERICAN PHENOMENON; IF YOU TRAVEL, PREPARE TO WALK.

NOT SO PAINFUL

But may the God of all grace, who called us to His eternal glory by Christ Jesus, after you have suffered a while, perfect, establish, strengthen, and settle you.

1 PETER 5:10

Years of preparation allow tour professionals to extricate themselves from the most difficult of golf's troubles.

Tough questions require us to be prepared as well. Among these is the old conundrum: If God is loving, why does He allow suffering in the world? Biblically, this question has a clear answer: God did not introduce suffering to the world. Man's disobedience established suffering, the natural result of sin.

But in our own quiet moments, a variation of that same question can haunt us. Why, if we have committed our lives to God, would He require us to endure suffering? Scripture gives at least three reasons. First, in our own suffering we identify with Christ. Second, through suffering God trains us. And third, our suffering helps us understand and soothe the suffering of others. Suffering still hurts. But these explanations do help us understand that God, above all, understands us.

TIP

"WINTER RULES" ARE FOR THE COURSE TO DECLARE, NOT THE INDIVIDUAL PLAYER.

ONE WAY

Teach me Your way, O LORD; I will walk
in Your truth; unite my heart to fear Your name.

PSALM 86:11

In the world of professional golf, the relationship between a player and his teacher can be precarious. If the player, who does the hiring, is not performing well, he may head off to find another mentor.

In life, however, if we have chosen God as our teacher, we must stick with Him. In the flawless world He created, trust was complete. Adam and Eve lacked no confidence in their Creator. Until the seed of independent possibility was sown in them—"Here's a decision you can make without God"—they had no gross pride or distrust.

Ever since that first I-can-do-this-on-my-own act of sin, God has worked to restore trust to His people. It is a simple message: "Follow Me, follow only Me, and you can count on knowing all you need to know." David, in Psalm 86, told God yes, he would follow.

Let's make David's decision our decision.

TIP

MAKE A FULL SHOULDER TURN, ESPECIALLY ON THE FIRST TEE.

FIRST STEPS

And Hezekiah received the letter from the hand of the messengers, and read it; and Hezekiah went up to the house of the LORD, and spread it before the LORD.

2 KINGS 19:14

Lay up or go for it, punch out or swing away. As golfers, we face challenges and enjoy taking the daring road.

But away from golf, we know the challenges are greater, even if not of the magnitude that Hezekiah faced from the haughty Sennacherib: "I'm coming to kill you—and all your people too!" Hezekiah went immediately to the Lord. Simply and literally, he lay history's most threatening letter before God. Hezekiah told God: "This one is Yours, Lord." And indeed, God made it His. Sennacherib lost 185,000 soldiers in the middle of the night; then he lost his life.

We have no guarantee that God's response to our circumstances will be as definitive as it was for Hezekiah. But we know now how Hezekiah gained such a response. He went to God first. When will we go to Him?

TIP

INCREASED WEIGHT ON YOUR FORWARD HIP AT ADDRESS WILL PROMOTE A DOWNWARD ANGLE OF ATTACK.

POWER PACKED

And while the crowds were thickly gathered together, He began to say, "This is an evil generation. It seeks a sign, and no sign will be given to it except the sign of Jonah the prophet."

LUKE 11:29

Scott Verplank, the longtime PGA Tour pro who has battled diabetes since childhood, offers a mighty encouragement to all others who aspire to rise above struggle to attain greatness. In offering hope, however, those who have overcome adversity will never be anything greater than examples: people who have dreamed, worked, and achieved earthly success.

In His own life, Jesus rejected requests for "signs" because He knew that's all they were—signs. He was disappointed that with the King among them, the people still sought the entertainment of magicians. In golfing terms, this would be like qualifying for the Tour, then continuing to walk outside the ropes. Our Savior is not about displays of power. He is power Himself. And He is ready to indwell you with that power. How much greater that is than simply seeing a miracle!

> **TIP**
>
> IMAGINE THE FLOW OF A POURED-OUT BUCKET OF WATER TO HELP READ THE BREAK OF A GREEN.

CONFIDENCE

> *"Be of good courage, and let us be strong for our people and for the cities of our God. And may the LORD do what is good in His sight."*
>
> 2 SAMUEL 10:12

Perhaps because golf is not the kind of sport where we set out to hinder our opponent, we don't get ourselves all charged up before the game has even started.

This may make it hard for us etiquette-minded golfers to understand the Old Testament warriors who fought fiercely for God. In battle they stood up to challenges that threatened God's place in their lives. Still, Joab was careful with his confidence. "Let us fight bravely," Joab told his brother, Abishai. "The LORD will do what is good in his sight" (2 Samuel 10:12 NIV).

That is the strange confidence of a leader committed to his calling. Joab knew he was called to obedience, not success. Sometimes we may do just as God has us do, and in the end it looks like failure. But if we know God and His calling on our life, we can proceed with confidence. We can leave the outcome up to Him.

TIP

EMOTION LESSENS YOUR POTENTIAL. TRY TO KEEP AN EVEN KEEL.

GETAWAY

Yet the news about him spread all the more,
so that crowds of people came to hear him
and to be healed of their sicknesses. But Jesus
often withdrew to lonely places and prayed.

LUKE 5:15–16 NIV

Like professional golfers who hone their games in silent solitude then must take large amounts of time to converse with the press, we all have little parts of our jobs that aren't so fun.

Although Jesus came to save the many, He did not always love to be surrounded by the many. It isn't easy teaching those who are not interested in learning. They come for the spectacle, or they come to disagree, or they come to be seen.

But Jesus had an out. It was the jump to solitude, to the comfort of silence. Even for those of us who are not famous, the crowds can seem too loud at times. But we have a Savior who stands above the crowd. He calls our name. And if we have ears to hear, we will take quiet time for Him alone, to listen and respond.

TIP

IMPROVING PLAYERS LOWER THEIR SCORES BY KNOWING HOW FAR THEY HIT EACH CLUB.

*But when His disciples saw it, they were
indignant, saying, "Why this waste?"*

MATTHEW 26:8

APRIL 16

A commitment can seem silly at times to those who do not make it. We forgive professionals who work hard at improving their game, but an amateur—well, why place such an emphasis on something with no payoff?

Such critical marveling went on when a woman came to Jesus and doused His feet with perfume. It was a perfume of great expense, a detail that did not escape the tongues of Jesus' disciples. Jesus was quick to rebuke them. This perfume, poured out in ludicrous excess, was a symbol of the woman's great love for Jesus and her understanding of the death Jesus would suffer. But the disciples were still blind to the things of heaven and too often distracted by the things of this world.

The woman was instead abandoned to Jesus, abandoning the economy of the world. In making her extravagant statement, she was discipling even the disciples.

> **TIP**
>
> TO SPEED PLAY,
> CALCULATE YOUR
> DISTANCE AND
> SELECT YOUR
> CLUB WHILE
> OTHERS ARE
> PLAYING.

TOO MUCH
OF A GOOD THING

So the children of Israel also wept again and said: "Who will give us meat to eat? We remember the fish which we ate freely in Egypt, the cucumbers, the melons, the leeks, the onions, and the garlic; but now our whole being is dried up; there is nothing at all except this manna before our eyes!"

NUMBERS 11:4–6

Why do we keep coming back to the golf course? Many would say it is a good score at the last or the one great shot on the nastiest hole. More likely, bad shots cause us to return. If we could replace all those ridiculous double bogeys with bogeys and pars, then maybe we could dream of more birdies.

It's a spiritual principle too. Our many failures keep us coming back to God, for in good times, we tend to elevate the value of our own worth. God gave the newly freed Israelites plenty of a good thing, and they insisted that they deserved better. But these people didn't need all the food, all the space, all the stuff. These people needed God. For only He can satisfy in rich times or in poor.

TIP
END YOUR WARM-UP WITH A STRING OF TWO OR THREE GOOD SHOTS, EVEN IF YOU LEAVE A FEW BALLS BEHIND.

*"Therefore do not worry about tomorrow,
for tomorrow will worry about its own things.
Sufficient for the day is its own trouble."*

MATTHEW 6:34

APRIL 18

Match play. For golfers, it is the ultimate gut check. In a significant match play event, such as the USGA championships, losers go home finished. Winners go home worried. In match play, the reward for each victory is to start over again and prove it once more. Night after night, the victors go to bed with the same nagging question, "Okay, but will my game hold up tomorrow?"

Oh, what tomorrow can do to our gut!

Jesus, too, spoke of tomorrow. He dismissed it. "Who of you by worrying can add a single hour to his life?" He asked His listeners (Matthew 6:27 NIV). It was a simple, piercing question.

You see, our time is today, the moment He has given us. Tomorrow is for Him. He knows it and He guards us against it. Sure, we can worry about it, but in the meantime we lose sight of all the blessings that already surround us.

TIP

HAVING YOUR CLUBS REGRIPPED CAN IMPROVE YOUR FEEL AND BOOST YOUR CONFIDENCE.

WHAT IS GOOD?

*All things are lawful for me, but not all
things are helpful; all things are lawful
for me, but not all things edify.*

1 CORINTHIANS 10:23

How much golf is too much? We might ask
Dana Quigley, who played every Champions
Tour event from August 1997 into the middle of
the 2005 season (278 consecutive events for which
he was eligible!). But what about you and me—
how often should we play?

Paul dealt with this question of excess when he
wrote his first letter to the Corinthians. Addressing
misconceptions that had arisen about freedom in
Christ, Paul did not condone a return to Jewish
legalism, but he did remind the people that wisdom
still mattered. If golf—or any other activity—has
become your master, although it is permissible, it is
not for you the right thing before God. Only Jesus
is to be your Master. When your
relationship with Him is right,
you'll know what else you are free
to do. And you'll know just how
much to do it.

TIP

PLAYING WHEN
YOU'RE HITTING IT
POORLY TEACHES
YOU TO SCORE
WELL ANYWAY.

MORE THAN ENOUGH

*And seeing the multitudes, He went up on a mountain,
and when He was seated His disciples came to Him.*

MATTHEW 5:1

How would you prefer to spend a weekend afternoon? On the golf course, playing the game? Or in the gallery, watching it? That's a tough decision, for generally the Tour stops in only once a year.

In biblical terms, we might say that the difference between watching and playing is the difference between being one of the crowd and one of the disciples. For the crowds, to see Jesus was enough. They yearned for Him to pass by, to bestow His favor on them. But rarely would they leave their place of comfort and follow Him wherever He might lead. For disciples, "enough of Jesus" was not enough at all. They wanted more. For this, they made sacrifices, like following Him up the mountain. They changed their schedule, changed their mind, changed their focus. They were not just people who watched the game. They were people who played it. And the game they played was the game of abundant life.

TIP

UNIQUELY MARK YOUR BALL WITH A PERMANENT PEN, AND YOU'LL NEVER SUFFER A PENALTY FOR HITTING THE WRONG BALL.

TRUE STRENGTH

We then who are strong ought to bear with
the scruples of the weak, and not to please ourselves.

ROMANS 15:1

It's hard, isn't it, to bear with the failings of the weak? There's nothing more frustrating than looking for a lost ball again when your own drive has split the middle and your approach shot awaits.

Paul's exhortation at the outset of Romans 15 is no easy matter either. In our walk of faith, there will be those who carry baggage from their life experiences, both inside and outside the church. And who, according to Paul, is responsible to look out for them? Those who are strong.

This is the self-sacrificing example that Christ set for us. We do not, as Paul explains, live to "please ourselves." We are no longer our own; we were bought at a price (1 Corinthians 6:19–20 NIV). And for the sake of Christ's body and those who are weak within it, we must sometimes pay a price too. We must reduce ourselves and lift up others.

TIP

FOR MORE POWER,
GET YOUR HANDS
HIGH ON YOUR
BACKSWING—BUT
DON'T STRETCH IT!

THE SEED

"Most assuredly, I say to you, unless a grain of wheat falls into the ground and dies, it remains alone; but if it dies, it produces much grain."

JOHN 12:24

Little as you know about it, you probably have a great appreciation for agronomy. Even when greens are punched and sanded, we know that it is a work that makes courses so much better. The greenskeeper's TLC sets up for a summer of great play.

Jesus understood agriculture and agronomy Himself. If His numerous references to sowing and reaping and seeds and weeds are any indication, He sincerely valued the farmers' work. He certainly knew how to speak their language.

But no passage stands out as strongly as this reference in John's gospel to Jesus' teaching about the kernel of wheat. For in speaking of the kernel's death, Jesus set the stage for His own. As one man in life, He was limited in His capacity to reach many. Only through His death would His life be given to all who came to receive Him.

> **TIP**
>
> WHILE GRIPPING THE CLUB, RIGHT-HANDED PLAYERS SHOULD SEE AT LEAST TWO KNUCKLES ON THEIR LEFT HAND.

MIGHTIEST PRAISE

*Sing to Him a new song; play
skillfully with a shout of joy.*

PSALM 33:3

 Tee it high and let it fly. Grip it and rip it. Drive for show.

These are the clarion calls of the power players, the big hitters, those who are "sneaky long" and those who are just plain LONG. These are their mantras, their adages, their mottoes.

And we hear them, yes we do. We hear them when we buy larger clubheads and harder balls. We hear them when we swing out of our shoes.

Those of us who love our God must also hear the power player of praise, King David. David never thought that sitting in the pew of quiet reflection was all there was to praise. He invoked his people to invoke a louder praise when it was fitting. He told them to shout. That's what passion and power do with joy—they unleash it!

TIP

DON'T "SCOOP" THE BALL INTO THE AIR; LET THE CLUB'S LOFT OF THE CLUBFACE DO IT FOR YOU.

SET STRAIGHT

Who shall bring a charge against God's elect? It is God who justifies. Who is he who condemns? It is Christ who died, and furthermore is also risen, who is even at the right hand of God, who also makes intercession for us.

ROMANS 8:33–34

There are two kinds of coaches in the world, those who lead with criticism and those who lead with praise. The first assess your swing and tell you what you're doing wrong. The second assess your swing and tell you what you're doing right.

This second coach is like our God. Although we know we come to Him ill equipped, He greets us eagerly. "Welcome!" He tells us. "I have specifically chosen you. And as a member of My team, there will always be a place for you." What a vote of confidence! Once we are in Christ, we will never be rejected by God. But like any good coach, God won't let us rest in complacency either. Through His Holy Spirit, He guides us daily by heightening our conscience, clarifying His Word in our hearts, and giving us the courage to minister to others like us.

TIP

LISTEN, RATHER THAN WATCH, FOR A PUTT TO GO IN THE HOLE.

THE GREAT ASSURANCE

O LORD, You have searched me and known me.
You know my sitting down and my rising up;
You understand my thought afar off.

Week after week on tour, a hundred obscure players chase glory. And every once in a while, one of these unknowns does what they all wish to do: he makes a name for himself.

We, too, can spend our lives pursuing a moment in which we gain "the ultimate prize" in our given profession or personal pursuit. It is that moment, we are convinced, that will redeem all the work we have poured into this passion, and all the sacrifice that it has required of us.

But there is no holy grail to be gained in this life. Even when we believe we have gotten our hands around it, its contents can be bitter. There is no holy grail, but there is a Holy God. And it is not being known by the world that matters; it is being known and loved by God that counts far beyond this life.

TIP

RELAXED BUT COMMITTED MAKES FOR THE BEST POSSIBLE SWING.

STEADY AS YOU GO

Weeping may endure for a night,
but joy comes in the morning.

PSALM 30:5

Tour professionals know not to grow too ecstatic over Thursday rounds. They often face difficulty and disappointment before the weekend is out. And yet, if they carry on in stoic fashion when great things happen, they will not be able to ride the adrenal momentum that can help win a tournament.

This is a marvelous lesson for life, where we must be careful to manage the emotions that God has given us. That's right; emotions come from God! God's people raised a cheer when Jerusalem's wall was rebuilt. Jesus wept upon seeing the grief of Mary and Martha over the loss of their brother, Lazarus.

By His Spirit, God will let us know when to press forward with vigor and when to slow down in contemplation. In this He may surprise us, for there are times when what looks like sadness will result in elation and praise. Such is the work of the King of redemption.

TIP

MAKE YOUR LAYUPS SMARTLY—YOU DON'T WANT TO RISK GIVING UP A SECOND SHOT.

THE REAL REASON

"For God did not send His Son into the world to condemn the world, but that the world through Him might be saved."

JOHN 3:17

It's only partly funny that we avoid practice with an excuse like this: "This course sets up well for my slice." In golf, we can laugh off the fact that the game has the better of us.

It's more difficult to laugh when confronted by an unbelieving friend who dismisses faith with flimsy excuses, including the argument that God is a finger-pointer out to catch us missing the mark.

But the Bible gives a true picture of God. He is not a God of condemnation. He is a God of justice. Nearly everyone respects earthly parents who govern their families kindly yet firmly with reasonable boundaries. Yet when it comes to our heavenly Father, they think He should let us run willy-nilly because He "loves" us.

He does love us, which is why He sent Christ: we need a Savior—not to condemn us, but to rescue us from our poor excuses.

TIP

LEAVE THE COURSE IN BETTER SHAPE THAN YOU FOUND IT. YOU'LL THANK YOURSELF NEXT TIME YOU PLAY!

TOTALLY COMMITTED

And [Amaziah] did what was right in the sight of the LORD, but not with a loyal heart.

2 CHRONICLES 25:2

Although a lot of us give golf more attention than we probably should, we know that our level of commitment is nothing compared with that of tour professionals. They are driven to excel, and that drive pushes them to work very hard for what they want.

As followers of Christ, we, too, are called to a life of work. It is not work for earthly gain. It is not even work for heavenly gain, for we know that we are saved by grace through faith and not by our own works (Ephesians 2:8–9). But we are called to commit ourselves to display the righteousness of Christ.

This is no small commitment.

It requires that we know what we are instructed to do. And it requires that we act. This can take courage, but if we surrender to the Spirit's authority, He will equip us with the gifts, the gusto, and the guts we need.

TIP

HARD SHOTS REQUIRE A SOFT TOUCH. DON'T FORGET TO HIT SHORT SHOTS ON THE RANGE.

READY OR NOT

"Now when they bring you to the synagogues and magistrates and authorities, do not worry about how or what you should answer, or what you should say. For the Holy Spirit will teach you in that very hour what you ought to say."

LUKE 12:11–12

Not even the best golfers all look alike—and neither do those who stand up for God.

You do not have to be a theologian, a seminary graduate, or even a Sunday school teacher to tell people the good news of Jesus Christ. You do not have to train as a lawyer, a preacher, or an orator to defend the faith. You do not have to be studied up, prayed up, or charged up. You need only to be in the hands of the Holy Spirit.

Yes, there is value in knowledge and preparation. But simply because we are not God, we will not have all the answers. His ways are beyond our comprehension (Isaiah 55:8–9). The time will come when we will be asked questions for which we have not prepared. This is when the Spirit will come, giving us wisdom that is not ours, the wisdom of the Father.

TIP

DON'T LET YOUR PRIDE BUY YOUR EQUIPMENT. BE REALISTIC ABOUT YOUR SWING.

BEYOND EXPECTATIONS

*The people were in expectation,
and all reasoned in their hearts about
John, whether he was the Christ or not.*

LUKE 3:15

Every avid golfer eagerly anticipates the chance to play a legendary course—a course seen beautifully depicted in magazines, a course that beckons us with its seaside settings or fantastic challenges.

Sadly, however, the chance at such excellent entertainment is one of the last places we find idealism these days. It is the state of a world that no longer expects God.

In the days before the coming of Christ, the Jewish people lived with the most marvelous of hopes. A Messiah was coming. No other people had such a promise in their hearts. It was a hope so sure that the Jews saw potential in each great man— could he be the One?

Now that hope has been realized. Christ has come, offering salvation to all. So for those of us who already believe, we have one grand calling: we, like John, must gladly point to Jesus.

TIP

ON WINDY DAYS, SWING WITH EASE IN THE BREEZE.

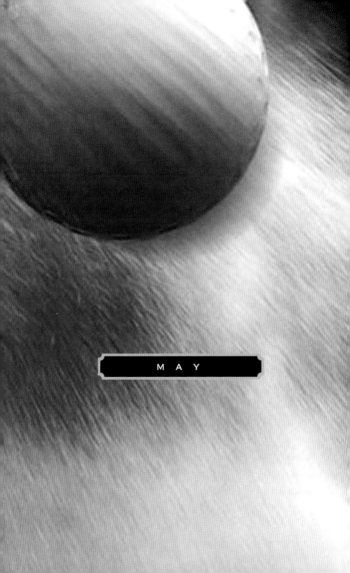

MAY

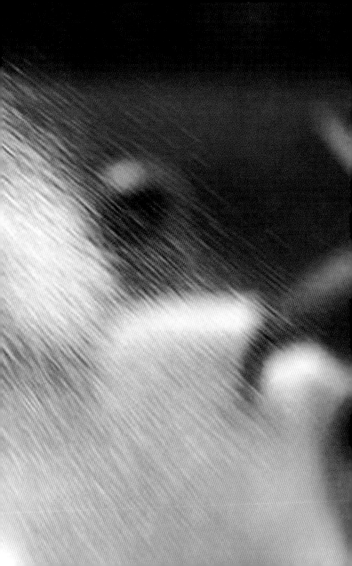

GUT FEELING

"Even so it is not the will of your Father who is in heaven that one of these little ones should perish."

MATTHEW 18:14

Think of that sad occasion when you hit a strong drive just slightly off line, following the ball nearly the entire way with your watchful eyes—but when you arrive to the place where your ball most certainly stopped, it is nowhere to be found. Search as you might, it is gone for good.

Now hold that feeling.

That's right. Hold that sinking, gut-burning feeling. Let the physical crunch be a lesson for your spirit. Because in our spirits, if we are growing in the image of our Savior, we will face that same feeling as we walk daily among those who are lost.

When we are grown in Him, we are called to the mercy that is born from such pain for those who do not know Christ. This mercy moves us to offer our lost friends the only comfort that will soothe their spirits.

TIP

BEFORE YOU START PLAY, BE SURE TO CHECK THE SCORECARD FOR UNIQUE "LOCAL RULES."

GOD'S WORK

Chenaniah, leader of the Levites, was instructor in charge of the music, because he was skillful.

1 CHRONICLES 15:22

When a pro golfer complains about the travel or the press, that athlete is no different from the rest of us. For we all complain about our jobs occasionally, even when we are doing what we love—even when we know that God has set us apart for what we are doing.

Look at Chenaniah, given responsibility for music because he was good at it. He could have been irked by the responsibility of it all, turning a blessing into a curse. Or he could have taken a tactical approach, where he handled well the patterns and designs of his responsibility—but causing his blessing to grow mundane.

With a right heart, however, Chenaniah took both the talent and the responsibility as blessings from the Lord. At times, Chenaniah likely mumbled and grumbled, but not for long. His eyes were on the Lord, and he was thankful for both the wonder and the work.

> **TIP**
>
> IF YOU'RE NOT GETTING A FULL SHOULDER TURN, TRY LIFTING YOUR CHIN A BIT AT ADDRESS.

TOGETHER WITH CHRIST

"For My yoke is easy and My burden is light."

Executive course, pitch-'n'-putt, three-par. Call it what you will, but if you're an average player it's still likely you've never shot par there. That's because short or not, it's the same game. You walk off the course feeling spryer than when you play the big ones, but the challenge remains greater than you.

Interestingly, Jesus' words about an easy yoke and a light burden take us down the same path. That is, we must still allow ourselves to be constrained, and we must still expect to carry burdens, but in the end these just won't feel the same.

Jesus doesn't remove us from the game. We still live here as He did, facing what the world throws at us. But rather than living it out alone, we serve with Him. That's how the work moves from drudgery to joy. His ever-presence eases our yoke and lightens our burden.

TIP

DON'T LASH AT THE BALL— "INTERCEPT" IT WITH A NICE, FULL SWING.

AT THE HEART

*"For where your treasure is,
there your heart will be also."*

As followers of Christ motivated to reach the hearts of others with the good news of Jesus, we want to reach out as effectively as possible. We must go to where people's hearts are.

A lot of places where our friends and acquaintances have set their hearts look more like trash than treasure. It can feel awkward to go where people who need Jesus are—unless we're talking about going to the golf course!

The Christ-centered life is still lived within the wild context of the world. This requires a thoughtful balance. But when we view our time on the golf course as God's time, the balance is right: one hundred percent of our time is spent in God's presence and one hundred percent of our time is given over to the people He places in our path. So we seek to know both of them— God and others—as well as we possibly can.

> **TIP**
>
> ROLLING THE BALL ACROSS THE FRINGE WITH A FAIRWAY WOOD OR DRIVER IS OFTEN YOUR BEST CHOICE.

JUSTICE AND LOVE

For He does not afflict willingly,
nor grieve the children of men.

In sports, we think nothing of the old adage "No pain, no gain." Even beginning golfers work through blisters on their way to a refined swing.

Yet in life, pain is a common theological sticking point. Why would a God of love allow grief for His people?

We would never suggest to a human parent that love consists only of giving children what they want. Indeed, although taking privileges from our children may "hurt" them, we know that such pain is necessary if we are to raise our children with the kind of love that properly prepares them for the world.

With much greater scope and understanding, God also gives us a full-scale love, not limited to lover as supplier. God's love includes His gifts. But it also includes His justice, His wisdom, His instruction, His protection, and His restriction. As a gardener may tend by pruning, God may care for us with pain.

TIP

ONCE YOU'VE CHOSEN THE LINE, ALL PUTTS ARE STRAIGHT PUTTS.

SALT THE EARTH

"You are the salt of the earth."

MATTHEW 5:13

Calling a person salty suggests a certain crusty boldness. A salty person will say just about anything to get your attention. On the golf course, a salty partner loves ribbing others—and not always good-naturedly. He may also have a few choice words for the ball, the course, and the nineteenth-hole attendants. Plainly, a salty person is not always nice.

Yet Christ picked salt as a trait of His followers.

Salt draws out the full flavor of the food it garnishes. Salty disciples of Christ do the very same thing. Sometimes we need to say things simply to call attention to God. Where a salty man normally makes a case for himself, salty believers make a case for our Master with the marvelously Christlike combination of knowledge and surprise.

Bring the extraordinary God into the middle of the ordinary world. You'll raise eyebrows—and open minds.

TIP

PRACTICE WITH MECHANICS IN THE FRONT OF YOUR MIND, BUT PLAY WITH THEM IN THE BACK OF YOUR MIND.

WHERE CREDIT IS DUE

David praised the LORD in the presence of
the whole assembly, saying, . . . "Yours, O LORD,
is the greatness and the power and the glory
and the majesty and the splendor, for everything
in heaven and earth is yours. Yours, O LORD,
is the kingdom; you are exalted as head over all."

1 CHRONICLES 29:10–11 NIV

You've seen it. And if your spirit is right with God, it does not set well with you: fans with arms extended, bowing in admiration to athletes who make a dazzling play. It's only partly serious, but it's an indication of something utterly significant—the dismissal of the one true God.

Before his death, David stood before an assembly of his people. If ever men and women were tempted to pay tribute to a fellow man, this was it. David had led this nation to preeminence over all surrounding nations. He would have seen all their bows of reverence. But David conveyed all credit where it was due. He praised the God who possessed all greatness and power and glory and majesty and splendor. David knew himself to be just a man under the one true God.

TIP

ON DOGLEGS
ESPECIALLY,
DOUBLE CHECK
YOUR ALIGNMENT.

JUST DO IT

He has shown you, O man, what is good; and
what does the LORD require of you but to do justly,
to love mercy, and to walk humbly with your God?

MICAH 6:8

When we show up for a tournament, we don't ask the pro if it would be all right if we carried fifteen or sixteen clubs this time. We don't expect a mulligan in the middle of the round. And we certainly put the clamps on the foot mashie!

Not only do we adhere to these rules, but so do a lot of folks who have abandoned the rules of life as designed by God—so many folks paying closer attention to the rules of golf than the law of love.

Over and over again, the Bible speaks of the strength that comes from joyful obedience. It is not an obedience born of guilt or obligation. Rather, it stems from a heart of thanks and a response of love to the One who first loved us. We obey because we want to do to what God wants us to do.

> **TIP**
>
> WHEN TENDING THE PIN, BE SURE TO HOLD THE FLAG TO KEEP IT FROM FLAPPING IN THE BREEZE.

KNOWING WHAT'S YOURS

"Is it time to receive money and to receive clothing, olive groves and vineyards, sheep and oxen, male and female servants?"

2 KINGS 5:26

If someone handed you a professional swing, what kind of dreams would start popping into your head? Pairings with the great players on Tour? Big winners' checks?

That new swing could change your life all right. But is a life change what you need? The grass may indeed be greener on the other side of the allurement. But God still may be calling you to the dirt.

Because amazing things happened when he was around, attractive enticements came the way of the prophet Elisha. When Naaman came to see this reputed healer, Elisha used God's power to end Naaman's incurable skin disease. But when Naaman offered Elisha the gifts he had brought—silver, gold, and clothing—Elisha said, "No, thanks." He knew that he had been called to something different. Under God, he was going to do just that and nothing else.

TIP

IF YOU WARM UP ON MATS, HEAD TO THE FIRST TEE EARLY AND GET IN SOME EXTRA SWINGS ON "THE REAL STUFF."

SWEAR IT OFF

But above all, my brethren, do not swear, either by heaven or by earth or with any other oath. But let your "Yes" be "Yes," and your "No," "No," lest you fall into judgment.

JAMES 5:12

James's day must have been much like ours, when opinions come from everywhere. In our time, the opinions of athletes and movie stars often count more than the opinions of those who study and think about the issues of the day. Advertisers especially love a celebrity endorsement.

In order to "strengthen" the truth, many people attach persons or things greater than themselves to their basic statements. Frequently, they swear by God.

But such oaths, no matter how fiercely sworn, weaken our words. An oath suggests that your normal *yes* and your regular *no* are not worth much. Each time you add a word-based guarantee, you sacrifice the chance to prove that your character is more solid than your ad campaign.

TIP

KEEPING YOUR CLUBS CLEAN— FROM GRIPS TO GROOVES—CAN HELP YOUR PLAY.

LET THE WIND BLOW

*We should no longer be children, tossed to and fro
and carried about with every wind of doctrine, by the
trickery of men, in the cunning craftiness of deceitful
plotting, but, speaking the truth in love, [we] may grow
up in all things into Him who is the head—Christ.*

EPHESIANS 4:14–15

One of the shortest par-3s on the PGA Tour—
the seventh at Pebble Beach—gains all its teeth
from the winds that whirl around it. The seventh
plays anywhere from a sand wedge to a 4-iron. Just
think, a 4-iron from 100 yards!

The apostle Paul warned that shifting winds
would come for us as well. These are the changeable
teachings of those who design new doctrines daily.
"Free thinkers," they call themselves, but their
thoughts are very costly! In golf, the wind experts
are Texans or Oklahomans or Brits. In life, those in
Christ who stand firm against all the airy teachings
that the world hurls at them are
grown-ups. That's right, if we are
fortified so that we bend but do
not break, so that we are resilient
and renewed, then we have become mature in Christ.

> **TIP**
>
> MOST PLAYERS
> NEED TO SHORTEN
> THEIR PRE-SHOT
> ROUTINE, NOT
> LENGTHEN IT.

NOT UNEXPECTED

For man also does not know his time: Like fish taken in a cruel net, like birds caught in a snare, so the sons of men are snared in an evil time, when it falls suddenly upon them.

ECCLESIASTES 9:12

An anonymous soul once said, "No one likes surprises." Of course, whoever it was meant bad surprises, the kind that show up on golf courses as balls nestled against tree trunks or buried under the lip of a steep bunker.

But there are far worse surprises. Solomon plainly called these evil. His words are poignant today as men without morals still cloak themselves in mystery and found their terror on ugly surprises.

Evil, however, is not unexpected. Christ warned of the wars and rumors of wars that would precede the last days. In fact, these would be only "the beginning of birth pains" (Matthew 24:8 NIV). Hatred, persecution, and death will follow. But Christ was not just some prophet of doom; He alone offered defense against it. He alone offered eternity.

TIP

"GOOD GOLFERS AREN'T WORRIED ABOUT WHAT ANYBODY ELSE THINKS OF THEM."
—BOB ROTELLA

GOD'S UNIVERSE

He made the Pleiades and Orion; He turns the shadow
of death into morning and makes the day dark as night;
He calls for the waters of the sea and pours them
out on the face of the earth; the LORD is His name.

AMOS 5:8

What you don't know may help you. For instance, on a new course, where you do not know the location of all the trouble, you let 'er rip with confidence. Your ignorance can produce bliss.

In life, knowledge can be the very thing that keeps us from God. Certainly, we know the universe is fascinating. But the cycle of secular science is this: Know. Explain. Humanize. Allowed to quantify the heavens, science believes it owns all knowledge of the universe. But look at the words of Amos, who saw the God of justice and righteousness as the same God whose creations filled the skies and covered the earth. What was in the heavens and what fell from the heavens came from His hand. Nature was, from the beginning, God's. Amos knew it. And that knowing surpassed knowledge.

TIP

IF YOU SEEK ADVICE, BE SURE IT ONLY COMES FROM YOUR PARTNER OR CADDIE IN TOURNAMENT PLAY.

ALTOGETHER DIFFERENT

> *For the LORD your God is God of gods and*
> *Lord of lords, the great God, mighty and awesome,*
> *who shows no partiality nor takes a bribe. He*
> *administers justice for the fatherless and the widow,*
> *and loves the stranger, giving him food and clothing.*

DEUTERONOMY 10:17–18

If we had no other description of our God, this passage alone would allow us to see the grand difference between the Holy One and those we so regularly place on pedestals today. And yes, we are a pedestal-building people. We choose icons on the basis of experience or appearance, talent or speech. Then we reward these chosen people with gold cups, cold cash, and camera time—keeping them on that pedestal until their actions or our distaste knocks them off.

Which is just about the time God shows up.

When the "mighty ones" have fallen, the Mighty One renders mercy. He stands with those who have been left to stand alone. And He welcomes those who have received no other welcome. There is no doubt that our God is different. After all, He is the pedestal, the very Rock of Ages.

TIP

"SOFTEN" YOUR ARMS FOR LONGER, STRAIGHTER DRIVES.

GROWN-UPS

Let no one despise your youth, but be an
example to the believers in word, in conduct,
in love, in spirit, in faith, in purity.

The youth movement in golf that began with Tiger Woods and Michelle Wie sure isn't slackening. Now it's Rory McIlroy, Yani Tseng, Rickie Fowler, and Ryo Ishikawa. Many welcome these young stars; others think they mar the game's traditions.

Certainly, we make mistakes in our lives that spring from our immaturity. Knowing God to be gracious and compassionate, David was one who asked for God's forgiving consideration in the matter of his youthful transgressions. But when it came to his protégé Timothy, Paul stepped up the instruction, writing two full letters to help establish this young man's role as a minister of the gospel. Not all youth are the same. Some are eager and ready for the next level of spiritual training. Would you inspire the young? Remember this twofold principle: patience and purpose. Forgive what is wrong but encourage toward what is right.

TIP

FINISH YOUR SWING STANDING TALL WITH YOUR BELLY BUTTON FACING THE TARGET.

OUT WITH THE OLD

Those from among you shall build the old waste places; you shall raise up the foundations of many generations; and you shall be called the Repairer of the Breach, the Restorer of Streets to Dwell In.

ISAIAH 58:12

If you really want to improve your game, maybe try losing your old favorite club. Really. Tour players are smart enough to keep up with technology—why aren't we?

When it comes to change, we truly are reluctant. How hard it is to surrender the old things in our life—even when they are no good!

That is why it is so good to know that our God is a God of regeneration. From the beginning, when we give our lives to Christ, the old passes away and the new comes (2 Corinthians 5:17). But we are not to be selfish with His renewing hand. We must come to the rescue of others, taking the loss in their lives and restoring it for all time. We must bring the salvation of Jesus—the One who makes hearts new—to those who do not know it.

TIP

KEEP HANDS AHEAD OF THE CLUBFACE FOR ALL CHIP SHOTS.

MAY 16

DEPTH IN FRIENDSHIP

*A man who has friends must himself be friendly, but
there is a friend who sticks closer than a brother.*

PROVERBS 18:24

It is difficult to exaggerate the relationship
between a professional player and his or her
caddie. A strong player-caddie relationship can
make a significant difference in the player's career—
and the caddie's too!

Solomon, too, knew that synergistic teamwork
was a thing to be prized.

Sometimes, he suggested, the team can be too
big. When we gather companions as though they
are commodities, we are often left to take the bad
with the good. Not all those we call friends are wise.
If their influence is destructive, sometimes we are
forced to end the friendship.

But there is another level of friendship. This is
the friend who can be trusted in any circumstance—
a friend who sticks closer than
a brother. Such deep friends encourage one another, pray with and
for one another, hold one another
accountable, and never leave when
the going gets tough. Seek such a
friend. Be such a friend.

TIP

GETTING
WRISTY WITH
YOUR PUTTER?
PRACTICE CROSS-
HANDED TO
REGAIN FEEL.

TOLERANCE

"Nevertheless I have a few things against you, because you allow that woman Jezebel, who calls herself a prophetess, to teach and seduce My servants to commit sexual immorality and eat things sacrificed to idols."

REVELATION 2:20

What idiosyncrasies do you tolerate in your golf game just because you're too lazy to work them out? Perhaps you have a hitch in your swing. Or maybe you use a beloved but sadly outdated wedge.

In Revelation, God praised the church at Thyatira for its love, faith, service, and perseverance. But then He went on to issue a direct statement toward a deceptive woman named Jezebel. Biblically, this could point to a specific woman, or it could represent a woman who woos men and then pierces their hearts with wickedness. Either way, God rebuked those in the church for tolerating this Jezebel. What a significant reminder in our time! We certainly can't be permissive with unrighteousness in our lives. But neither can we permit unrighteousness or deception in those around us who act as though they have spiritual influence—even if it means being called intolerant ourselves.

> **TIP**
>
> POSITIVE REINFORCEMENT LEADS TO CONFIDENCE; NEGATIVE REINFORCEMENT LEADS TO DOUBT.

SKILLED LABOR

*Then the LORD spoke to Moses, saying: "See, I have
called by name Bezalel the son of Uri, the son of Hur,
of the tribe of Judah. And I have filled him with
the Spirit of God, in wisdom, in understanding, in
knowledge, and in all manner of workmanship."*

EXODUS 31:1–3

All Tour players have one thing in common:
they are more skilled than the rest of us. And
those who have their priorities in line recognize
that this skill is God-given.

When God spoke to Moses about the skills
of Bezalel, He admitted freely that He had made
one man more skilled than the rest in particular
artistic crafts. This is the way of the Lord—to
bestow particular gifts, particular talents, particular
measures of faith upon each one of us.

Now, if you play golf, you may get to wishing
that God had made you a bit more like some tour
favorite. But you may not be
doing what God has in mind for
you. Like Bezalel, be filled with the
Holy Spirit, with skill, ability, and
knowledge that come from God.
Then you will be satisfied with
whatever God has for you, even if
it means more bogeys than pars.

NAMELESS AND FAITHFUL

Still others had trial of mockings and scourgings,
yes, and of chains and imprisonment. They were
stoned, they were sawn in two, were tempted, were
slain with the sword. They wandered about in
sheepskins and goatskins, being destitute,
afflicted, tormented—of whom
the world was not worthy.

HEBREWS 11:36–38

You may enjoy looking for stories of courageous men and women who have chosen to follow Christ against the odds. But here in Scripture, such people often are not even named.

Shouldn't such brave servants of God at least have their names recorded in the annals of history? Perhaps. But to a one, they would surely tell you that their names are written in a much finer place: the annals of eternity. We should not aspire to be Aaron Baddeley or Katherine Hull. But we should aspire to speak boldly of our faith, as they do of theirs. We should not aspire to be Abraham or Moses, but we should aspire to act in boldness of faith. We should not be concerned whether our names are known by men, but whether our faith is known by God.

TIP

TEACH CHILDREN EARLY HOW TO PLAY SAFELY AND RESPECT A GOLF COURSE.

UNCOMMONLY COMMON

*He is despised and rejected by men, a Man of
sorrows and acquainted with grief. And we hid,
as it were, our faces from Him; He was
despised, and we did not esteem Him.*

ISAIAH 53:3

We have all been paired with players who have more sideways than "frontways" to their shots. They are novices, and we are usually thankful that we do not have to play with them tomorrow.

Popular as it has become to paint Jesus more nobly, more powerfully, more like the Savior that He was, this simple fact cannot be denied: those noble and powerful in His time thought little of Him. The amazing thing about Jesus was not that He was stronger than a gladiator, more attractive than a Greek statue, or richer than a king. What was amazing about Jesus was that He was noticeably human.

And yet there was something about Him. This was not just a man among men. This was God among men, Im-manuel. He had come for no marquee reason, but with a simple purpose: to seek and to save. That doesn't require a special look—just a special One.

TIP

TO IMPROVE
PUTTING TEMPO,
PRACTICE TO
"ZONES" ON THE
GREEN RATHER
THAN TO HOLES.

TOGETHER AS ONE

*Only let your conduct be worthy of the gospel
of Christ, so that whether I come and see you
or am absent, I may hear of your affairs, that
you stand fast in one spirit, with one mind
striving together for the faith of the gospel.*

PHILIPPIANS 1:27

Paul was never afraid to couch the advancement
of the gospel in competitive terms. He knew
there was a battle to be won. It was a battle in the
hands of many who came together as one, and he
offered a threefold strategy for victory.

First, take a firm stance, making a commitment
of longevity. Second, use our multiplied strength:
the oneness of spirit, centering ourselves around
God's eternal purpose. And third, our center must
be the gospel. We have no message of our own; we
have only the fight for the faith.

In golf your partner may be more or less skilled
than you, but your goal is the
same: score as low as you can.
And when the time comes to
team up for Christ, we set aside
the matters of preference and
battle as one for the good news
of Jesus Christ.

TIP

IF YOUR SWING
SPEED IS SLOW,
YOU'LL GET
MORE LOFT FROM
FAIRWAY WOODS
THAN LONG IRONS.

RISK-REWARD

*But we are not of those who draw back to perdition,
but of those who believe to the saving of the soul.*

HEBREWS 10:39

In that great company of tour professionals, do you ever wonder if there really is such a thing as a Risk-Reward hole? For such great players, the emphasis is certainly on the Reward.

Not so with most of us. We can't help but see the water and the sand. Without the ability to hit the ball straight nearly every time, the emphasis is on the Risk.

But not in life. In Christ, our life is empowered by the Holy Spirit, so that we may love, worship, and serve God without fear. The Spirit-filled follower of Christ is like the tour professional. The emphasis is on the Reward. And well it should be, for that Reward was earned by One much greater than we—One who has in turn given it to us to give again to others. Life in Him is simply this: Reward—Reward—Reward—Reward. So let's go for it!

TIP

STRETCHING PRIOR TO PRACTICE OR PLAY WILL IMPROVE YOUR FLEXIBILITY AND REDUCE INJURY.

IT DEPENDS ON GOD

The Spirit Himself bears witness with our spirit that we are children of God.

ROMANS 8:16

Perhaps you know the story of Andrew Buckle, the Australian professional who once won a tournament when his final approach shot struck a marshal's raised *Quiet, Please* sign and bounded back onto the green. Buckle then two-putted to win.

The marshal's action was wholly unintentional, but it gives us a marvelous picture of God's unsolicited mercy—which is most definitely intentional.

God sees that we have missed the mark, and He steps in to rescue us. It's a far cry from the treatment we deserve as wayward sinners, but it is precisely the treatment we would hope for from someone who loves us. And God certainly loves us. So in spite of sin and in spite of our human effort at rectifying that sin, He steps in to do the work we cannot do—He makes us holy through His Son.

> **TIP**
>
> THE RULES OF GOLF PERMIT JUST FOURTEEN CLUBS. ADHERE TO THIS RULE AND YOU'LL LEARN WHICH CLUBS ARE MOST VALUABLE FOR YOU.

NO OFFENSE

A brother offended is harder to win than a strong city, and contentions are like the bars of a castle.

PROVERBS 18:19

Banter is common stock among golfers, particularly men. Golfing buddies who frequently play together usually know what they are in for when they head out together. Will the competition be fierce or friendly? Will the chatter be idle or pointed?

Some people are far more comfortable with banter than others. But all have lines that, when crossed, lead to offense. Although invisible, these lines are very real, especially when they are crossed. As followers of Christ, we must be cautious not to play near these lines.

If an offended brother is "harder to win than a strong city," we must steer clear of offending those with whom we are building relationships. Sensitivity, although not normally noted as a "manly" concept, is of great priority for the believer. If others do not trust us, especially with their personal stories and feelings, they are very unlikely to trust the God we proclaim.

TIP

FOR A FREE-FLOWING SWING, THINK, "EYES ON THE BALL" INSTEAD OF "KEEP YOUR HEAD STILL."

THE PRICE OF GRACE

For by grace you have been saved through faith,
and that not of yourselves; it is the gift of God.

EPHESIANS 2:8

Maybe you've noticed those small money clips worn by PGA Tour players. They are badges of privilege, allowing them access to the course, clubhouse, and locker room, and earned at considerable sacrifice. That same sacrifice—years of single-minded practice—earns nice passes for family and friends too. It's a sweet piggyback deal for those who haven't worked nearly so hard.

In the same way, we gain the ultimate privilege of eternal life through Jesus Christ, not because of what we have done, but because He paid the ultimate price. The price of criticism, judgment, and death. The price of sins cast upon Him. The price of physical, emotional, and spiritual pain.

We can never forget that price, for if we ignore the cross, we ignore what made us His once and for all. We paid nothing, yet we have received all. So let us keep praising Him who paid our way.

TIP

GRIP THE CLUB JUST FIRMLY ENOUGH—AS YOU WOULD HOLD A STEERING WHEEL ON THE OPEN ROAD.

GOD'S WAY TO PERFECT

And let endurance have its perfect result, so that you may be perfect and complete, lacking in nothing.

JAMES 1:4 NASB

One day you play the third hole with a drive down the middle, an approach to the center of the green, and a lag putt that settles inches from the hole. Easy par. The next time you knock your drive under a tree, punch the ball down the fairway, hit an ugly wedge that stops twenty-five feet from the hole, and drain the long putt—par again.

Golf's many ways to "perfect" help us remember what God's standard for us is really all about. In the Sermon on the Mount, Jesus implored us to "be perfect . . . as your Father in heaven is perfect" (Matthew 5:48). Daunting.

But some translations couple "perfect" with its more literal definition from the Greek: "complete." God is perfect because He is utterly complete, and He is equipping you in the same way. By His Holy Spirit, He brings you closer to completion, according to the purpose He has for your life.

TIP

TO WHIP YOUR WEDGE GAME INTO SHAPE, PLAY A PAR-3 COURSE TWO OR THREE TIMES IN SUCCESSION.

TALK IS PRICEY

The lips of the righteous know what is acceptable,
but the mouth of the wicked what is perverse.

For every fish that grows through the telling, there is a birdie putt just like it. And for every sailor whose tongue runs bluer than blue, there is a misfiring golfer to match. Yes, the mouths of many golfers get them into as much trouble as their swings.

But for the follower of Christ, such a reputation would be out-of-bounds. We are called to tongues both true and appropriate.

Solomon's proverb warns us against all kinds of perverse talk. To lie is to pervert the truth. To gossip is to pervert another's character. To bark back in anger is to pervert love. To blaspheme is to pervert the image of God.

The Bible offers three better choices for a righteous tongue. When we are pulled toward gossip or lies or insults or anger or flippant cursing, we can turn to these—prayer, praise, and encouragement. Make your tongue ready.

TIP

PRACTICE PUTTING TO A TEE STUCK IN THE GREEN AND YOU'LL REALLY FOCUS YOUR AIM.

THE WILL TO WIN

And He said, "Therefore I have said to you that no one can come to Me unless it has been granted to him by My Father." From that time many of His disciples went back and walked with Him no more.

JOHN 6:65–66

Always in sports there is the ridiculous discussion of "who wants it more." But if desire were the key ingredient in every victory, ten-year-olds would be world champions—for oh, how they dream! Championships, we forget, are won by a precarious mixture of ability and adrenaline and fortuitous bounces and weather and concentration and "team chemistry" and putts that didn't go in on Friday suddenly falling on Sunday and, yes, desire.

But since the beginning of sinful time, desire has reigned supreme in the enemy's training ground of pride. Satan wants us to be convinced that we are capable of fashioning our own salvation. On the surface, a little bootstraps theology seems fine—you know: God helps those who help themselves. But there is no such scripture. God alone is our source of strength. His Son is our only salvation. Even our desire comes from Him.

> **TIP**
>
> ALWAYS MAKE YOUR LAST SWING THOUGHT A POSITIVE ONE. THEN THINK OF NOTHING AS YOU SWING.

THE LONG AND THE SHORT OF IT

His love endures forever.

PSALM 136 NIV

Maybe you have one of those remarkable memories. You can recall each shot from your last round of golf, each business transaction this month, each argument made at the last congregational meeting.

Why are we like this? Why do we remember the incidentals of our lives, when there are simple, foundational, transcendent truths that just won't stick in our heads?

God's love endures forever. Twenty-six times this truth is repeated in Psalm 136, and yet it so often escapes us that He is there, not just looking at us, but looking out for us. In our redeemed souls, this is what we really want. But in our flesh, we want that ugly shot back. We keep grasping for something bigger when perhaps what we need to do is remember something marvelously basic.

His love endures forever.

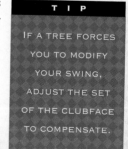

TIP

IF A TREE FORCES YOU TO MODIFY YOUR SWING, ADJUST THE SET OF THE CLUBFACE TO COMPENSATE.

UNITED

Bear one another's burdens,
and so fulfill the law of Christ.

GALATIANS 6:2

The NCAA Golf Championships may stand alone as the most emotionally grueling of sports contests. In an inherently individual game, players face not only the heightened emotions that surround their own game during a national championship, but they also take on the concerns of their teammates.

Eventually, nearly every player stumbles. But because each member of your team has experienced this same failure, they can stand by you in your pain—even if it is by simply saying nothing.

Herein lies a great example for those of us who profess oneness in Christ. We must remember our own days of struggle when we hear of the burdens carried by others. How painful it was for us—and how incredible to have others come alongside!

We must also be ready when it is our turn to carry the burden, looking for those around us who are facing trouble. Let's offer them humble, loving help.

TIP

TO AVOID DAMAGING BUNKERS, ENTER FROM THE LOW SIDE NEAREST THE BALL.

JUNE

THE ULTIMATE TEST

*The refining pot is for silver and the furnace
for gold, but the LORD tests the hearts.*

PROVERBS 17:3

In professional golf, the majors—and particularly the Open Championships—are the sport's ultimate tests, fitting stages for the ultimate players.

Tests come in all forms. The final exam is a well-known rite of academic passage. The litmus test informs a scientist of a chemical's nature. The "test of time" is associated with products of design and their ability to hold cultural respect as fads come and go.

Solomon knew that in his time, the finest elements were tested by fire. And he knew that we would be tested with similar force. But Solomon's God—and our God—is familiar with fire. Christ baptizes "with the Holy Spirit and fire" (Luke 3:16).

So we need not fear the refining fire of difficult times. For the God who refines us also protects us. As the crucible shielded the silver from the flame, God tests our hearts with His hands lovingly around them.

> **TIP**
>
> TODAY'S ROUND IS YOUR BEST PRACTICE SESSION FOR TOMORROW'S. LEARN FROM TODAY.

POCKET CALCULATORS

"Therefore I say to you, do not worry about your life, what you will eat or what you will drink; nor about your body, what you will put on. Is not life more than food and the body more than clothing?"

Tour professionals rely heavily on their yardage books. When the heat of battle is on and there are so many other factors to consider—wind, lie, adrenaline, and the way they struck the ball on the range—these players place utter confidence in their calculations.

Through years of practiced living and self-preserving routine, we, too, place exaggerated confidence in calculations. When we are buffeted by the unexpected, we seek comfort in the things we have built for ourselves. And because in our heart we know that these are of our own making, we fall into worry, like a player changing clubs again and again. There is only one cure for worry, and it is the topic that received the most attention in Christ's Sermon on the Mount: prayer. To stop worrying, we must fix our eyes on the loving, providing God of heaven. We must take to Him our worries.

TIP

A GOOD SWING OUTWEIGHS BAD EQUIPMENT MORE THAN GOOD EQUIPMENT HELPS A BAD SWING.

BETTER THAN WINNING

Instead of your shame you shall have double honor, and instead of confusion they shall rejoice in their portion. Therefore in their land they shall possess double; everlasting joy shall be theirs.

ISAIAH 61:7

Despite the hassles tour players face, you probably wouldn't mind giving it a try for a tournament or two. Play a dream course. Have a seasoned caddie tote your bag. And—here's the big one—take your chances at one of those huge purses. Hmm. Not bad.

But not best. As followers of Christ, we are always awaiting something better. We await the promise of heaven. Heaven is not someplace you go because your friends say nice things about you at your funeral. Nor is it someplace you go because your family can't wait to see you there someday. No, heaven is where you go because you have made an investment in eternity.

You have given your life to Jesus Christ. The happiness of this world is a happiness with strings attached. Always, it will be tainted by hassles. But not the joy of eternity with our Savior. That joy will be everlasting and perfect.

> **TIP**
>
> THANK EVERY COURSE WORKER YOU SEE—THEY MAKE YOUR DAY ENJOYABLE.

DYING BY DEGREES

*There is therefore now no condemnation to those
who are in Christ Jesus, who do not walk
according to the flesh, but according to the Spirit.*

ROMANS 8:1

How good is good enough? If you can practice till you're black and blue and you're still only as good as the next guy, at what point does "Hang in there" give way to "Hang it up"?

You may find yourself asking these same questions in your spiritual life. In those moments when you realize that you're never going to reach holy, it's easy to consider moving on to something else.

Indeed, the spiritual mirror can be a most unkind device. Vanity lingers before a mirror, first admiring. But the longer it stays there, the more imperfection it sees, the more pained it becomes.

Through Christ, God has removed the mirror, replacing it with the portrait of a man on a cross, bearing all that imperfection and carrying it once and for all to the grave. His work is finished, complete, perfect. There is nothing more that needs to be done.

> **TIP**
>
> THE RULES PERMIT A FREE DROP WHEN YOUR BALL RESTS IN A DANGEROUS SPOT (LIKE NEXT TO A BEEHIVE!).

ONE ACT

Therefore, as through one man's offense judgment came to all men, resulting in condemnation, even so through one Man's righteous act the free gift came to all men, resulting in justification of life.

ROMANS 5:18

Although we may be reluctant to admit it, a round of golf is not made in one shot. If a tournament is won by only a stroke, a birdie at the first is as important as a birdie at the last. And to suggest that just one moment in history is more critical than another is equally fallacious, isn't it?

Not according to Scripture.

In response to the single tragic act of sin, through which Adam led all humanity into a pattern of sin resulting to death, Paul set apart another single act as the most important in history. It was the act that brought life—the hope of heaven—to all. It happened in just a few hours' time, but this one act of righteousness, the death of Jesus Christ, can turn our lives in an entirely different direction.

TIP

THINK "DRIVE" THE BALL TO THE TARGET. DON'T "LIFT" IT.

NO OTHER

"Look to Me, and be saved, all you ends of the earth! For I am God, and there is no other."

ISAIAH 45:22

The greatest golfer of all time? It's open to debate, although most knowledgeable folks point to one of just three men: Hogan, Nicklaus, Woods.

But we can't let the arguments stop there these days. "Open to debate" is the prevailing philosophy of our lifetime. And issue by issue, there may be little danger in lively discussion.

But lumped together, all this adds up to a dangerous new value: absolute equality. Although all people were created with equal worth in the eyes of their Creator, all ideas are not equal—especially ideas about that Creator. Plainly put, there is truth and there are lies. A holy God is not capable of lying, so we must hold fast to the words He has said about Himself. He alone is God. Although many of us were brought to that truth by open discussion, it is not an item up for debate.

TIP

SWING TO PROPEL THE BALL FORWARD AND LET THE LOFT GET THE BALL AIRBORNE.

EXPECTATIONS

My voice You shall hear in the morning, O Lord; in the morning I will direct it to You, and I will look up.

PSALM 5:3

How do you head into your golf lessons? For most of us, these lessons are few, so we look forward to them as hours of possibility. There is a certain hope to them.

And how do you head into your times of prayer? Above all, David attached this trait to his requests: expectation. His prayers, he knew, did not fall on deaf ears. He did not give them up into powerless hands. David's God heard and David's God acted. And David's God is our God. We, too, should come to Him with expectation—more expectation than we have of our employees or our investments or even our families. From God, we can expect anything.

No wonder David prayed in the morning! It gave him all day to sit back and watch God answer his prayers. And no wonder so many of his psalms were filled with praise!

TIP

FOR HIGH PITCH SHOTS, THINK OF AN UNDERHANDED TOSSING MOTION.

SHIELDED

But You, O LORD, are a shield for me,
my glory and the One who lifts up my head.

If you take time each summer to watch the U.S. Open, you know well how "golf's toughest test" claims its victims. Many players go home looking for refuge from what they have endured.

Life, too, claims its victims. Not that it does so at a place so beautiful as a U.S. Open venue. Rather, it claims us anyplace our prestige, our priorities, or our personhood is on the line, anyplace our relationships can be stirred or strained.

Maybe you know all this right now. Maybe you need a refuge. But the refuge you need is not a better place, for sometimes you will be forced to walk where you do not want to go. The refuge you need is the One who will walk with you in all of these places. He is the God of heaven, who will shield you and lift your head.

> **TIP**
>
> ON TOUR, THE PUTTING STATISTICS GENERALLY LINE UP WITH THE MONEY LIST.

HEADS UP

But they thought to do me harm. So I sent messengers to them, saying, "I am doing a great work, so that I cannot come down. Why should the work cease while I leave it and go down to you?"

NEHEMIAH 6:2–3

You may be uncomfortable with the modern practice in sports of intentionally rattling one's opponent. In golf, this includes the "gamesmanship" of giving short putts early to keep the opponent's confidence down for when he or she will really need those putts later.

Like them or not, to be successful against such ploys you must maintain a sense of your own mission. A wavering confidence can turn to a stumbling performance.

In life, too, we have an opponent. His name is Satan, and he delights in thwarting our movement in the direction of God. To combat this enemy, we must

TIP

MENTALLY CALL YOUR SHOT—TARGET, SHAPE, AND TRAJECTORY— BEFORE YOU HIT IT.

be as focused as Nehemiah, who refused to pulled from what God had called him to do. When we know and pursue what God desires from us, both in general obedience and specific purpose, it is so much easier to proceed with confidence.

LAWLESS

*"Their throat is an open tomb; with their
tongues they have practiced deceit";
"the poison of asps is under their lips."*

ROMANS 3:13

J U N E 1 0

There are myriad ways to mishit a golf ball. You can roll it, blade it, chunk it, hook it, slice it, whiff it, and shank it! Maddeningly, for all the ways to hit a ball badly, there is just one good place to hit it. But it is something we submit to in golf. Strike the ball solidly on a square clubface, or deal with the consequences.

In the world, however, this philosophy prevails: make your own set of rules, and you don't have to face any consequences for breaking them. It's a sweet deal from the human perspective. But our sin forces us to pay a price in guilt and trouble.

There is just one true righteousness. It is the righteousness of Christ, which sets us free from the law of sin and death. In Him, we pay no price, for He has already paid it.

TIP

THE GOAL IN GOLF IS SIMPLE, BUT THE PATHS TO IT ARE MANY. CHOOSE WHICH ONE IS BEST FOR YOU.

A COMPELLING REASON

And see, now I go bound in the spirit to Jerusalem, not knowing the things that will happen to me there.

You hear it at nearly every lesson: "Now, this will feel funny at first, but trust me, it will really make a difference in your swing." When you have spent your golfing life grooving your swing, any change feels uncomfortable at first. But trusting your professional, you are compelled to go on into this peculiar territory, certain that it will be for the better in the end.

And in life, you would do well to remember this: although Jesus promised that we would be comforted, He never promised that we would be comfortable. Jesus was crucified for His deity. The apostles died martyrs' deaths. Certainly, this was not comfortable. But it was a compulsion they could not get around. They were led there by the Holy Spirit. In the end, because they were willing to go, their commitment made an eternal difference.

TIP

LEARN THE PROPER WAY TO FIX A BALL MARK, PUSHING IN FROM ALL SIDES.

THE GOD WHO TRUSTS

*For prophecy never came by the will of
man, but holy men of God spoke as they
were moved by the Holy Spirit.*

2 PETER 1:21

Imagine God entrusting the authorship of His
Word to mere men. In an exchange about as likely
as Phil Mickelson switching places with his caddie on
a major championship Sunday, God turned over His
sacred and eternal instruction to imperfect shepherds,
reluctant prophets, adulterous kings, murderous perse-
cutors, and despised tax collectors.

From our perspective, it was a major risk. From
His preeminent throne, it was nothing of the kind.
That Word was not spoken to the writers; it was
breathed into them and exhaled from them (2 Timothy 3:16).

How brave is our God! How trusting! But more
than that, how knowing. You see, despite sin's power,
God is most certain of Himself.
He has no doubt that His grip
is greater, His deliverance more
sure, His hope most irresistible.
He knows precisely when a man
or woman is His own, changed by
salvation inside and out.

TIP

"SEEK TO
UNDERSTAND
YOUR SWING, THEN
SPEND YOUR LIFE
PERFECTING IT."
—MANUEL
DE LA TORRE

DARKNESS TO LIGHT

*He has delivered us from the power of
darkness and conveyed us into the kingdom of
the Son of His love, in whom we have redemption
through His blood, the forgiveness of sins.*

COLOSSIANS 1:13–14

You know the difference between a good golf round and a bad one, don't you? A good golf round is drawn in straight lines, long distances, close proximities. Bad golf rounds look more like a child's scribbled drawing, with slants and curves and skews.

The difference between a rich life and a troubled one is equally clear. And fortunately, how we can experience the one over the other is also plainly spelled out for us in Scripture. A rich life, an abundant life, is a life in Christ, the Light of life (John 8:12). Perhaps it is no coincidence that in English, at least, when we say that we have broken through to understanding, we often use the expression "Finally, I see the light." Now, in deference to the One who illuminates righteousness for us, we simply need to learn to write that with a capital letter: "I see the Light!"

TIP

READY TO INVEST IN NEW CLUBS? HAVE A PROFESSIONAL FIT YOUR SWING FIRST.

FIT TO PREACH

And when they had prayed, the place
where they were assembled together was shaken;
and they were all filled with the Holy Spirit,
and they spoke the word of God with boldness.

ACTS 4:31

Perhaps you're a serious golfer with the natural talent to encourage you along. So you practice hard and enjoy success.

The ability to speak the word of God boldly has little to do with your practice as a speaker. In the past, you have perhaps excused yourself from telling others about Christ because of your lack of experience. Well, until the Holy Spirit's descent on Pentecost, Peter was an expert at saying all the wrong things. Suddenly, overtaken by the Spirit, he preached a message for all time. The knowledge of God's Word, locked up within him, simply poured out.

Is it time for you to be as eager in bringing good news as you are at improving your golf game? Pray that God fits you with His Spirit's boldness to be so outspoken.

TIP

INCREASE YOUR ENJOYMENT BY PLAYING FROM THE TEES MOST APPROPRIATE FOR YOUR GAME.

BAD TO GOOD

But the chief priests plotted to put Lazarus
to death also, because on account of him many
of the Jews went away and believed in Jesus.

JOHN 12:10–11

The last man to win consecutive U.S. Opens, Curtis Strange, once said that handling a 6-iron is so simple that you could eat pasta with one. Yet Strange badly misstruck a 6-iron in falling to Nick Faldo during the 1995 Ryder Cup matches, and it pained him for years.

Like sin.

That's right, no matter how "good" we become, below the surface is that "old man," the one who leads us down the path of sin-induced pain. Even God's chosen leaders knew the grip of sin and the weight of its consequences.

The only way out for sinful people is a sinless Savior. We need One who "has been tempted in every way, just as we are," but who was—absolutely unlike us— "without sin" (Hebrews 4:15 NIV). That One, of course, is Jesus. He alone can do what we cannot— save us from sin.

> TIP
>
> LOOSE IMPEDIMENTS, SUCH AS LEAVES OR ROCKS, MAY BE REMOVED FROM AROUND A BALL.

THE HOME COURSE

And this is eternal life, that they may know You, the only true God, and Jesus Christ whom You have sent.

JOHN 17:3

When a player shows exceptional understanding of a course—the ideal places to drive the ball, how to read the unreadable putts, the composition of the sand—we say, "He just knows the course." What a simple analogy for the relationship we are to have with God. We are not to know *of* the Lord. We are not to know *about* the Lord. We are to know the Lord.

When we only know *of* the Lord, we are like pagans who cluster all their gods into a nameless crowd of "deities." They hope that some particular one out there will hear their cry and come to their aid. When we only know *about* the Lord, we give ourselves over wholly to the pursuits of the mind.

Instead, know the Father. Know the Son. This is eternal life. It is how we walk the Home Course.

TIP

YOU CAN REPAIR YOUR SLICE BY WORKING TO KEEP YOUR ELBOWS CLOSER TO YOUR BODY.

CHAMPION OF THE PEOPLE

*For thus says the High and Lofty One who
inhabits eternity, whose name is Holy: "I dwell in
the high and holy place, with him who has a contrite
and humble spirit, to revive the spirit of the humble,
and to revive the heart of the contrite ones."*

ISAIAH 57:15

Thanks to the worldwide appeal of players like Charl Schwartzel, Jiyai Shin, and Angel Cabrera, golf is reaching people and places it has never reached before.

We must remember, however, that athletics are like many other endeavors. They are amoral. In the hands of a tyrant, a bigot, or a fool, athletics and business and education and the arts and even religion can grow in wickedness. But in the hands of those who see God first, those venues all can carry righteous compassion to a hurting world. Those of us who love golf can bring more than the game to people interested in this wonderful sport. We have the chance to bring the high and holy God to those who are lowly and contrite, those who have been resistant, or those who have never heard.

TIP

FOR A BALL BELOW YOUR FEET, FLEX YOUR KNEES MORE THAN USUAL TO GET NEARER TO THE BALL.

GIFTED CHILDREN

And He Himself gave some to be apostles,
some prophets, some evangelists, and some pastors
and teachers, for the equipping of the saints for the
work of ministry, for the edifying of the body of Christ.

EPHESIANS 4:11–12

Each of us has been gifted with a particular gift of the Spirit. Our God is a lavish God, who has loved us first and instilled in us a response of love. He equips us not only with the ability we need to contribute to His kingdom but also with the eager joy to employ that talent.

It does not matter where your church is located or how many people attend. It does not matter if you are a teacher without her notes or an evangelist without his tracts. God has equipped you beyond the tools of the trade to speak for Him, to serve Him, to live for Him.

A wise golfer once said, "A good putter can putt with anything." So also, because God has instilled His gifts in you, you can serve Him energetically, no matter the circumstances around you. This is not like school—in God's kingdom, all of His children are gifted.

TIP

IN YOUR SHORT GAME, DON'T GET LAZY. ACCELERATING THROUGH IMPACT WILL KEEP YOU HITTING IT FIRM.

WISE TO THE GUISE

*For Satan himself transforms himself
into an angel of light.*

2 CORINTHIANS 11:14

Funny as it seems, resort courses look as lovely
as they do because they dress up their trouble.
The edges of the bunkers are tidily kept, the sand
is immaculately raked, and the water is graced by
dancing fountains.

This beautiful ugliness is so like the work of
our enemy, it is almost eerie. For Satan himself, the
one who has for ages contended with God, could
not tempt us with gross attractions. A master of
disguise, he lures us into disgrace.

Anyone can recognize evil when it is sold as evil.
But Satan markets little that way. Instead, he offers
it to us as tolerance, freedom, or personal expression.
Certainly these are noble ideas. But when we tolerate
immorality, or ask for freedom to pursue our selfish
endeavors, or express our feelings
above the feelings of others, what
is beautiful becomes a light that
blinds rather than a light that
illuminates.

TIP

AFTER READING A
LONG PUTT, PICK
A MARK CLOSE
TO YOU ALONG
THE LINE AND
START THE BALL
ROLLING.

WELL MARKED

Clearly you are an epistle of Christ, ministered by us, written not with ink but by the Spirit of the living God, not on tablets of stone but on tablets of flesh, that is, of the heart.

2 CORINTHIANS 3:3

Do you carry a Sharpie in your bag? These permanent markers are used to uniquely identify golf balls, virtually eliminating the chance of hitting a wrong ball. Players use all variations of lines and dots and words. In any case, the IDs say, "This ball is mine."

God has marked us as well, not with external markings but with His Spirit in our hearts. That was wonderful not only for Paul's readers, the Corinthians, but for Paul and Timothy as well. The Corinthians, living for Christ, provided evidence of the work that the two ministers had done among them.

As modern followers of Christ, we should still be seeking to make that kind of impact.

Each day in Christ provides new ministry opportunities. We don't need a program. We just need to allow the Spirit of God to help us step out in encouragement, teaching, and prayer.

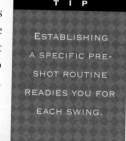

TIP

ESTABLISHING A SPECIFIC PRE-SHOT ROUTINE READIES YOU FOR EACH SWING.

A BIGGER GOAL

Brethren, I do not count myself to have apprehended;
but one thing I do, forgetting those things which are
behind and reaching forward to those things which
are ahead, I press toward the goal for the prize of the
upward call of God in Christ Jesus.

PHILIPPIANS 3:13–14

Here is a passage enjoyed by athletes everywhere. Paul struggled to push ahead with
resolve and discipline to collect the victor's prize.
He set behind him the things that hurt him, and he
went forward in seeking this goal, which he knew
he had not yet reached.

Sometimes golf makes for lousy metaphors
when it comes to Scripture. Sure, we do our best to
follow the mental coaches' advice and put that triple
bogey behind us when we tee it up at the next hole.
But ask any golfer how the round went and what
comes to mind? Those ugly holes.

So we must ask God to help
us press on toward the goal to
win an eternal prize. With God,
when we have reached our place
with Him, we will not be asked
to start again next week. We will
have made it, once and for all,
into the arms of Jesus.

> **TIP**
>
> IF YOU CAN'T
> CARRY THE
> TROUBLE, LAY
> BACK TO WHERE
> YOU HAVE
> A FAVORITE
> DISTANCE INTO
> THE GREEN.

TRUTH ABOUT TROUBLE

*Yea, though I walk through the valley of the
shadow of death, I will fear no evil; for You are
with me; Your rod and Your staff, they comfort me.*

PSALM 23:4

Trouble lurks on every course. And par is made
by surviving it. By going through the valley, in
other words, a golfer's joyous goal is reached.

The idea of walking through the valley,
especially the deathly valley of David's psalm, is in
no way appealing. And yet, David wrote of willingly
following his Shepherd through this dark place. But
David knew there is only one reason why God would
lead us down such a path—He knows this is the only
way to get us to the goodness on the other side.

Although God warns us that rich and easy times
can lead us away from Him, Scripture contains no
such warning about trouble. Although we deserve
the trouble that we bring upon ourselves through
sin, God will allow us to face
other trouble as well. Indeed, He
reserves His trouble for those He
wishes to discipline, to develop,
and to bless.

TIP

NEW GOLFERS
LEARN ETIQUETTE
FROM THE REST
OF US; LET'S
TEACH THEM
WITH WORDS AND
EXAMPLES.

A FORGETFUL GOD

"I, even I, am He who blots out your transgressions for My own sake; and I will not remember your sins."

ISAIAH 43:25

If anyone knows the great chasm between perfection and imperfection, it is we golfers. After all, it was a golfer who said that a shank is the closest thing to a pure shot! We know we need forgiveness.

But more than something we need, God's forgiveness is something He desires. God loves people. In fact, He created us to enjoy our company. He walked with Adam in the garden; He called Abraham His friend. But our sin keeps us from His presence. Holiness and unrighteousness do not mix. So, for His own sake, God chose to blot out our transgressions, to forget our sins.

Because of the coming of the Savior, Jesus Christ, we may all become God's children. We may turn to Him for the ultimate relationship, a relationship of eternal communication with the one true God. This is the wonderful message we must receive and the wonderful message we must pass on.

> **TIP**
>
> MAKE MINOR ADJUSTMENTS ON THE COURSE AND MAJOR OVERHAULS ON THE RANGE.

SOMETHING TO SAY

*And always be ready to give a defense to
everyone who asks you a reason for the hope
that is in you, with meekness and fear.*

1 PETER 3:15

Men have one standard question they ask new partners on the golf course: "So what do you do?" And keeping with our terse ways, a quick "I'm in real estate" or "I teach" or "I run a machine shop" does the trick when it comes to a response. Following the almost obligatory, "And you?" the conversation is pretty much over if you don't know what to say next. And many of us don't.

To move a conversation to the spiritual, we must be ready. Practice telling yourself or a trusted friend the story of how you were made new in Christ. Hearing the story again yourself just might be your biggest encouragement! And find a partner who will tell his story too. Together you can be bearers of good news—so good it can lead a troubled heart to the One who came expressly to heal the eternally sick.

TIP

IF YOU PLAY WHERE IT'S WET MUCH OF THE YEAR, MAKE A GOOD PAIR OF GOLF SHOES A TOP PRIORITY.

THROUGH CHRIST

He . . . was manifest in these last times for
you who through Him believe in God, who
raised Him from the dead and gave Him
glory, so that your faith and hope are in God.

1 PETER 1:20–21

Good golf comes down to this: trust your swing. When you take the club back, confident that it will do what you have trained it to do, your swing will be good, and your scores will be lower. Trust one thing, get another.

True Christ-centered faith is the same way.

Today, many people believe they will get to heaven if they simply believe there is one. A place so wonderful, they think, could not exclude them. But just because there is a mountain does not mean we will climb it, and just because there is a heaven does not mean we will go there. To get to heaven we must believe in Him who makes it possible to get there. We must trust one Man, who died to give us our hope. In this way, we will attain all that He offers, including heaven.

TIP

COUNT YOUR STROKES AS YOU TAKE THEM; IT'S TOO TEDIOUS TO TALLY THEM AT THE END OF THE HOLE.

ANOTHER KIND OF MASTERY

*By faith we understand that the worlds were framed
by the word of God, so that the things which are
seen were not made of things which are visible.*

HEBREWS 11:3

Likely, you are missing some essential piece for becoming a great golfer: strength, flexibility, coordination, concentration, or perhaps just all the time that it would take to get each of these.

Perhaps you want to ask, why? Why does someone else get all the goodies needed to be the very best? Calculate as we will, we cannot come up with a formula for God's purposes.

In the same way that you will probably never find yourself among the world's best golfers, you almost surely will never sit in the think tanks where the world's finest minds congregate. Still, you can give a friend a golf tip that changes his or her game for the better, and you can still offer an amazing statistic or story that gets your friends thinking.

We cannot unlock the mysteries of the universe, but humbly we can share the wonders of the One who can.

TIP

YOU MAY ASK A PLAYING PARTNER FOR HELP INTERPRETING A RULE, BUT THE FINAL CALL IS YOURS.

THE PERFECT GAME

*For such a High Priest was fitting for us, who
is holy, harmless, undefiled, separate from sinners,
and has become higher than the heavens.*

HEBREWS 7:26

Just what is golf's perfect round? Eighteen
birdies? Perhaps. But great players make eagles,
sometimes two or three in a round—so we're still
guessing. Of course, there never will be a perfect
round.

When we are honest with ourselves about life,
we know that there will be no perfect game there
either. Yet we strive to attain ultimate righteousness
on our own. It is something we cannot do. Only One
has ever been blameless: Jesus. And His perfection
uniquely qualified Him to make an eternal way for
us by offering the final sacrifice.

You can spend your days kicking yourself
because you try and try to do "something beautiful
for God." Through Jesus, we
don't do something beautiful *for*
God—we do something beauti-
ful *with* God. That switch in understanding changes everything. It
makes us completely dependent
on Him, which is the only way to
get life right.

TIP

AIM WITH
YOUR USUAL
SHOT SHAPE IN
MIND, NOT FOR
THE ELUSIVE
"CAREER" SHOT.

SURPRISE, SURPRISE

For you yourselves know perfectly that the day of the Lord so comes as a thief in the night.

Alertness is a principal characteristic of followers of Christ. Although Christ's return will be unmistakable, it will not be scheduled ahead of time, neatly tucked into our day planners, right after that one last dental appointment. The Lord Himself said that no one knows the day or the hour. For that reason, we must always be ready, attentive to how we are living.

Each round of golf is so very different. But the player who is prepared, the one who has thoroughly practiced all facets of the game, is the player who is ready for each unique shot.

So it is with life. Each round is so very different. But the end is the same. We will each be trumpet-called to heaven. Those who are prepared, those who are alert, will be those who are ready to answer it.

TIP

CLOSE YOUR STANCE AND THE CLUBFACE SLIGHTLY TO HIT A LOWER SHOT.

IN YOUR RIGHT MIND

Set your mind on things above,
not on things on the earth.

COLOSSIANS 3:2

Not once in the day have you hooked a tee shot. Then somewhere in the middle of the back nine, on a hole where the only real trouble is left, an instant before you take the club back, you hear this in your mind: *Don't hook it.* And what do you do? Hit it three city blocks to the right!

For this very reason, many professional golfers now employ sports psychologists or "mental coaches" to help them prevent the invasion of damaging swing thoughts.

But in life we have One much mightier than a mental assistant. We have the Holy Spirit. And the more we surrender to Him, the more we can count on His grip on our life. Our prayers will stay prayers, and our meditations will remain focused on Christ. Our minds will be set in a Godward direction.

TIP

FOR MID-RANGE PITCH SHOTS, GAUGE YOUR DISTANCE BY THE TOP OF THE FLAG, NOT THE BOTTOM.

CLOSE TO HOME

Therefore we must give the more earnest heed to the things we have heard, lest we drift away.

HEBREWS 2:1

Oh, what a verse! A good golf teacher would end every lesson with it. Of course, if he did so, we would probably give him a curious look and think, *Who gave you the wisdom of Harvey Penick?*

But the writer of Hebrews had a greater purpose in mind than continued attention to the fundamentals of a golf swing. He wanted his hearers to be ever mindful of the salvation that was worked for them by Jesus Christ, confirmed by those who heard Him and by the signs and wonders performed by the Holy Spirit (Hebrews 2:2–4). In other words, this was an undeniable message—undeniable and irrevocable.

No wonder, then, that it is so significant that we cling to this message. But not only to the message—we must also cling to the Savior Himself. Disciplined in the faith, with a recurring exploration of our salvation in Christ, we can set our feet so that we do not drift away.

TIP

DEADEN A SLICK DOWNHILL PUTT BY PLAYING THE BALL TOWARD THE TOE OF A PUTTER.

THE GOLF SEASON

It's a joy to play a game that is so different each time. Even when you play the same course regularly, even when you finish with the same score, today and tomorrow can look quite different. Today you drove each ball right down the middle—but where were all those putts you made yesterday?

Life is like this too, of course. You get out of the same bed each day, but considering what happens from that point on, you'd never know. And when you're ready for it, when you're feeling well and high on confidence, this array of little challenges can even be fun. You make it back to that same bed at the end of the day, satisfied with all that's been accomplished.

Nehemiah and Ezra led such an effort, when they managed the rebuilding of Jerusalem's wall. Facing sinister enemies and tough physical labor, the people worked on with courage until the wall was completed. And in the end, overjoyed with the fruit of their labor, they celebrated with praise and honor for God.

J U L Y

DO THE DEW

Brethren, join in following my example, and note those who so walk, as you have us for a pattern.

PHILIPPIANS 3:17

Summer golf brings early play, and if you're early enough, you'll get some help from those who go before you. You'll see the lines of their putts—missed and made—etched in the dew on the uncut greens.

Sometimes we wish the next steps of our lives could be lined out so clearly. In a way, they can.

The broken lives of people who reject God should be for us very much like that line in the dew that misses the hole—a clear warning how *not* to live.

But the pattern of how to live is equally clear. It is spelled out in Scripture and it has been lived out by many godly men and women who have formed for us Christlike examples. Take note of those who live according to this godly pattern. It can be your pattern too!

TIP

PREPARE FOR GOLF'S REALITIES. EVERY SHOT WON'T GO WHERE YOU WANT IT TO GO.

ALL FOR US

But He was wounded for our transgressions, He was bruised for our iniquities; the chastisement for our peace was upon Him, and by His stripes we are healed.

How about a free golf lesson? Say Butch Harmon, longtime teacher of successful tour pros, called one evening and offered to teach you—for free! You'd certainly want to know why. "I've seen your swing," he would answer. "You need me. And I'd be happy to do it."

Butch Harmon is offering to pay a debt that is not his. After all, he's not the one who let your swing go to the dogs.

Of course, this would not happen. Strangely, however—and God is so strangely different than our world thinks—it has been done in the spiritual realm. Christ paid a debt that was not His. Our sin has left us irreparably damaged before God. But Christ came to our rescue. By His death, He has called us to Himself. By His grace, we answer, "Yes, Lord, I'm coming!"

> **TIP**
>
> YOUR BEST GOLF IS PLAYED BY ELIMINATING DISTRACTIONS AND FOCUSING ON THE TARGET.

RECOVERING THE SPLINTERS

And this I say for your own profit, not that I may put a leash on you, but for what is proper, and that you may serve the Lord without distraction.

1 CORINTHIANS 7:35

Ever wonder what to practice next? Golf leaves us with so many choices, from straightening out our drives, to heightening the trajectory of our irons, to softening our touch around the greens, to honing our aim with the putter. There's too much to choose from.

Your attempts to walk with the Savior can seem like this: Sunday's commitment to two services, Wednesday Bible study, Thursday's father-daughter activity, Saturday's outreach. You can spend so much time being "Christian" that you lose sight of Christ!

Paul was convinced that men and women of God could serve Him exclusively, with "undivided devotion." This is hard to imagine in our society, but the encouragement remains: do whatever you can to limit the splintering of your life. Give Christ lots and lots of room.

> **TIP**
>
> WHEN RAKING A BUNKER, MAKE SMOOTH WITH THE RAKE TO LESSEN THE NUMBER OF FURROWS.

FIRST THINGS FIRST

And now abide faith, hope, love, these three; but the greatest of these is love.

1 CORINTHIANS 13:13

Junior golfers arrive at their first clinic with all states of inventive swings: sideways, cross-handed, flailing, you name it. There is so much to correct. But a good pro doesn't worry about changing it all right now. The pro helps the child take it one step at a time.

Jesus' chosen Twelve were no angels either. At least one came to Jesus with an undesirable reputation. Another prejudicially criticized Jesus before he had even met Him. And in the end, one of them ended up being the devil's own agent. Jesus chose them anyway.

When it came to people, Jesus put first things first. He permitted their weaknesses and their sins because He did not see people for what they were. He saw them for what they could become. And He taught them the faith, hope, and love they would need for eternity.

TIP

FINISH YOUR WARM-UP BY VISUALIZING AND "PLAYING" THE COURSE'S FIRST FEW HOLES.

ROCK SOLID

"Do not fear, nor be afraid; have I not told you from that time, and declared it? You are My witnesses. Is there a God besides Me? Indeed there is no other Rock; I know not one."

ISAIAH 44:8

Face it: golf is anything but simple. By the time you calculate the distance to the green, the position of the hole, the weather conditions, and the rhythm of that yappy dog in the yard near the tee, it's pretty tough to remember your swing thoughts. Then you must put them to work.

The same thing can happen in your walk with the Lord, for life also has a lot of distractions. Satan, our enemy, loves to elevate the importance of lesser things and attract our eyes from God's love for us. When we trade *the* Rock for the world's many lesser rocks, we find that we are standing on sand, just like the builder in Christ's parable. His house collapsed because he did not pay first attention to its foundation. God is the one true Rock. Your security depends on standing on His great promises.

> **TIP**
>
> A TOWEL IS ONE OF YOUR MOST USEFUL TOOLS, ESPECIALLY IN CLEANING YOUR BALL ON THE GREEN.

NEW AND NEW AGAIN

So also is the resurrection of the dead. The body is sown in corruption, it is raised in incorruption. It is sown in dishonor, it is raised in glory. It is sown in weakness, it is raised in power. It is sown a natural body, it is raised a spiritual body. There is a natural body, and there is a spiritual body.

1 CORINTHIANS 15:42–44

At times on the golf course, we feel a long, long way from our potential. We want to get to the driving range and take out our frustrations or fly as far away from this dumb old game as possible.

There are times in life when we feel much the same. Our focus has fizzled, our backs ache, our phones ring all the time or not at all. Christ has given us abundant life, but there are always times when that abundance seems awfully meager or overwhelming. These are the times when we must remember that life abundant is about life eternal.

Our bodies, remember, are dying seeds. But what goes to the ground in death, dishonorable and weak, will be raised in Christ, glorious and strong. What an overwhelming hope!

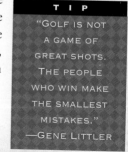

TIP

"GOLF IS NOT A GAME OF GREAT SHOTS. THE PEOPLE WHO WIN MAKE THE SMALLEST MISTAKES."
—GENE LITTLER

GOOD WORK

Therefore, my beloved brethren, be steadfast, immovable, always abounding in the work of the Lord, knowing that your labor is not in vain in the Lord.

1 CORINTHIANS 15:58

A day at the practice range can be the cure for a number of ills. Or it can be a source of frustration. How often have you hit the ball well on the range, only to have your swing fall apart on the course? Now, *that* is work done in vain.

Catastrophic loss can steal our life's work too. Only if our work is work of eternal significance are we insured against catastrophe—not only that, but also against fear and hatred and malice.

The apostle Paul knew all about such troubles. His enemies sought to shut him up and tear him down, jail him and murder him. Yet he was strong in encouraging us all to do the work of the Lord, because he knew that such labor was not done in vain.

TIP

TO WALK A COURSE, YOU ONLY HAVE TO GO ABOUT ONE MILE EACH HOUR. TRY IT MORE OFTEN!

THE POWER OF LOVE

Set me as a seal upon your heart, as a seal upon your arm; for love is as strong as death, jealousy as cruel as the grave; its flames are flames of fire, a most vehement flame.

Each of us who plays golf can spout off a rapid-fire list of reasons we love it, from the chance to begin each hole afresh to the joy of being outdoors with little else to think about.

But could we do the same with God's love? Or has His presence in our life become so esoteric that we speak of His love as a teenager babbles about some musician she has seen and heard but never met?

Let us be careful to know the love of our Father for the reality that it is. For His love is "as strong as death," perhaps the mightiest metaphor in Scripture. Like death, God's love is inevitable, coming our direction even when we are negligent to return it with our obedience. And God's love is conclusive. We can spend our lives denying it, but in the end it will reign regardless of us.

> **TIP**
>
> REMEMBER THESE BASIC RULES: PLAY THE COURSE AS YOU FOUND IT AND THE BALL AS IT LIES.

UNDERSTANDING

The eyes of your understanding being
enlightened; that you may know what is the
hope of His calling, what are the riches of the
glory of His inheritance in the saints, and what is
the exceeding greatness of His power toward us who
believe, according to the working of His mighty power.

EPHESIANS 1:18–19

Your non-golfing friends probably cannot imagine the appeal of swatting a ball from tee to green to hole, hole after hole and round after round, or how you spend so much time and so much money doing something that causes so much frustration.

Your nonbelieving friends probably don't understand you either. They cannot imagine the appeal of Bible study, worship, and prayer, or how you give so much time and money to a church steeped in an ancient tradition. The truth is they will never understand until the Holy Spirit reveals salvation to their hearts. In the meantime, Paul suggested praying that people would know three wonders: the hope, riches, and power of Christ. It is a prayer we can pray for those friends in our own lives who still don't understand.

TIP

A FLATTER SWING PLANE TENDS TO PRODUCE A DRAW; AN UPRIGHT PLANE PROMOTES A FADE.

ON AND ON

But as for you, brethren, do not grow
weary in doing good.

2 THESSALONIANS 3:13

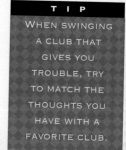

Especially when riding a cart, golf is not a physically demanding sport. But take one look at a serious player coming in from the range, face drenched in sweat, and you'll get a different idea. Serious golf requires serious work.

Our spiritual bodies are built similarly. As sinners, we are not conditioned to doing right. Before Christ enters our lives, we readily surrender to the appetite of our flesh. And the more we succumb to the flesh, the less able we are to combat its demands.

Living for Christ can be tough, then. Paul was no taskmaster requiring fifteen buckets of spiritual range balls. But he knew that we must be disciplined, putting aside all that seeks to hinder us and persisting in love-marked obedience. Jesus gave us this example, right through to the cross. His work has made ours so much easier.

TIP

WHEN SWINGING A CLUB THAT GIVES YOU TROUBLE, TRY TO MATCH THE THOUGHTS YOU HAVE WITH A FAVORITE CLUB.

IN THE FACE OF UNBELIEF

The foolishness of a man twists his way,
and his heart frets against the LORD.

PROVERBS 19:3

We have all witnessed the infamous golf scene where a player takes an awful swing resulting in an awful shot, then in awful fashion invokes the name of God in an unholy way. Perhaps (shamefully, we know now) we have been that golfer.

It's an odd sequence of events, really. Why, for our own stupid or stubborn acts, would we blame God for the consequences? Or why, when faced with the obvious working of God's hand, would we reject His preeminence? It's hard to know, but Scripture mentions just such episodes.

Jesus knew that men would doubt, disbelieve, and even betray Him. Even those closest to Him doubted and denied Him. But He sent them the Holy Spirit, and their unbelief changed to understanding, their folly to wis-dom. Like them, we also must move from persecution to praise.

TIP

YOU CAN HELP YOUR SHORT GAME BY ADDING A GAP WEDGE AND SUBTRACTING A RARELY USED LONG IRON.

MORE THAN A FEELING

But be doers of the word, and
not hearers only, deceiving yourselves.

JAMES 1:22

Suppose you show up for your second golf lesson and the instruction the pro gives you is exactly the same as the week before. Would you demand your money back? You might deserve it back—unless you have not hit a practice ball since the previous session.

How many passages of God's Word have we read, impressed by their import, only to leave them behind, eagerly reading on to see what the next passage inspires in us? Without a doubt, the Bible does inspire. But confidence without commitment goes nowhere.

The Word of God in our lives is meant first of all to give us a glimpse of what God has done for us. But the Word is also intended to move us in a Godward direction. We must let it change our very actions.

> **TIP**
>
> PRACTICE HITTING
> EACH OF YOUR
> WEDGES TO
> THREE DIFFERENT
> DISTANCES,
> CREATING
> BROADER ABILITY.

LEFT BEHIND

"Peace I leave with you, My peace I give to you;
not as the world gives do I give to you. Let not
your heart be troubled, neither let it be afraid."

JOHN 14:27

Are you one of those players who "leaves it all on the golf course" when you have finished a round? Athletes who do this have nothing left over in the way of competitiveness—at least for that day—when they have finished.

Certainly we can say the same of Jesus. When He left His disciples staring up into the sky, wondering what could have become of Him, He had done all that He had come to do. He had made a way again for God's people to know their heavenly Father.

But in leaving, there was much that He left behind, including His peace. The world will come against us, but because Jesus had so much to give, we can know what the world does not—a day without worry.

TIP

KEEP AN EYE ON WHERE YOUR PUTTS ARE MISSING. IF THEY'RE ALL LOW, PLAY MORE BREAK.

"DO AS I HAVE DONE"

*"For I have given you an example,
that you should do as I have done to you."*

JOHN 13:15

If you're looking to improve, you go to those who best know the game. You go to the professionals. Even just watching a pro on television, particularly getting a sense of his or her tempo, can bring greater steadiness to your own efforts.

From the time we are infants, we base much of ourselves on the examples of others. If our parents are nurturing people, their examples become our habits. Other mentors provoke the best in us too. In this way, we learn from life's professionals.

But those we follow most closely must be those who follow Christ earnestly. We will recognize them as we recognize Him: by the way they love and serve others without qualification or exception. They—and we—will do as He has done.

TIP

AS YOU TAKE YOUR
PUTTER BACK
AND THROUGH,
KEEP THE V
OF YOUR ARMS
CONSISTENT.

WINNING RESPECT

*Aspire to lead a quiet life, to mind
your own business, and to work with
your own hands, as we commanded you.*

1 THESSALONIANS 4:11

What a wonderful excuse to head to the golf
course! The next time someone is tormenting
you about the time you spend on the golf course,
you just point to Paul's instruction here to the
Thessalonians. Tell them that your golf game
fulfills a biblical teaching: it is quiet; it is a solitary
business; it is work done with your hands.

Honestly, what could Paul have meant by emphasizing these three particular characteristics of life and
work as characteristics to which we should aspire?

Plainly put, we are to be people with a point.
We are to speak purposefully, focus on the work
that has been given to us, and "get our hands dirty"
through disciplined commitment. We are God's
people, called to live as Christ
did. Jesus never lost sight of His
purpose. There was a point to
His person—and there should
be one to ours.

> **TIP**
>
> "PAINT"
> YOURSELF INTO
> A MENTAL BOX
> TO ELIMINATE
> DISTRACTIONS
> BEFORE
> YOU SWING.

DRAWN LINE

*Then many of the Jews who had come
to Mary, and had seen the things Jesus did,
believed in Him. But some of them went away
to the Pharisees and told them the things Jesus did.*

JOHN 11:45–46

In a casual round of golf, the normally stringent rules of the game are relaxed. Short putts become "good," players agree upon mulligans, and many bags hold extra clubs.

In our casual world, Satan does all he can to turn our eyes from God by clouding the issue about who God really is. Thus, we are pounded with the ubiquitous message that God is who we make Him to be. The lines have been softened.

But when Jesus raised Lazarus from the dead, the responses came on either side of a definite line: faith or rejection. Those who believed the miracle trusted Christ. Those who did not raced off and extracted a shocking verdict from the high priest: Jesus must die. It was a stark line, but it set the stage for the rest of us. We either stand for Christ or against Him.

> **TIP**
>
> IT'S HARD TO CONTROL DISTANCE FROM THE ROUGH, SO CONCENTRATE MOST ON HITTING IT STRAIGHT.

THE GREATEST TEST

Examine yourselves as to whether you are in the faith. Test yourselves. Do you not know yourselves, that Jesus Christ is in you?—unless indeed you are disqualified.

2 CORINTHIANS 13:5

There is just one sure way to know whether someone is a good golfer. We must get out on the course with him or with her. When we have seen the distance and shape of the shots, and tracked the score, we know just how good this player is.

Writing to the Corinthians, Paul spoke of a test of authenticity. Paul challenged them to examine themselves, to give themselves the test of faith.

This test is not in the talk or in the planning. It is a test of your walk. Do you walk as one eager to do what Christ would have you do? If so, your faith is alive, for as James wrote: "Faith without works is dead" (James 2:26).

Although we are saved by grace "through faith" (Ephesians 2:8), our works reveal the authenticity of that faith—just as the golfer is revealed through his game.

FALSE GODS

*And the word of the LORD came to me,
saying, "Son of man, these men have set up
their idols in their hearts, and put before them
that which causes them to stumble into iniquity.
Should I let Myself be inquired of at all by them?"*

EZEKIEL 14:2–3

We know what an idol is. An image made of stone or wood, an idol is ascribed a power it does not really possess.

Today, as in Ezekiel's time, we are more likely to honor idols of the heart. These are the things that charm those of us who may be called "avid" (as in "avid golfer"). Thinking there is room in our hearts for both, we pursue simultaneously things of this world and things of God.

Yet although "everything is permissible" (1 Corinthians 10:23 NIV), it is certain that some things, when given a place in our hearts, will cause God to ask of us, "Shall I allow this one to inquire of me?" It is not right of us to loudly chase idols of false promise, then wonder why God is silent when we inquire of Him.

> **TIP**
>
> IF YOU PREFER AN UNRUSHED GAME, ASK YOUR PRO SHOP TO SUGGEST LESS CROWDED TIMES WHEN YOU CAN PLAY.

Now it came to pass, as He was praying in a certain place, when He ceased, that one of His disciples said to Him, "Lord, teach us to pray, as John also taught his disciples."

LUKE 11:1

How's your putting? It's not a trick question. But it sure feels like one. For with putting (and the rest of golf), there is always room for improvement.

There's an equally cumbersome spiritual question: How's your prayer life? Talk about putting the dagger in a conversation!

No wonder that disciple asked Jesus to teach them to pray. And knowing the disciple's honest dilemma, Jesus answered him: Direct your prayer to the heavenly Father, Jesus began. Present your needs to God, the physical needs and the spiritual ones. Forgive and seek forgiveness.

Study the Lord's Prayer, and you'll gather much more rich instruction. But spend some time in prayer, and you'll gain a wealth of other riches too: encouragement, forgiveness, empowerment, provision . . .

TIP

DON'T CONFUSE WARM-UP WITH PRACTICE OR YOU'LL WEAR YOURSELF OUT BEFORE YOU START.

A SAVED LIFE

"For whoever desires to save his life will lose it, but whoever loses his life for My sake will save it."

LUKE 9:24

Have you ever grabbed a club ferociously, let your mind replay every swing thought from your last six lessons, and swung with all your mechanical might? Sure you have. And where has the ball gone?

Often we try to grab hold of our lives in this same way. We want what we want, and we hold on with all our stubborn strength. At least it has the look of strength. But Jesus wasn't fooled. And He didn't want His disciples fooled either.

God, through Christ, offered another way: you gain life by losing it. We can only follow such a teaching because Jesus has gone before us. For His sacrifice, He was raised to the right hand of the Father, His throne established forever. So we gain life by living in His strength rather than ours. We trade our lives for His.

TIP

PRACTICING TROUBLE SHOTS WILL BETTER PREPARE YOU FOR THEM ON THE COURSE.

GOING ON

Do not let the sun go down on your wrath.

EPHESIANS 4:26

When we look down the line and see that guy inching his way onto the range to rake in a nearby ball, we know exactly what he has done: he has flubbed his last ball—and he isn't about to leave the range with that shot on his mind!

It is among our callings as followers of Christ to end our days in tune with the love of God. Carrying sin into tomorrow is to wake up "separated" from God.

God has promised that He won't leave us, and He wants us to desire that we never leave Him. So it is important to Him that our encounters with Him and with others end right, with His love repairing and sustaining every relationship. How much better this is than to walk away angry or jealous or worried—all feelings that can stand between us and our loving Savior.

TIP

TEST NEW BALLS BY COMPARING YOUR BEST SHOTS AGAINST WHAT YOUR REGULAR BALL GIVES YOU.

RIGHTLY JUDGED

But Daniel purposed in his heart that he would not defile himself with the portion of the king's delicacies, nor with the wine which he drank; therefore he requested of the chief of the eunuchs that he might not defile himself.

DANIEL 1:8

Daniel bore in his name the standard that would guide his life. The name *Daniel* meant "God is judge." On the surface, this meaning intimidates us. But perhaps this is because we do not have the eyes of Daniel.

Daniel was set free by making God his only judge. His commitment freed him from breaking God's law, and his superior health bound the other young men to his godly diet. His commitment freed him from the lions' den and bound his accusers within the teeth of those beasts. Who is your judge? Is it your playing partner, that instructor you read faithfully, or the memory of some parent who always demanded your "best effort"? Next time you play, do this: make God your judge. Your entire perspective will be changed. You'll want to play that way all the time—and live that way too!

> **TIP**
>
> TO TEST THE VERSATILITY OF YOUR GAME, GET AWAY TO DIFFERENT COURSES NOW AND THEN.

WHAT DO YOU KNOW?

Pilate said to them, "You have a guard;
go your way, make it as secure as you know how."

MATTHEW 27:65

If you want to get yourself in a lot of trouble on a brand-new golf course, make all kinds of assumptions. Assume the greens are soft. Assume you know the distances. Assume the wind is swirling.

This is how the Pharisees got themselves into trouble too. After Jesus' death, they blockaded His tomb, assuming they were thwarting the distraught followers of a dead man. They were not. They were dealing with the God of the universe, who released His Son with a violent earthquake and an angelic visitation. Despite their assumptions, Jesus our Savior was raised from the dead.

It is a lesson to us all. Assume what you will, but know this: Jesus Christ was, is, and always will be God as Man, the risen King. Never think that by your own dismissal of Him, you will ever box Him up. He has already broken every chain.

> **TIP**
>
> A COURSE'S SLOPE, NOT ITS RATING, TELLS YOU HOW TOUGH IT IS FOR THE AVERAGE PLAYER.

EQUIPPED TO STAND

*No temptation has overtaken you except
such as is common to man; but God is faithful,
who will not allow you to be tempted beyond what
you are able, but with the temptation will also make
the way of escape, that you may be able to bear it.*

1 CORINTHIANS 10:13

As I drove with a friend past a golf course recently, he spoke of his respect for the course and how much he enjoyed playing it. But quickly he added: "Of course, I have yet to play an easy course." His words told what many of us are reluctant to say: the game is beyond us to master.

Life, too, is beyond our ability to master. Inevitably, we face times of confusion and sadness and temptation and sin. Where is the power of God then? Right where it always is. At His fingertips. Touching us just as we need to be touched.

Always our strength must come from Him. The more time we spend with God and the more purposeful we are in those times with Him, the more readily we will draw on His incredible, faithful power. The more equipped we will be to stand and then, victoriously, to march.

> **TIP**
>
> GENERATE CREATIVITY IN YOUR SHORT GAME BY PRACTICING DIFFERENT SHOTS OFF VARIOUS LIES.

SPEAK UP

So Jesus stood still and called them,
and said, "What do you want Me to do for you?"

MATTHEW 20:32

On the practice tee, when our golf teacher asks, "What do you want me to do for you?" we respond nobly, "My short game stinks" or "I'm hooking my driver." What we really want to say is, "I want to beat Carolyn. I'm sick of losing to her!"

When Jesus asked the two blind men what they wanted from Him, they could have listed lesser cures—pennies for dinner or a family that cared. But this was their one chance. Before them stood the Healer, who could give them what would really satisfy them. So they yelled mightily, and then with His power He opened their eyes and changed their lives.

How blessed we are that He still walks among us! Let's not content ourselves with whispered petitions. It is time to set aside our decorum and shout: "Jesus, we want to see!"

TIP

DON'T RUSH YOUR DOWNSWING.

INSTEAD, ACCELERATE SMOOTHLY THROUGH THE BALL.

BIGGER AND BETTER

Moreover the law entered that the offense
might abound. But where sin abounded, grace
abounded much more, so that as sin reigned in death,
even so grace might reign through righteousness to
eternal life through Jesus Christ our Lord.

ROMANS 5:20–21

In early 2003, seventy-four-year-old Jack Gosch made back-to-back aces on the tenth and eleventh holes of his home course, right after what he called his worst front nine in several months.

We all go through seasons resembling Mr. Gosch's front nine—weeks or months of dashed hopes, incalculable losses, or reckless trials. In fact, our life before Christ is like that front nine. The consequences of sin mount, and we discover we are on the entirely wrong road.

Don't take this lightly. Sin is a formidable force in the universe. Its earthly consequence is physical death. And without salvation, its ultimate power is in separating us eternally from the very God who created us and loved us since the beginning.

No wonder grace is so amazing. We must have it!

TIP

AT THE TOP OF YOUR BACKSWING, YOU WANT YOUR THUMBS UNDER THE GRIP.

LAST CHANCE

*"And when those came who were hired about the
eleventh hour, they each received a denarius."*

MATTHEW 20:9

Those familiar with the recurring double-
or-nothing wager right down to the last hole
should be able to quickly recognize a lesson in the
way gambling golfers play their bets to the end.

Many people live their lives with little concern
for the course they follow, assuming there will be
a final opportunity to clean everything up before
God. On their deathbeds, they can "press and break
even." In this regard, they are right, as we know
from Jesus' parable of the eleventh-hour workers.

But life's gamblers miss something else entirely.
There is no need to wait for heaven to experience
the fullness of life. God offers it to us beginning the
moment we give our lives to Jesus.

TIP

KEEP YOUR
LOWER BODY
"QUIET" WHEN
HITTING SHORT
SHOTS AROUND
THE GREEN.

END OF DISCUSSION

Therefore God also has highly exalted Him and given Him the name which is above every name, that at the name of Jesus every knee should bow, of those in heaven, and of those on earth, and of those under the earth.

PHILIPPIANS 2:9–10

Cast aside by the increasing number of athletic tour players with strict practice and workout regimes, the question that lingered far too long is gone: *Is golf a sport?* Of course, the answer didn't really matter that much.

The most important questions have to do with our lives, not just with life. What is our purpose? Who will help us fulfill it? And when our lives have ended, will anything we have done been worth it?

Many people today do not believe there are definitive answers to these questions. The prevailing philosophy says that what you find to be true for you is what you should call truth. Just don't call it truth for others. But Paul wrote that in the end *all* will bow; *all* will know the answer. How much richer their lives will be if we can give them the answer long before the end!

TIP

IF YOU LIKE YOUR STANDARD PUTTER BUT ARE MISSING SHORT PUTTS, TRY A CROSS-HANDED GRIP.

THE LONG RUN

There is no wisdom or understanding
or counsel against the LORD.

PROVERBS 21:30

It's match play and you have just watched your opponent chip in to steal an obvious win from your hands. Defeated, you mutter, "This match is over," as you make your way to the second tee.

No smart golfer would give up on a round of golf so quickly! Yet we regularly take stock of our lives according to yesterday. Or this morning. Or just now. We forget to "walk circumspectly" (Ephesians 5:15 KJV), and instead we sprint or stumble, buffeted by the latest winds.

God, although with us each moment, is a God of forever. His wisdom, His insight, His plans come from His ability to view the entirety of history—past, present, and future. To Him, failure and disaster are only steps along the way. We will not win all of life's "matches," but we can always keep gaining on His plan.

TIP

COPY THE
GOOD YOU SEE
FROM THE
GREAT PLAYERS.

DON'T SAY IT

Death and life are in the power of the tongue, and those who love it will eat its fruit.

PROVERBS 18:21

If you're worth your salt at admitting your faults, you'll jump right in here. Nearly all golfers would have to. Somewhere, sometime, you have said something on the golf course you wish you had never uttered (or shouted). And off the golf course, you've done the same, probably this week.

Oh, those tongues of ours! What a nasty tendency they have to precede our brains! And in a world that loves noise, volume is golden.

So let's stop today, short of our usual stopping place. Let's say, "Enough said." Let's think instead— think for some minutes how we will use our tongues today for the glory of God.

TIP

WHEN IN DOUBT, LAY UP. PLAYING IT SAFE MAKES YOU CONFIDENT TO STICK YOUR APPROACH IN THERE TIGHT!

THE GOOD SIDE

Rejoice in the Lord always. Again I will say, rejoice!

Here's a great golf tip: "Remember the birdies and forget the rest." It's not about improving your swing. It's about improving your enjoyment of the game.

Paul gave the Philippians a similar tip for life: "Rejoice always." It kind of makes you wonder if Paul lived on planet Earth, doesn't it? Rejoice in everything? He couldn't have possibly been serious.

But because Paul knew his God so very well, because he knew the fullness of grace so intimately, Paul was something very few of us are. Paul was a "glass all full" kind of person. He knew that if he could count on Christ to undo all that he, Paul, had done in his sinful self, then he could count on God for anything. And if you count on God for anything, you can rejoice in Him for everything.

TIP

NEAR THE GREEN, PARK YOUR CART ALONG THE WAY TO THE NEXT HOLE.

AUGUST

THE CASE FOR CHRIST

The first one to plead his cause seems right, until his neighbor comes and examines him.

PROVERBS 18:17

While relaxing with friends after the round, do you enjoy a lively debate about which Tour player is best in one facet of the game or another? It's easy to get caught up in such a conversation.

In today's world, a case is being made against Jesus Christ. It plays the biblical role of "the first to present his case." It is a popular argument, exalting the ability to think for ourselves and the freedom to do what is right in our own eyes.

But one certain riff plays in the heartbeat of every human. It is guilt. This cut in our conscience asks each of us that critical question: *If what I am doing is not wrong, why do I feel bad about it?* Guilt is God's rebuttal to sin, and it burns in our hearts, even when we say He does not exist.

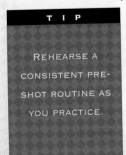

TIP

REHEARSE A CONSISTENT PRE-SHOT ROUTINE AS YOU PRACTICE.

SHUN EVIL

"And to man He said, 'Behold, the fear of the Lord, that is wisdom, and to depart from evil is understanding.'"

Sometimes the most satisfying of feelings is finally to understand. Certainly, it is among the most esteeming. We often lose confidence when we cannot figure out a problem that appears so simple on the surface. That's partly why golf can be such a frustrating game. Just last week your putting was excellent; now nothing will go in.

The world is certainly no less confusing. Our best friend runs off with another woman. Our trustworthy neighbor is convicted of embezzlement. Our happy-go-lucky colleague checks into a rehab center. What's with all this evil? How can "good" people be sucked into its grasp?

Yet it is not our place to "figure out" evil. It is our place to recognize it and to run from it. In this way we show that we understand . . . that evil is not of God . . . that evil tears apart people and relationships between them . . . that evil is to be shunned at all costs.

TIP

TO LOOSEN UP BEFORE YOUR ROUND, SLOWLY SWING YOUR DRIVER WITH ITS HEADCOVER ON.

KNOW IT ALL

And He is the head of the body, the church,
who is the beginning, the firstborn from the dead,
that in all things He may have the preeminence.

COLOSSIANS 1:18

AUGUST 3

If you are a golfer, you know a lot about golf: the swing, the courses, the professionals. If you are an investor, you know a lot about business: fifty-two-week highs, the effects of prime rate adjustments, the best no-load funds. Teachers know children; pastors know theology; mechanics know engines; doctors know medicine.

But how much do you know of the Savior? It's a question we must all answer in the same way: *not enough.* We do not know enough of Him, for our sin-turned hearts are used to looking at ourselves first. And we cannot know enough of Him, for He is mighty and infinite.

But we know where to begin looking. We look at the Word of God. And if we are as committed to this knowledge as we are to the other endeavors in our lives, we will keep looking intently until the day we see His wonderful face.

TIP
GOLF GIMMICKS ABOUND, BUT NONE OF THEM BEAT SOUND FUNDAMENTALS AND REGULAR PRACTICE.

TOWARD PERFECTION

As you know how we exhorted, and comforted, and charged every one of you, as a father does his own children, that you would walk worthy of God who calls you into His own kingdom and glory.

1 THESSALONIANS 2:11–12

One of the many reasons golf serves as such a great metaphor for the spiritual life is that no one has ever played the perfect game. In spite of the continual lowering of scores on the professional tours, the rarest of feats is a tournament played without a bogey. Even Tour winners must deal with failure.

God is not deceived about our failures. He knows we will wander from Him, for a moment or a season. Yet He looks for us to choose Him and His plan for our lives. Knowing that our flesh will fall, He wants our hearts, as David gave Him his.

The biblical idea of perfection is more accurately translated "completeness." To become perfect in Him is not to become perfect. Not in this lifetime. But it is to become complete, a goal achieved only if we are resolute in gaining daily in Him.

TIP

OBVIOUS SWING FLAWS ARE OFTEN RELATED TO POOR GRIP OR ADDRESS POSITION.

NO CRISIS HERE

We are children of God, and if children, then heirs—heirs of God and joint heirs with Christ, if indeed we suffer with Him, that we may also be glorified together.

ROMANS 8:16–17

Everyone is seeking an identity these days. In fact, plenty of people are content to possess their identities in something outside of themselves: their jobs, their cars, their contacts, even their addictions and their struggles. And you know golfers whose identities are based on what clubs are in their bags or what balls they place on the tee!

The Bible, too, speaks of seeking our identity from outside ourselves. But rather than coming from some*thing*, Scripture teaches that our identity must come from Some*one*. We can identify ourselves directly with God's Son, Jesus Christ.

It may be uncomfortable to give up your own identity in favor of another. But, oh, what Another! And what really were our identities before? By giving ourselves to Christ, we receive the glory He offers in return.

TIP

A NUTRITIOUS SNACK AT THE TURN WILL HELP KEEP YOUR ENERGY UP FOR THOSE LATE HOLES.

BOLD WORDS

"Yet who knows whether you have come to the kingdom for such a time as this?"

ESTHER 4:14

Little-known Mordecai made himself large by confronting his goddaughter Esther, queen in Xerxes's vast kingdom. She alone could save the Jews, her people.

Strict laws made this risky business, however. Although a queen, Esther could be executed for initiating a hearing with the king. Like Esther, we would be tempted to preserve ourselves. But our spirits rightly prod us. We cannot turn them on and off simply by moving from one activity to the next.

Sovereignly, God has placed us wherever we are, from the royal court to our tiny corner offices, from the Tournament Players Course of this weekend's PGA event to the local muni where we pay our eighteen bucks and miss easy putts on bumpy greens. Our spirits, placed in us by God, go with us to each of these places. And our spirits embolden us to speak for Him.

TIP

NO GREAT GOLFER IS ONLY A "FEEL PLAYER." GREAT GOLFERS ALL HAVE GREAT MECHANICS TOO.

GRATITUDE

Oh, give thanks to the LORD! Call upon His name;
make known His deeds among the peoples!

1 CHRONICLES 16:8

As a simple exercise in faith, let's give thanks today.

Thank God today for the provision He has given you. Even in the basics—food and drink and clothing and shelter—we are blessed. Beyond that are the many "bonus prizes" of life: comfortable cars, evenings at the show, sunny rounds of golf. Each comes from God.

Thank God today for the people He has given you. Family, friends, coworkers, neighbors, pastors, mentors—easy or difficult, they all shape our lives. And because they, like we, have eternal souls, we can make a grand difference in their lives too.

Finally, thank God today for the purpose He has given you. As men and women born to sin, we started in one hell-bent direction. Through Christ, our courses changed. We are bound for hea-ven. What a great way to live!

TIP

IF YOU ENJOY THE TIPS IN MAGAZINES, DON'T GET OVERLOADED. WORK ON ONE NEW THING AT A TIME.

THE MAIN THING

"Concerning the hope and resurrection of the dead I am being judged!"

ACTS 23:6

With so many things to think about before each golf swing, it can be rather difficult to determine which is the main component of good execution. Not so with the good news of Christ, where the main thing is made very clear to us.

Before the Sanhedrin, in the harshest of courts, challenged by his peers, Paul went straight to this greatest hope: the truly powerful resurrection of Jesus Christ.

Without the resurrection, we worship a Savior who has not really saved us. For if we cannot be raised from the dead, we have no chance for heaven. And if we cannot go to heaven, then we are doomed simply to die. Without the resurrection, not only do we have no chance at heaven; we cannot even hope for it—our dreams would have died with Christ.

> **TIP**
>
> UNLESS WEATHER HAS MUDDIED THE COURSE, DON'T BUMP THE BALL. LEARN TO PLAY IT AS IT LIES.

BIG AS CAN BE

God thunders marvelously with His voice;
He does great things which we cannot comprehend.

JOB 37:5

Although few of us have ever shot par on any course, we are more inclined to move back to the longer tees than forward to the shorter ones. We like challenges that go beyond us, and we dream of someday meeting those challenges.

When it comes to God, however, our reckoning is somewhat different. Our spirits know the truth of God's immensity. But the sin nature that still dwells within urges us to reduce Him to a manageable size.

If you are guilty of shrinking God, you must give God space. You must go to where the thunder rolls and hear the voice of God. You must go to where the lightning strikes and sense the enormity of His power. For in such a place, He will not just indwell your heart—He will expand it.

TIP

PLAN TO LEAVE YOUR CHIP SHOTS WHERE YOU'LL HAVE THE EASIEST PUTT.

THE RIGHT WORDS

He who walks with wise men will be wise,
but the companion of fools will be destroyed.

PROVERBS 13:20

How good it is to be standing on the range, beating balls, when someone knowledgeable in the game walks up and speaks a sentence of helpful instruction! You take that bit of golfing wisdom and instantly put it into practice to find that, sure enough, it changes everything.

Any wise word can bring that kind of aid, Solomon wrote. And as believers with continual access to the Word of God and the indwelling guidance of the Holy Spirit, we have the marvelous privilege to impart such words.

We may give, like the golf teacher, words of instruction. Encouragement to those who need a gentle push. Confirmation to those who have already taken brave steps. Admonition to those who are missing the mark. As ambassadors of Christ, we may give words of life.

TIP

POSITION YOUR EYES DIRECTLY OVER THE TARGET LINE WHEN ADDRESSING A PUTT.

QUITE RIGHT

*But now the righteousness of God apart from
the law is revealed, being witnessed by the
Law and the Prophets, even the righteousness
of God, through faith in Jesus Christ, to all
and on all who believe. For there is no difference.*

ROMANS 3:21–22

An old golf book, sometimes called the epistle
to the Romans, includes these sad but true
words: "There is no one who does good, not even
one. . . . Their mouths are full of cursing and
bitterness" (3:12, 14 NIV).

To be fair to those who are gripped by this game,
golf is not the only endeavor that reveals shameful
character. How about that moment when your boss
says you are not living up to expectations? When
the pipe breaks under the kitchen sink? When your
teenage daughter has "something" she needs to tell
you? Life gives us plenty of opportunities to display
what is within us. It is a good thing
that we are not trying to get to
heaven by our own righteousness,
but by the righteousness of Jesus.
Everything we do on our own is
just not good enough.

> **TIP**
>
> TO IMPROVE YOUR
> PUTTING FEEL,
> PRACTICE SIX-
> FOOTERS WHILE
> LOOKING AT THE
> HOLE INSTEAD
> OF THE BALL.

BELIEVE IT

And [Abram] believed in the LORD, and He accounted it to him for righteousness.

GENESIS 15:6

Have you ever played in a pro-am? Before you even step on the tee, you know this will be your best golfing day ever. The pro's scores will be credited as your scores, and you believe that he or she is better than you.

Now, this is an imperfect analogy, because the pro may let you down, soaring into the mid-70s and leaving your team back in the pack. But God is completely reliable. To believe in Him is to receive credit for righteousness, and to receive all He has promised for those who worship Him in spirit and in truth.

Your mind may be telling you that this idea is too easy, that you must *do* something to be recognized by the Father for your actions. But Abram's righteousness did not come through anything he had done; it came through believing that through the Savior, something would be done.

TIP

SEE GOLF'S OBSTACLES AS CHALLENGES RATHER THAN SETBACKS.

RULING IN RIGHTEOUSNESS

"The God of Israel said, the Rock of Israel spoke to me: 'He who rules over men must be just, ruling in the fear of God. And he shall be like the light of the morning when the sun rises, a morning without clouds, like the tender grass springing out of the earth, by clear shining after rain.'"

2 SAMUEL 23:3–4

Although golf's appeal is broader these days, courses are still a chosen hangout of those who make their living in business, politics, and medicine. To speak of the attributes of leadership among golfers is to hit an appropriate target.

Among King David's last words, he chose to share God's own words to him about two great qualities of leadership. First, leaders must rule with righteousness. They must know the laws of the land and the mandates of Scripture, adhering to them unwaveringly. And they must instill this same respect for absolute propriety among their charges. Second, leaders must fear God, knowing that what they have today can be lost tomorrow.

Rule righteously. Fear God. In this way, you will go from appointed one to anointed one.

TIP

GREAT SWINGS DON'T ALWAYS PRODUCE GREAT SCORES. BE SURE YOU KNOW HOW TO MANAGE THE GOLF COURSE.

STRAIGHT AND NARROW

The integrity of the upright will guide them, but the perversity of the unfaithful will destroy them.

PROVERBS 11:3

Like a professional and a hacker side by side on the driving range are the person called upright and the one called unfaithful.

The person who lacks integrity will do all he can to appear righteous. But in the end, his sins find him out, and so do his friends. He will either find himself lonely or find himself looking for the next poor fool who will—at first—believe him.

Integrity, however, is a singular course in a godly direction. The rules are set beforehand, and people of integrity choose always to play by them—even when it is not easy to do so. The one who chooses integrity also chooses truth, perseverance, and confidence. No wonder others look to such people to lead them! It is easy to commit to those who are so committed themselves.

> **TIP**
>
> IF YOU CAN'T REPLACE OR FILL YOUR DIVOT, GENTLY KICK IN THE SIDES TO REPAIR THE DAMAGE.

CHANGE FOR THE BETTER

*"Woe to you, scribes and Pharisees, hypocrites!
For you travel land and sea to win one proselyte,
and when he is won, you make him twice as
much a son of hell as yourselves."*

MATTHEW 23:15

When we talk one game and play another, it doesn't take long for our true skill to be revealed. The course will show us for what we are.

Christ unveiled hypocrisy in the Pharisees too. Their fault was not that they were without passion. Rather, their passion was so great that it blinded them to compassion. And they passed this legacy of haughty intolerance on to those who were their followers.

Following Christ means taking a different course altogether. It is a course away from religion and into forgiving, honest relationships with those who disciple us and those we wish to disciple. We go out in understanding rather than judgment.

TIP

TAKE SOME
SWINGS WITH
YOUR EYES
CLOSED TO FEEL
WHAT THE CLUB
IS DOING.

AT THE READY

Your word I have hidden in my heart,
that I might not sin against You.

PSALM 119:11

In the waning light, after you've completed your "serious" practice, you stand on the range and try things you'd rarely expect to use—punch shots, left-handed shots, one-legged shots. You do it for fun, and because one day you just might need a funny little miracle shot on the golf course.

Scripture memory is similar to the purposeful practice of the accomplished golfer. Some Scripture we memorize because it instructs us in the essentials of our faith. But other Scripture we memorize because it is a resource and a comfort to us in troubled times.

Like any discipline, Scripture memorization can lead to weariness. But when we remember the purposes behind memorizing Scripture, and when we let Scripture inform our lives at every possible turn, we will be armed and ready for whatever odd or unrighteous circumstance might come our way.

TIP

MAKING PRACTICE SWINGS WITH YOUR FEET TOGETHER CAN HELP IMPROVE YOUR BALANCE.

HOLIER-THAN-THOU

"By that will we have been sanctified through the offering of the body of Jesus Christ once for all."

HEBREWS 10:10

Here's the bad news: try as he or she might, your teaching pro can't turn you into a Hall of Famer. Odds are, you simply have too far to go and you've started much too late.

Without knowing the full assurance of Scripture, getting yourself all the way to holy can be as dreamy a thought as becoming Ben Hogan. When you come across that Old Testament command, "Be holy because I, the LORD your God, am holy" (Leviticus 19:2 NIV), your head starts shaking.

Thank God for the new covenant between Him and us through Jesus Christ! Through it, we have been made holy—right now. After all, a Holy Spirit cannot dwell in an unholy temple! Thus, in beautiful progression, the Son has made us holy by His sacrifice so that the Holy Spirit may indwell us and prepare us for the day when we will meet the Father.

TIP

FOR OTHERS ON THE COURSE, YOUR MOST IMPORTANT PIECE OF GOLF EQUIPMENT IS YOUR DIVOT REPAIR TOOL.

GROW ON!

As newborn babes, desire the pure milk of the word, that you may grow thereby, if indeed you have tasted that the Lord is gracious.

1 PETER 2:2-3

If age has mellowed you, you may find that even if you don't love golf as much as when you were more competitive, you still love going to the golf course. You enjoy being with people and getting away from your regular routine. It's a total change in your perspective.

How like life in Christ! When we come to Him, deciding that the lives we have been living are full of holes, He forgives us and cleanses us from our sin. It's complete salvation.

Immediately, God begins to rewrite the code that is in us. It is no longer we who hold the place of prominence. It is *He*. And as long as we actively pursue what He has in mind for our lives through the study of His Word and the conversation called prayer, He moves us in a God-focused direction.

TIP

PLAYING ON A HOT DAY? START DRINKING WATER LONG BEFORE YOUR ROUND.

SPIRITUAL DISCIPLINE

*Thus Hezekiah did throughout all Judah,
and he did what was good and right and true
before the LORD his God. And in every work that
he began in the service of the house of God, in
the law and in the commandment, to seek his
God, he did it with all his heart. So he prospered.*

2 CHRONICLES 31:20–21

So you want to be a great golfer? Well, here's
all it takes: discipline. You will need a focus so
singular that other areas of your life must be set aside.

But when your discipline is directed toward the
King of heaven, nothing else will suffer.

This is what Hezekiah, king of Judah, discovered.
He committed himself to God's principal vision:
reverence for His temple and obedience from His
people. He made no small commitment, no quick trip
down to the tabernacle. No, Hezekiah sought God
wholeheartedly. He went after God, reading His laws
and studying His decrees. Then
he did what God commanded.
Hezekiah's work was neither hap-
hazard nor heartless. He knew
God's Word and he knew God's
work. He committed himself, and
for that he prospered.

TIP

TO KEEP YOUR
FOCUS SHARP,
PLAY YOUR
ROUND IN SIX
THREE-HOLE
"MINI-COURSES."

ONLY ONE

[God] has . . . spoken to us by His Son, . . . who being the brightness of His glory and the express image of His person, and upholding all things by the word of His power, when He had by Himself purged our sins, sat down at the right hand of the Majesty on high.

HEBREWS 1:2–3

If you're a golf-shop junkie, you've stood overwhelmed before the boxes and boxes of golf balls. There are so many to choose from!

More than a few people have tried to make the matter of faith similar to other free enterprise. "Choose what you want," says this idea, "and I'll choose what I want. And neither of us can go wrong." That may work for choosing golf balls, but when it comes to choosing the focus of our faith, our position must be much more severe: there is only one right choice. It is both sad and ironic that advertisers are praised when they present any product they wish as better, newer, stronger, best— while theologians are criticized. But the writer of Hebrews was no mere theologian. Inspired by the Holy Spirit, he made it clear: the Son, Jesus Christ, is "the exact representation" of God's being.

TIP

IF CONDITIONS ARE BAD, REMEMBER IT'S THE SAME FOR EVERYONE, AND SIMPLY DO YOUR BEST.

READY FOR ROUGH

But know this, that in the last days
perilous times will come.

2 TIMOTHY 3:1

In each round of golf, we face unexpected challenges—experts say three on average—like shots from behind trees or severe lies in bunkers. Practice prepares us for these.

Paul wrote to his protégé, Timothy, that trouble will come in life too. We must not be surprised by it. We must be prepared for it. Paul went on to list some of the ways people will act unrighteously in the end times—they will be boastful, unforgiving, self-serving, and abusive. They will lack self-control, act brutally and with treachery, and they will love pleasure rather than God.

But in Christ we are a different people. The more we know of Him, the more we are able to recognize the folly before us. This is important. We want always to be clear on the difference between righteousness and unrighteousness. We want to be trained in the truth.

TIP

INVOLVE YOUR WHOLE FAMILY IN THE GAME; YOU CAN PLAY TOGETHER FOR A LIFETIME.

GOOD AND BEST

And the LORD said to Samuel, "Heed the voice of the people in all that they say to you; for they have not rejected you, but they have rejected Me, that I should not reign over them."

1 SAMUEL 8:7

Teaching pros must swallow hard sometimes. We come to them wanting something worked out in our game that they know is about six steps beyond us. We pay them to give us what we want, but they wish they could teach us what is best.

God swallowed hard this way when His people requested a king. He was not grieved that they were seeking a king over a prophet. Both could be great in the hands of God. What truly struck the Lord was that they were not choosing Him. They were asking for an earthly ruler, which, He said, "they have done since the day that I brought them up out of Egypt" (1 Samuel 8:8).

In our lives, anything short of God is less than best. Only a faith in God first and God best will make us rich in Him.

> **TIP**
>
> RULES FOR MATCH PLAY AND STROKE PLAY ARE NOT THE SAME—BE SURE YOU KNOW THE DIFFERENCE.

GAINING ON IT

*We are bound to thank God always for
you, brethren, as it is fitting, because your
faith grows exceedingly, and the love of every
one of you all abounds toward each other.*

2 THESSALONIANS 1:3

On the golf course, when we have hit the ball
well and scored low, we know that teeing it up
again probably wouldn't result in any better score.
So we just wish we would have made that one extra
putt or that the ball would have kicked left rather
than right on that one key hole.

There is always room, as they say, for improvement.

Although Jesus is the same yesterday, today,
and forever, we are not. Temptation we resisted
yesterday can capture us today. Likewise, the prayer
that has gone unspoken far too long we now pray
with fervency—and God answers us demonstrably.
We will never in these present bodies get it all right.
But that doesn't mean we choose
to stop growing in faith or
increasing in love. We "press on,
that [we] may lay hold of that for
which Christ Jesus has also laid
hold of [us]" (Philippians 3:12).

> **TIP**
>
> THINK SPEED,
> NOT DIRECTION,
> WHILE STROKING
> A LONG PUTT.

EMERGENCE

We went through fire and through water;
but You brought us out to rich fulfillment.

PSALM 66:12

There is no prouder golfer than the one who makes birdie from "the gunch." Yep, the golf holes that lead to the best stories are those where we start out in big trouble, then come away smiling.

We delight as well in hearing the salvation stories of men and women whom God has fully changed. Although we fall into the habit of praising God only when life is easy, the biblical writers knew that sometimes God's greatest blessings come when the darkness surrounds us.

This is why the psalmist could look at fire and flood and see the victorious emergence rather than the hardship. The blessing is in the destination, which means we can't judge the journey until it is through.

TIP

PREVIEW THE
ROLL OF THE BALL
IN YOUR MIND
BEFORE
YOU PUTT.

THE FRIEND OF THE DAY BEFORE

Confess your trespasses to one another, and pray for one another, that you may be healed. The effective, fervent prayer of a righteous man avails much.

JAMES 5:16

If you have ever hit balls after a round, you know that everything you can't make happen on the course starts clicking on the range. It leads to the inevitable question: "Why couldn't I get this going before?"

Unfortunately, life can be just like this. The day after he sins, your friend lays the weight of consequences upon your shoulders. It is no good being a day-after friend, one who must help clean up the mess after it is made. We often pride ourselves on how God miraculously heals the hurt of wayward souls. But why not work to prevent sin and its consequences in the first place? Infidelity doesn't have to happen—nor embezzlement, abortion, or gossip. But to prevent them, we must become a day-before friend. With love and encouragement, we must delve into each other's lives before it is too late.

TIP

DON'T TRY TO DEFEAT NEGATIVE THOUGHTS; REPLACE THEM WITH POSITIVE ONES.

LOOKING FOR GOD

Then Laban and Bethuel answered and said, "The thing comes from the LORD; we cannot speak to you either bad or good."

GENESIS 24:50

Avid golfers regularly hear golf's great refrain when a player makes a great shot or finishes well: "That will keep you coming back." In a world increasingly bent on cynicism, it's nice that golf has such a positive adage.

These days, there is no greater remedy for negative, negative, negative than to fix our eyes on what God is still doing in our time.

Laban and Bethuel must have had such God-fixed eyes when Abraham's servant suddenly walked on the scene and suggested that Bethuel's daughter, Rebekah, was just right for Abraham's son Isaac. Talk about far-fetched stories! But Laban and Bethuel had learned to look for God. Immediately they said, "This is from the Lord."

We must think differently than our colleagues of the world. Men and women of Christ must look first for the influence of God.

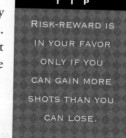

TIP

RISK-REWARD IS IN YOUR FAVOR ONLY IF YOU CAN GAIN MORE SHOTS THAN YOU CAN LOSE.

PAYING ATTENTION

If someone says, "I love God," and hates his brother, he is a liar; for he who does not love his brother whom he has seen, how can he love God whom he has not seen?

1 JOHN 4:20

Love others to show that we love God. Love God to show that we love others. Did John really mean to write such conflicting demands?

If you have trained under a challenging golf instructor, you know the feeling of being pulled in different directions. Just when you think your driving is shaping up, the instructor says, "All right, let's move to the bunker and work some more." Never a break.

God's Word is like that instructor. Each time we read it, it reminds us that there is more to this life in Christ. There is upward attention, outward attention, inward attention. Indeed, many people tire of such attention to the spiritual. But the beauty of our relationship with Christ is that He does provide for us the respite of Himself, those times in prayer when we can unashamedly say, "Lord, help me know what to do next."

> **TIP**
>
> PLAY CONSERVATIVELY EARLY IN THE ROUND AND WATCH YOUR CONFIDENCE BUILD.

UPRIGHT MAKES RIGHT

By the blessing of the upright the city is exalted,
but it is overthrown by the mouth of the wicked.

PROVERBS 11:11

All of us in business are certain to put before the public the best our company has to offer. All of us in sports put our best team on the field or floor. And all of us, when we go to church, show up in our "Sunday best"—be that clothing or faces or suddenly cleaned-up speech.

As you can see from Solomon's Proverbs, this Best Foot Forward Principle is a biblical truth. The city is exalted not by its lowest element but by its finest. Perhaps this is the very reason we call those who are marked by leadership "pillars."

What is God's measure of a pillar? One who is upright, able to stand unconvicted and serve with conviction all at the same time. Men and women whose eyes are set on Christ act surely and capably, knowledgeable of God's desire for them. In this way they bless all those around them.

> **TIP**
>
> IF YOU'RE IN BETWEEN CLUBS, GO WITH THE LONGER CLUB AND SWING IT SMOOTHLY.

CONTENTMENT

Let your conduct be without covetousness; be content with such things as you have. For He Himself has said, "I will never leave you nor forsake you."

HEBREWS 13:5

And now, the Golfer's Promise: "Next time . . ."

Next time, I'll take longer over that short putt. Next time, I'll lay up. Next time, I'll carry my 2-iron instead of three wedges. Next time . . .

It's a shame, really, that in golf and in life, we're better at bragging about what we lack than about what we have.

But there is a secret to breaking this habit: do not be satisfied with the seen but with the Unseen. When the writer of Hebrews said that we should be content with what we have, he was not pointing to what was in our houses, our automobiles, or our golf bags. He was pointing to what was in our hearts. Because if God is in our hearts, He will never leave—no matter what else we do or do not have.

> **TIP**
>
> AFTER THE GRASS HAS GROWN ALL DAY, GREENS WILL BE SLOWER IN THE LATE AFTERNOON.

SEND IN THE REPLACEMENTS

*For God has not given us a spirit of fear,
but of power and of love and of a sound mind.*

2 TIMOTHY 1:7

Ready to trade in your golf swing? If you're a weekend player, you likely spend much of the week replaying your Saturday round. And for whatever sinister reason, the DVR of our minds seems only to play back the "lowlights."

God knows our minds work in such negative ways. After all, our minds, like our bodies, were once bent on sin. But God has removed our sin, and He desires greatly to replace it as well. He will give you the characteristics necessary to exchange your defeat for victory in Him.

Take fear, for instance. Paul wrote specifically of what God offers in exchange for our timid approach to life: power, love, and a sound mind. That means we must be ready. Our God is not stagnant. His life for us comes in exchange for the life we once craved. It requires our willingness to give Him the old, never to see it again!

TIP

INQUIRE ABOUT A COURSE'S DRESS CODE WHEN YOU RESERVE YOUR TEE TIME.

ROLE MODELS

When [Barnabas] came and had seen the grace of God,
he was glad, and encouraged them all that with purpose
of heart they should continue with the Lord. For he was
a good man, full of the Holy Spirit and of faith. And
a great many people were added to the Lord.

ACTS 11:23–24

You may be one of those who enjoy golf because of all the "nice" people who play the game. Even the Tour has focused on how "good" its players are.

But what makes a person "good"? What causes us to identify certain individuals as classy, nice, or admirable?

Luke sure knew what qualities he would identify when he described his fellow minister in Christ, Barnabas. Luke saw that Barnabas . . . looked for grace among the people of God . . . encouraged the disciples to remain true to the Lord . . . was full with the Holy Spirit, displaying the fruit of love, joy, peace, patience, kindness, and goodness . . . was full of faith, sure of His Savior . . . and infectiously brought others to the Lord.

Now that we know what "good" is in Christ's kingdom, let's go grab some for ourselves!

TIP

IF YOU'RE USING COINS TO MARK YOUR BALL, CHOOSE SMALLER, DARKER ONES.

SEPTEMBER

STEERING CLEAR

*And do not be conformed to this world, but be
transformed by the renewing of your mind,
that you may prove what is that good and
acceptable and perfect will of God.*

ROMANS 12:2

The hardest part of the mental game of golf may not be concentrating on our swing thoughts for the day. Rather, it may be "unconcentrating" on the many other things going on around us. What we bring to the course and what we talk about during play can lead our minds away from the game, resulting in bad swings, bad shots, and bad scores.

In your former life, you didn't struggle with sin—you surrendered to it (often gladly). Now these temptations have become an unholy distraction, pulling you from God. Tell God that you recognize this. Ask the Holy Spirit to renew your mind, blowing away what was old so there is room for newness in Christ. Then fill your mind with the rich treasures of God's Word. "Then," as Paul added in Romans 12, "you will be able to test and approve what God's will is—his good, pleasing and perfect will" (v. 2 NIV).

> **TIP**
>
> PRACTICE FEWER SHOTS EACH WITH MORE CLUBS RATHER THAN JUST REPEATING YOUR FAVORITES.

FIRM FAITH

Watch, stand fast in the faith, be brave, be strong.

1 CORINTHIANS 16:13

You may be one of those who once played golf more seriously than you do now. One way or another, greater concerns have carved their way into your life. Serendipity defines your average score these days.

An unattended spiritual life is like an unattended golf game—it leaves a whole lot to chance. In contrast, Paul encouraged us to stand firm in the faith.

Standing firm requires attention to our position and our surroundings. Therefore, we must put our entire weight (that is, all of our being) on the foundation laid by Christ through His saving death and empowering resurrection. We must repeatedly return to this great truth. For above all else, salvation firm in Christ is what gives us courage and makes us strong.

> **TIP**
>
> WORK ON YOUR CREATIVITY: PLAY A ROUND WITH THREE CLUBS AND A PUTTER.

ON OUR WAY

Hear this, you who swallow up the needy,
and make the poor of the land fail, saying: "When
will the New Moon be past, that we may sell grain?
And the Sabbath, that we may trade wheat?"

AMOS 8:4–5

It is wonderful to see a window of time in our week large enough to fit a round of golf. But we must be careful that that window isn't something we force open. Especially on God's days.

When Amos brought the Sabbath reminder to Israel, too many of God's people were just waiting for the day to end, so they could get to the "more important" things in life. Through Amos, God was making it clear again exactly what was important.

Today, the New Testament frees us from legalism. Freely, you may choose to take a portion of your rest on the golf course. But remember Jesus' words: "Unless your righteousness exceeds the righteousness of the scribes and Pharisees, you will by no means enter the kingdom of heaven" (Matthew 5:20). Ours is still a higher calling. We must spend God's time carefully.

TIP

IF WEATHER TAKES YOUR ROUND AWAY, IMPROVE YOUR GAME WITH LIGHT WEIGHT TRAINING INDOORS.

FOLLOW ME

Imitate me, just as I also imitate Christ.

1 CORINTHIANS 11:1

Teaching professionals lose business each year to their best students. These players haven't turned professional themselves. It is just that they get asked, as good players, to "take a look at my swing and tell me what you think." Rightfully, these amateurs should plug their favorite local pro. After all, they are walking testimonials for those who have helped them hone their games.

Handing off credit is precisely what Paul did when he wrote to the Corinthians that they should follow his example. Paul knew he was a sinner, but he never hesitated to place the attention where it belonged—on God. What God had done for Paul, He would do for any who asked: He would give them His grace.

Are you willing to allow others to see God in you as well? Paul is no longer here. But Christ certainly is! Ask God to make you a Paul—an example of the living, forgiving Christ.

TIP

YOUTH AND NATURAL ABILITY STILL WIN THE DAY IN GOLF; DON'T BEAT YOURSELF UP IF YOU DON'T FIT IN THOSE CATEGORIES.

GOD'S DISTANCE

For as the heavens are high above the earth,
so great is His mercy toward those who fear Him;
as far as the east is from the west, so far has
He removed our transgressions from us.

PSALM 103:11–12

If you're worried that you're the only one who can't see the flag from the tee anymore, worry not! The obsession with distance seems to be going to any length these days to keep us from getting to the green.

But distance isn't always a bad thing. David stretched the eyes of his people with two similes declaring God's vastness. First, David saw the heavens as distant—and the space between here and there, immense. That's how big God's love is. Then, David compared God's forgiveness to an endless line. He has removed our sins so far that we can stand in the infinite east and know that they have been sent to the infinite west.

Has it been a long time since you last played the back tees? Maybe it would be worth doing again, just to remind yourself how giant God is. After all, isn't golf as beautiful as poetry?

TIP

ONE FOOLISH SHOT WON'T BE FIXED BY TRYING ANOTHER ONE.

CHRIST AS LORD

But in your hearts set apart Christ as Lord.

1 PETER 3:15 NIV

How about those golfers who spend more time around the trade-in barrel than they spend on the range, working with what they already have? Uncertain of the strength of their game, they switch clubs as often as they lace up their spikes.

So it was with the people Peter had in mind when he wrote this first epistle. He knew they were driven more by the winds of worldly change than they were by the fresh, cleansing wind of the Holy Spirit. For three chapters, he fired a barrage of straight admonitions: Set your hope on the grace of Christ. Be holy. Live in harmony. Be sympathetic. Love like brothers. Be compassionate and humble.

But when he arrived at this fifteenth verse, he distilled these many directions into one: make Christ Lord. That is, give Him supremacy. Nothing shines brighter, we sing in the old hymn. Nothing is purer. Nothing is fairer. And nothing should ever be higher.

TIP

LISTENING TO TV COMMENTATORS ANALYZE PROS' CHOICES CAN MAKE YOU A SMARTER PLAYER.

CONVICTED BY CONVICTIONS

*"For I say to you, that unless your righteousness
exceeds the righteousness of the scribes and Pharisees,
you will by no means enter the kingdom of heaven."*

MATTHEW 5:20

It doesn't take much to rattle your convictions. The suggestion of a heavy wager on the first tee is often enough to do it.

We Christians are not afraid of convictions. A lot of us talk high and mighty about principles. We figure we've got the Bible on our side. But oddly, in most translations, the word *convictions* is entirely absent, and *principles* shows up only in basic terms, most often referring to the principles of the world.

What we are called to be is a *righteous* people, more righteous even than the most religious of leaders in Jesus' time. This is not a righteousness that comes from ourselves; our righteousness is Christ's righteousness, the result of our being in Him. It produces a faith we could never muster alone. For this very reason, it is a righteousness that is humble, not one that constantly spouts its convictions.

TIP

DON'T GET SLOPPY WITH YOUR SHOTMAKING. THE RULES REQUIRE A CLEAN STRIKING OF THE BALL.

LITTLE AND BIG

*And [Naaman's] servants came near and spoke
to him, and said, "My father, if the prophet had told
you to do something great, would you not have
done it? How much more then, when he says to you,
'Wash, and be clean'?" So he went down and
dipped seven times in the Jordan, according to the
saying of the man of God; and his flesh was restored
like the flesh of a little child, and he was clean.*

2 KINGS 5:13–14

Drives you crazy, doesn't it, how a simple
adjustment can get your out-of-whack swing
right back in tune?

Such was the general Naaman's experience with
Elisha the prophet. Naaman was ill and sought a
mighty cure. So what a great disappointment it must
have been when Elisha told Naaman merely to dip
himself in the river. But Naaman's men urged him
to obey. Perhaps it took simpler men to respect
Elisha's simple instruction. The
lesson is plain: in seeking the amazing, we can miss the rich rewards
of determined obedience to simple
instructions. Often the simple solutions—like "trust and obey"—
really do bring the finest results.

TIP

SWINGING
"BIGGER" CAN
WORK AS LONG AS
YOU MAINTAIN A
FLUID TEMPO.

HAVING IT ALL

"Rejoice greatly, O daughter of Zion! Shout, O daughter of Jerusalem! Behold, your King is coming to you; He is just and having salvation, lowly and riding on a donkey, a colt, the foal of a donkey."

ZECHARIAH 9:9

No good golfer can survive the variety of excellent courses with only one facet of the game in shape. The best players must have "all the tools."

Likewise, we must also seek balance as followers of Christ. Our Savior was anything but single-faceted. Indeed, Zechariah's prophecy identified three key traits of our Lord. First, *Jesus Christ was righteous*. He knew the law of the Father, and He followed it purely. Second, *Jesus possessed salvation*. He never let His own righteousness separate Him from the people. Finally, *Jesus was gentle*, acting in righteousness, not judging by it. We are an error-prone people who will not always act righteously, offer the gift of salvation, or be kind. But by the Holy Spirit, we will show more and more of Jesus in our lives—and people will praise our Father in heaven. Now, that's a well-rounded game!

> **TIP**
>
> AT SETUP, SQUARE THE CLUBFACE FIRST; THEN STEP INTO YOUR STANCE.

TIME FOR GOD

[Daniel] knelt down on his knees three times that day, and prayed and gave thanks before his God, as was his custom since early days.

DANIEL 6:10

Maybe you are one of those who cannot play just nine holes. You're an all-or-nothing golfer.

As much as we try to be the same way in our time with God, looking to give Him a full chunk of devotional attention, some days dominate our time with unexpected crises. When we finally catch our breath, we feel guilty. We look at the life of Daniel and are shamed by his discipline. Let's not forget that there were many other hours in Daniel's day, hours when he was working, answering the concerns of the king.

So don't say, "I can't give God only five minutes. I'll keep working and talk to Him later, when I have some real time." No! Give God whatever minutes you have. Read a psalm; sing a hymn; say a prayer. You'll learn in those times—and you'll get in a bit of "practice" for when you have hours to be with Him.

TIP

INDOORS, HONE YOUR WEDGE PLAY BY PITCHING WIFFLE BALLS TO DIFFERENT LEVELS OF A BOOKSHELF.

THE VERY BEST

"Let not the wise man glory in his wisdom,
let not the mighty man glory in his might, nor
let the rich man glory in his riches; but let him
who glories glory in this, that he understands and
knows Me, that I am the LORD, exercising
lovingkindness, judgment, and righteousness in the
earth. For in these I delight," says the LORD.

JEREMIAH 9:23–24

Golf is a nice sport. That is, people who play golf, typically, are nice. For instance, you probably don't fear the day when sportscasters start identifying which Tour professionals are the best trash-talkers.

Such nice people make it easy to get uppity about our game, however. In fact, it doesn't matter what the source of our pride is—wisdom, strength, or riches—we are not to boast about it. Rather, our boast is in God, the One who has given us all these blessings. So we boast in our knowledge of God. We know where we have come from, we know who has saved us, and we know where we are headed—thanks only to God.

TIP

NARROW YOUR STANCE AND OPEN YOUR BODY ON CHIP SHOTS.

IN GOOD HANDS

*Get wisdom! Get understanding! Do not forget,
nor turn away from the words of my mouth.*

PROVERBS 4:5

It is easy to see why Solomon was so convinced about the ultimate value of wisdom. In God's economy it is a perpetual resource, constantly renewed by Him for those who already have it.

Athletes, including golfers, are much like this. Once they find a steady source for motivation, production, or performance, they return to that source time and again. They are assured it will not let them down. They are wrong, of course. No worldly thing can stand by them forever.

But God stands by us forever. He gives us the wisdom we need to face each day, and He gives us the knowledge of Him that we may gain confidence in His deliverance. So start today with wisdom—and go on in it until we meet Him one day in heaven!

> **TIP**
>
> FEEL MORE
> COMFORTABLE
> TAKING A LONGER
> PUTTING STROKE?
> PLAY THE BALL
> NEARER THE TOE
> OF YOUR PUTTER.

GODLY INDEPENDENCE

Lord, all my desire is before You;
and my sighing is not hidden from You.

We who love sports love our heroes. We reserve our highest accolades for those who reach down through the muck in which their boots are mired and pull themselves from the grip of trouble. From the ashes, they emerge victorious.

In this frame of mind, we struggle with the kind of scripture in which we see strong men whimper. Psalm 38 is a prime example of such scripture. David, conqueror of giants, soother of kings, leader of warriors, and chosen king of God's people, is broken before God.

But this is godly independence. God, the essence of strength, makes His greatest strength from our weakness. So godly independence, rather than passing the blame, admits personal responsibility for one's own failings—in spite of how it looks before "stronger" men. Godly independence is fully dependent on the only One who can make us truly stronger: God Himself.

TIP

PRACTICE STRAIGHT, LEVEL PUTTS TO GAIN FEEL AND CONFIDENCE.

THE GREATEST BLESSING

When I consider Your heavens, the work of Your fingers, the moon and the stars, which You have ordained, what is man that You are mindful of him, and the son of man that You visit him?

PSALM 8:3–4

Golf gives us much for which we can be thankful—time outdoors, time with friends, time away from the office, the joy of a well-played shot.

It would be hard to choose golf's greatest blessing, as it can be hard to select among life, liberty, and happiness. When people say, "God bless you," they often mean these very things: May God give you health. May God give you the freedom to do what you want. May God give you the things that make you happy.

Yet David wrote of a still greater blessing, greater than the vast and glorious heavens and all things on earth. The greatest blessing is that God has cared at all. Although we have sinned our way into trouble from the beginning of time, although we have doubted and wavered and reasoned against Him—He has chosen to make His loving, merciful way into our lives. Nothing is richer than that!

TIP

IT IS HARD TO BLOCK OUT DISTRACTIONS; TRY TO REPLACE THEM INSTEAD.

TEAMWORK

"And the glory which You gave Me I have given them, that they may be one just as We are one: I in them, and You in Me; that they may be made perfect in one, and that the world may know that You have sent Me, and have loved them as You have loved Me."

JOHN 17:22–23

The Ryder Cup, the Solheim Cup, the President's Cup. These biannual events take an individual sport and turn it into a high-fiving team game. Players feed off one another's successes, and the momentum of confidence can carry a team to victory in an afternoon.

Interdependence is a key biblical concept. As a group of believers, we are to function organically, as a healthy body would.

When we give ourselves to Christ, we give ourselves to unity among believers as well. We must be cautious regarding doctrine, yes, but we must come together in the most essential things: We have all partaken of the same saving grace. We have all been given the same glory that was given to Christ. We all possess the same hope for the world to come. These are things that unite us.

TIP

FRIENDLY MATCHES ON THE PUTTING GREEN PREP YOU FOR PRESSURE PUTTS ON THE COURSE.

COPIOUS AMOUNTS

My cup runs over.

PSALM 23:5

Sam Torrance, victorious European Ryder Cup captain in 2002, assessed his leadership and his team's performance in this eloquent way: "All I did was lead them to the water, and they drank copious amounts." It sounds almost like Scripture. But although we know what Scripture sounds like, less often do we live it. When was the last time you drank copious amounts of the Father's love?

He gives it to you, you know. David's cup was not the only one that overflowed its brim. But he was one of the few to notice.

Saved by God's Son, we are the recipients of living water. If we do not drink this water, we will just go on in spiritual thirst. And His abundant love will just spill on the floor. There is only one way to beat an overflowing cup: keep drinking—copiously.

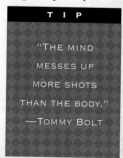

TIP

"THE MIND MESSES UP MORE SHOTS THAN THE BODY."
—TOMMY BOLT

THE GOOD AND THE BAD

"Then you say in your heart, 'My power and the might of my hand have gained me this wealth.' And you shall remember the LORD your God, for it is He who gives you power to get wealth, that He may establish His covenant which He swore to your fathers, as it is this day."

DEUTERONOMY 8:17–18

Golf sure keeps us humble. Average bragging time for a good round: one day. The chances are that tomorrow will undo the good that today has done.

In real life, however, we don't like being humbled. Failed business ventures, dismantled relationships, crippling addictions—how much better to be successful! Or so it would seem. But painful humility that drives us to God is far better than easy success that causes us to forget Him. Humility reminds us to give Him the credit that He deserves—which is all of it.

Every season, whether it brings success or failure, comes from Him. We must praise Him for both. And we must pray for the humility to handle either.

TIP

IF YOU THINK YOU CAN HIT A 7-IRON OVER THAT TREE, GO WITH AN 8-IRON AND REDUCE YOUR RISK.

Therefore, whether you eat or drink,
or whatever you do, do all to the glory of God.

1 CORINTHIANS 10:31

Golf is a one-goal game: get the ball in the hole. Because of varying abilities and interests, however, it's easy to get distracted. For the player afraid of penalties, lakes and white stakes come into clear view. For the nature enthusiast, birds and deer can capture the attention. For aspiring course designers, the shape of a green or the placement of a hazard becomes a topic of discussion. All of these are powerful fascinations; not one is the goal.

Our world, too, is full of powerful fascinations. Some of these, like the beauty of nature or the development of creativity, are worthy of our attention. Others, like shiny extras on a new car, don't hold much real value. But all can serve to deter us from our great goal.

We were made to serve and glorify God. As His workmanship, we are created to do good things in Him.

TIP

LETTING A FASTER GROUP PLAY THROUGH MAKES IT BETTER FOR THEM AND FOR YOU—NOW YOU'RE NOT RUSHED!

MERE MEN

Are you not carnal and behaving like mere men?

1 CORINTHIANS 3:3

The apostle Paul was never afraid to voice his opinion, maybe even to a fault. But when it came to comparing men, in Paul's eyes, some men were "mere" and others were not. That's right, for Paul there was a second best.

Athletes, even we good-natured golfers, have a hard time settling for second best. But each time we act like "mere men," we reflect something inferior. In the Corinthian church, Paul saw jealousy and quarreling. These, he said, were entirely inappropriate behaviors for those with a higher calling.

Men and women of God are supposed to act much differently than those of the world. We are to appreciate the work of others. Sports, when they are about one person beating another, are a poor metaphor for the kingdom of God, where all of us work for the same King, as members of one team.

TIP

IF YOU MUST CARRY A CELL PHONE, CHECK YOUR MESSAGES EVERY FEW HOLES RATHER THAN LEAVING THE RINGER ON.

CAREFUL CHOICES

Now I urge you, brethren, note those who
cause divisions and offenses, contrary to the
doctrine which you learned, and avoid them.

ROMANS 16:17

It is a sad fact of life: not everyone plays fair. Surely you know those who employ "gamesmanship" to knock their opponents off their game.

When Paul wrote to the Romans, he offered a warning, for he had found that even in church, some play maliciously. Paul told the Romans to look out for people who would intentionally work to undermine the very things they had been taught. Paul issued a simple directive: "Stay away from them."

Thus, it is so important that we know the truth. Like bank tellers who recognize counterfeit bills because they have worked so extensively with the real thing, we will be quicker to recognize those who desire to damage the truth if we know what Scripture teaches. Then we will be the ones who establish the line of division: the line between those who have the truth and those who only seek to destroy it.

TIP

BEFORE A COMPETITION, PRACTICE SHORT GAME, SHORT GAME, SHORT GAME.

ABSOLUTELY NOTHING

Who shall separate us from the love of Christ? Shall tribulation, or distress, or persecution, or famine, or nakedness, or peril, or sword? . . . In all these things we are more than conquerors through Him who loved us.

ROMANS 8:35, 37

Which club defines your game? If you are one who constantly switches putters, that wouldn't be it! But what about your driver—the one you have finally figured out how to hit longer and straighter consistently? Whatever the club is for you, you likely harbor a secret fear of losing it.

Harbored fears are tough to live with. They range from the fear of divorce to the fear of death, the fear of losing touch with our teenagers to the fear of losing it all. Most of all, perhaps, we fear losing the life to which we have grown comfortably accustomed.

But one surety remains. We can never be separated from the thing that strengthens us most. That list in Romans 8 is inclusive. Nothing, absolutely nothing, can separate us from the love of Christ.

TIP

TO GET THE MOST FROM YOUR LESSON, ASK QUESTIONS.

INSIDE OUT

"The good man brings good things out of the good stored up in his heart, and the evil man brings evil things out of the evil stored up in his heart. For out of the overflow of his heart his mouth speaks."

LUKE 6:45 NIV

Any player's game reveals just how much he or she has put into becoming a golfer. Certainly, natural ability can carry one newcomer further than another, but skilled flop shots, power fades, and miraculous undoing of troubles usually point to a golfer who has spent hours preparing for the toughest competition.

Christ spoke of a similar revelation that can be found in each of us: the words that we speak unveil what we have carved in our hearts.

Words can harm or they can heal. We must look to speak words of good medicine—preventive and curative—into the lives of those God brings to us. From God's Word, we can encourage others with the assurances and directions that God has used to awaken us to Him. And we can only speak such words if we have them ready in the storehouse of our hearts.

> **TIP**
>
> BUY YOUR CLUBS FROM A SHOP THAT ASSESSES YOUR FIT AND ALLOWS YOU TO TEST THE CLUBS.

A FULL LIFE

And there are also many other things
that Jesus did, which if they were written one
by one, I suppose that even the world itself could
not contain the books that would be written. Amen.

JOHN 21:25

Do you have a friend who loves to tell you about his most recent golf round, complete with details and descriptions that just keep going? "Perhaps," you dream of saying, "you could give me the condensed version."

Believe it or not, thick as it is, the Bible is only the condensed version of God's interaction with us. In the time before microchips, the full account of Jesus was the most complete set of scrolls John could imagine. This could only be because Jesus lived among people, not among books and colleagues, like other teachers. Jesus knew that a doctor among doctors wasn't doing much doctoring—so He went to the sick. When you work among people as Jesus did—physically, emotionally, spiritually, relationally—the accounts of your life grow exponentially. People couldn't contain the stories He'd put within them.

TIP

YOUR GREATEST GOLF ENJOYMENT WILL COME FROM PLAYING WITH PEOPLE OF COMPARABLE ABILITY.

HARDY FOOLS

But God has chosen the foolish things
of the world to put to shame the wise,
and God has chosen the weak things of the
world to put to shame the things which are mighty.

1 CORINTHIANS 1:27

To those who do not play golf, we who enjoy the sport are definitely among the foolish ones of this world. After all, what kind of game is it? All you do is beat a ball around a bunch of tricked-up grass and soil, trying in frustration to get that little ball to go in that little hole.

In God's view, foolishness, however, is no detriment. In fact, those who are foolish in the ways of the world are more likely to be made wise in the ways of heaven. It's yet another paradox of God's economy. Sarah the barren became Sarah the mother of countless descendants. Moses the exile became Moses the deliverer of the exiles. David the small became David the mighty. Jesus endured the horrible to produce the wonderful. And God takes the foolish and instills His wisdom in them.

TIP

STRENGTHEN YOUR LEGS AS WELL AS YOUR ARMS WHEN CONDITIONING; BOTH ARE GOOD FOR GOLF.

HUMBLED

That very hour the word was fulfilled
concerning Nebuchadnezzar; he was driven
from men and ate grass like oxen; his body was
wet with the dew of heaven till his hair had grown
like eagles' feathers and his nails like birds' claws.

DANIEL 4:33

Your swing was grooved, the par putts were going in, and you were enjoying this career day. Then, "from nowhere," you hit a shot unlike any you'd hit in six months. It hooked severely, bounced off a mound, and rolled out-of-bounds. Game over. Even if you did not get angry, your swing disappeared for the rest of the day. Your score ballooned, and it was just another humbling day on the golf course.

Humility can be hard to come by, in golf and in life. But it is the perfect product of the fear of God, remembering that our Father orders our days. He does so not at whim but out of His remarkable love for us. He wants our hearts. By giving them to Him, we will always walk in proper humility before Him. Sometimes, however, He must take us "into the rough" to get them.

TIP

KEEP A CHECK ON YOUR EXPECTATIONS—ESPECIALLY AFTER A GREAT ROUND.

WHAT WE HAVE

"For assuredly, I say to you that many prophets and righteous men desired to see what you see, and did not see it, and to hear what you hear, and did not hear it."

MATTHEW 13:17

Just think what early golfers would have given for metal woods to drive high-tech golf balls down resort fairways onto flawlessly manicured greens! How much we have that they did not.

We should feel as fortunate when it comes to our spiritual lives too. When Jesus spoke to the Pharisees, who were plainly dissatisfied with His claims to be the Messiah, He told them they were blind to the very things so many before had longed for. God was standing amid them and they could not recognize Him because their vision was clouded by their own ideas of what was good. In our own time, the world often tries to dictate what should look good to us: newer, bigger, better stuff. We must never grow enamored with what is shiny, lest we, too, become blinded and unable to see the Savior for who He is.

> **TIP**
>
> IF YOU PLAY GOLF FOR BUSINESS, BE SURE TO MAKE IT A PLEASURE FOR YOUR PARTNER.

THE NARROW WAY

"Enter by the narrow gate; for wide is the gate and broad is the way that leads to destruction, and there are many who go in by it. Because narrow is the gate and difficult is the way which leads to life, and there are few who find it."

MATTHEW 7:13–14

Like golf, our spiritual life was designed to be lived down the middle, away from the thicket. Yet like a golfer whose eyes are too big for his fairway wood, we often "go for it" when we should be laying up. We take foolish risks.

The primary risk is to *abandon the Word of God*. When we stop reading the Bible, we forget its irreplaceable instruction. A second risk is to *abandon the people of God*. Jesus Christ was misinterpreted, misrepresented, and mistreated countless times during His ministry. But He never left the people. A final risk is to *abandon conversation with the Father*. As your closest friend, God is communicative—He wants to hear from you, and He wants you to feel free to tell Him everything. Yes, our walk with Christ is a narrow one. But that is because we are playing Follow the Leader.

TIP

DON'T COST YOURSELF PENALTY STROKES BY GROUNDING YOUR CLUB IN A HAZARD (INCLUDING SAND BUNKERS).

SALVATION'S MARVELOUS BREADTH

*"Behold, God is my salvation,
I will trust and not be afraid."*

ISAIAH 12:2

Don't kid yourself. The golf swing is a complicated set of physical commitments, one after the other in controlled but rapid succession. No one piece holds it all together. Say it just comes down to the clubhead being in position at impact, but you can't deny that several correct actions lead to pure contact.

God is not like the golf swing. He is so infinite and yet so simple. One thread runs through all that matters between Him and us. Latch on to this one thing and we will live abundantly and eternally with Him. What is the one thing? Salvation.

For salvation alone, Jesus Christ came to man. We cannot be tough enough or true enough or tenacious enough to come to our own rescue. But, oh, if we know Christ, we have hope for the greatest promise of all—the promise that we will live with Him.

TIP

BETWEEN REGRIPPINGS, USE SOAP AND WATER TO RENEW YOUR GRIPS' TACKINESS.

QUICK-CHANGE ARTISTS

*My brethren, count it all joy
when you fall into various trials.*

JAMES 1:2

Mentally trained to envision their shots, Tour players shape their drives in their minds, seeing the ball land in the best possible spot for an approach to the green. But when their drives go awry, and all mental plans are buried in the rough or dead behind a tree, these players have a remarkable ability to adjust. They are experts at dealing with a change of plans.

Likewise, our faith must stand up in troubled times.

God wants to know if you will have faith even when you cannot see where you are going. Better yet, He wants to know if you will trust Him when you can see where you are going but you don't like what you see. These times are called trials. These times are the times we must consider pure joy. That's easier to do in God's hands.

TIP

THE BEST DEFENSE AGAINST PRESSURE IS TO HAVE A ROUTINE FOR PREPARING AND HITTING EACH SHOT.

CHARACTERS IN CONFLICT

He who is slow to anger is better than the mighty,
and he who rules his spirit than he who takes a city.

Imagine that proverb embroidered on your golf bag! Unless you play alone, announcing such a philosophy should go far in helping you keep your attitude in check, for an unchecked temper has long been the bane of serious golfers.

And yet, temper is often a by-product of passion. It is an expression of frustration from one who cares deeply. Jesus' love for the house of God led Him to drive the moneychangers from the temple. His commitment to His mission caused Him to rebuke Satan harshly when the enemy tried through Peter to lighten Jesus' spiritual load.

So Solomon's words are accurate. Honorable people do not suppress their tempers—they control them. A good golfer uses the disappointment of one hole to create extra power on the next tee. And patient people know when it is right to be upset.

TIP

IF YOUR PARTNER IS STANDING WHERE IT MAKES YOU UNCOMFORTABLE, DON'T BE AFRAID TO ASK HIM TO MOVE.

THE SILLY SEASON

When professional golf's regular season comes to a close, many of the popular players embark on what has come to be known as the Silly Season. A series of unofficial made–for–TV events, it includes Skins Games and Father–Son Challenges and Three–Tour Show-downs. It's pressure–free golf, where the players collect checks just for appearing and then add to that by coming out on top.

The end of the year may seem to you like the Silly Season as well. But rather than relieving the pressure, the lineup of holiday activities seems to grow more daunting each year. It's hard to find God in the midst of the madness.

Jesus' own life must have seemed like a perpetual Silly Season. The demand for miracles from people who did not really believe, the expectation to speak each time He went to synagogue, and the foibles of His disciples must have made Him shake His head and chuckle. But in obedience Jesus did just what was asked of Him, right down to the end—and His obedience gave Him the last laugh.

OCTOBER

BLESSED BELIEF

Jesus said to him, "Thomas, because you have seen Me, you have believed. Blessed are those who have not seen and yet have believed."

JOHN 20:29

We have all heard the story of the hacker who makes a hole in one. It is a story always retold with an unmistakable tone of voice that says, "Whoever would have believed it?"

Thomas made the error of not believing what he had not seen. But his asking to see some verification is hardly what we would consider skeptical today, simply cautious. After all, the disciples had been so lately burned. Christ, whom they were certain was the Messiah, had been put to death. It was the last thing they had expected.

Jesus understood Thomas's thinking. Indeed, He immediately gave Thomas what he had asked for: the invitation to see and to touch the thing he doubted. But there is a greater blessing, Jesus confirmed, for those who believe although they have not seen. We are those people, and as long as we believe, that greater blessing is ours!

TIP

TO RELIEVE NERVES ON A TOUGH TEE SHOT, EXHALE DEEPLY JUST BEFORE SWINGING.

ALL THE KNOWLEDGE IN THE WORLD

Knowledge puffs up, but love edifies.

1 CORINTHIANS 8:1

If you have ever been the anchor on a scrambles team, you know well the most egregious error you can make: leaving a putt short. After seeing just what the putt should do, you never give it a chance. All the knowledge in the world hasn't made the least bit of difference.

We must be careful in our walks with God to prevent the same mistake. For knowledge alone, if not altogether worthless, is no better than one of those myriad Top Ten lists. It's interesting and entertaining, but without value until something is done with it.

Let's take the truth and love that God has given to us and give them away to others. Edify them. Encourage them. Teach them. In God's kingdom, that is how knowledge is used righteously—not as a weapon or a trophy, but as a gift humbly received and humbly given.

TIP

FROM FAIRWAY BUNKERS, IT'S BETTER TO BE SHORT NEAR THE GREEN THAN CATCH THE LIP AND JUST TRICKLE OUT.

GRACE AND PEACE

*Grace to you and peace from God
the Father and our Lord Jesus Christ.*

GALATIANS 1:3

It was Paul's stock greeting. He used it in every letter he wrote. He began with this dual blessing—grace and peace from God Himself, and from Jesus Christ.

Golfers appreciate grace. They know their day will be full of human error, and they take all the help they can get. If their ball skips out of a bunker, golfers don't apologize. They rejoice! Such grace is always welcome. Yet God's grace is so much greater, given to us at every crossroad. His mercy is new each morning.

And golfers appreciate peace. Unlike the stoic face of the undaunted pro in the wake of a costly mistake, God's peace transcends a relaxed countenance. It is a peace from deep inside, passing understanding.

We who know God's grace and peace know life abundant. Let's bless others with what we've been given!

TIP

"SOFT HANDS" ON A PITCH SHOT WILL ADD LOFT AND ENSURE A SOFTER LANDING.

STICKING WITH IT

*Therefore let that abide in you which
you heard from the beginning. If what you
heard from the beginning abides in you,
you also will abide in the Son and in the Father.*

1 JOHN 2:24

Golf has its basics: Place your feet shoulder
width apart. Close your fingers around the grip,
and be sure the Vs of the thumbs and forefingers
point in the same direction. Turn your shoulders
under your chin and begin your backswing low
and slow.

If ever you have strayed from these very basic
principles, your game probably has taken a severe
turn for the worse. These first lessons are essential.

The basics are never very difficult. They don't
clutter your thinking. They don't paralyze you with
particulars. They just take you back to what is most
clear. Spiritually, that isn't merely a big help; often,
it is a big healing. How often we
could end our own struggles and
our own stresses if we simply
remembered that the Victor did
His work long, long ago. Our
job is only to remain in what has
been so beautifully done.

> **TIP**
>
> WORK MOST ON
> LAGS AND SHORT
> PUTTS, NOT MID-
> RANGE PUTTS, TO
> IMPROVE YOUR
> PUTTING.

SOUNDS OR SILENCE?

And they sang responsively, praising and
giving thanks to the LORD: "For He is good,
for His mercy endures forever toward Israel."

EZRA 3:11

In some ways, a golf course is much like a church. One certain similarity is this: silence is greatly appreciated. In fact, those who dare to yell in either place can normally expect disapproving stares.

So, what do we do with this Old Testament business of shouting to the Lord? Twenty times the psalmists wrote of shouts of joy and triumph. Isaiah spoke of such joyful shouts twenty more times. The Israelites shouted for the ark of the covenant, shouted for their king, and shouted at the rebuilding of the temple. Didn't these people know they were making a racket?

God's people didn't hold back their joy when He answered their cries. When we fall into routines, we risk a stale faith that features no such joy. Far better it is to be on the lookout for times when we can shout too—times when God faithfully answers our prayers.

TIP

FOCUS ON YOUR TARGET, NOT THE TROUBLE THAT SURROUNDS IT.

NEARER TO THEE

Draw near to God and he will draw near to you.

JAMES 4:8

Although just one of a twosome playing through, the man spoke an interesting truth. He narrowly missed a long putt, and my own partner said with compassion, "Almost." The fellow responded, "A lot of almosts."

It sounded as though he were giving us the story of his life—and of yours and mine. Life is filled with almosts. We have felt the pain of falling short. And we have paid the penalties that have been pinned on us for these errors.

How great our God is that He knows our faults and yet has not cut us off from His perfection! Through James, He has told us that we may still draw near to Him. Our lives do not have to be a tale of almosts—just off the bull's-eye in that zone archers fittingly call the sin line. In Christ, we can press in to the center of God's will.

TIP

PUTTING IS ABOUT FEEL, AND A NEW PUTTER MAY GIVE YOU JUST THE CHANGE IN FEEL YOU NEED.

THE BRIGHT SIDE

Do all things without complaining
and disputing, that you may become blameless
and harmless, children of God without fault
in the midst of a crooked and perverse generation,
among whom you shine as lights in the world.

PHILIPPIANS 2:14–15

I golf; therefore I complain.

But along comes Paul. Honestly, it must have sickened the Philippians to be told they must rejoice in everything—the plowing, the weeding, the cooking, the cleaning, the kids, the neighbors, the government. And what is all this about blamelessness and purity and being lights in the world? Who could ever expect sin-bent humans in a sin-ridden world to live without blame, to never argue, to never grumble? It's a ridiculous idea. And a godly one. Paul had no other option. He had to call us to a life of purity. Anything less would be less than Christ. It would be open to our own self-loving, complaint-filled interpretation. Can we live up to such a standard? Not on our own. But Jesus offered this assurance: "All things are possible with God" (Mark 10:27 NIV). Even the end of complaining.

TIP

AT A NEW COURSE, LET THE PRO SHOP KNOW YOUR HANDICAP INDEX AND THEY'LL RECOMMEND THE RIGHT TEES FOR YOUR GAME.

THE WHOLE STORY

For all have sinned and fall short of the glory of God, being justified freely by His grace through the redemption that is in Christ Jesus.

ROMANS 3:23-24

Working with a beginner, no competent professional would cover only the grip, the stance, or the swing—a good golf shot requires proper knowledge and execution of all of these working together.

Yet when it comes to Scripture, we frequently make the mistake of learning only pieces of biblical truth. This often happens with Romans 3:23, which begins, "For all have sinned and fall short of the glory of God." Preachers insist that if people are to know their need for salvation, they must first recognize that they are sinners. This is sound reasoning, but it's incomplete. This very verse gives us so much more, offering not only the truth about sin but also God's provision in removing sin from us. We must read the whole passage. God sees us not as sinners to be punished, but sinners to be forgiven. That's the whole story—one with a grace-full ending!

> **TIP**
>
> YOU'LL OFTEN FIND MORE TROUBLE OVER THE GREEN THAN SHORT OF IT.

FUNDAMENTALS

*Now, brethren, concerning the coming of our
Lord Jesus Christ and our gathering together to
Him, we ask you, not to be soon shaken in mind
or troubled, either by spirit or by word or by letter,
as if from us, as though the day of Christ had come.*

2 THESSALONIANS 2:1–2

Belly putters. Tungsten core golf balls. Long-shafted drivers. Setting your Pro V1s on their seam. These innovations can work, but none of them will revolutionize your game. The hype that surrounds them isn't too good to be true, but let's put it this way—if you aren't good, they won't be true.

In church, a lot of folks get worked up about the end times. The end times are fascinating, no doubt, but we must encourage each other to keep our eyes, our hearts, and our minds on the fundamentals: Christ *will* come, but we must not speculate beyond our ability to know. Our eyes must be open, but they must also be trained. God will continue to do amazing things. But He is not a God of trickery. When Christ comes in His glory, we'll know it. Until then, let's fix our eyes on loving Him and teaching others to do the same.

TIP

ON THE GREEN, KEEP YOUR FEET AND THEN YOUR SHADOW OUT OF YOUR PARTNER'S LINE TO THE HOLE.

GO FOR THE GREEN

SMART FOOLS

Let no one deceive himself. If anyone
among you seems to be wise in this age,
let him become a fool that he may become wise.

1 CORINTHIANS 3:18

Every once in a while, we would do ourselves a big favor if we froze at the top of our backswing and said, "Let's try that again." One writer put it this way: "Better to look like a fool before you hit the ball than after."

Being called a fool is not always an insult. When we say that someone is "a golfing fool," for instance, we do not mean to suggest that person is stupid about the game. Instead, we are saying that player is ridiculously committed to golf.

We should be ridiculously committed to Jesus Christ. We should be so ridiculous about it that we talk to Him and about Him. So ridiculous about Him that we give up what we've been in exchange for what we can become. So ridiculous about it that . . . well, you get the idea. Now, what kind of fool do you want to be?

> **TIP**
>
> KEEP MOVING
> BETWEEN SHOTS
> AND YOU'LL HAVE
> THE TIME YOU
> NEED WHEN IT'S
> YOUR TURN
> TO SWING.

STEP RIGHT UP

Let us therefore come boldly to the
throne of grace, that we may obtain
mercy and find grace to help in time of need.

HEBREWS 4:16

It is a common ploy of beginners to sneak a range ball out to the course for those holes where trouble lurks. As novices, we think we have the right ball for the job. Our game is not good; our ball is not good—so it is okay if our shot is not good.

All too often this is how we approach God. Aware that even our best is not good enough for Him, we come with something less, hiding the things we treasure, fearful that He will reject them. If He rejects our "stuff," we fear, He will reject us.

But the author of Hebrews encouraged confidence when approaching the throne. Our heavenly Father is a God of redemption. He takes what is weak and worthless, what is shy and shameful, and He makes these things new. Our God alone can create the best from our worst. That is what grace is all about.

TIP

WHILE WATCHING YOUR SWING ON VIDEO, LOOK FOR THE GOOD MORE THAN THE BAD.

EYES ON LIFE

Let us fix our eyes on Jesus.

HEBREWS 12:2 NIV

Ever read course descriptions intended to entice you to come enjoy a round? They possess a curious commonality. They all yearn to tell you how many bunkers the courses feature.

There seems something diabolical about the idea that a large number of bunkers is supposed to attract you to a golf course. After all, the game's mental coaches tell you repetitively to focus on what is good.

As men and women of God, we live in a world fraught with trouble. Viruses run unchecked, unwarranted blowouts cause traffic deaths, women and children are victimized, and evil abounds. We can't ignore these worries completely. But we don't face evil alone; we face it with the only One equipped to defeat it on all fronts. No wonder we must keep our eyes on Him!

> **TIP**
>
> HAVING CLUBS THE RIGHT LENGTH FOR YOU IS CRITICAL TO PROMOTING PROPER POSTURE AT SETUP.

UNTANGLED

*For if, after they have escaped the pollutions
of the world through the knowledge of the
Lord and Savior Jesus Christ, they are again
entangled in them and overcome, the latter
end is worse for them than the beginning.*

2 PETER 2:20

Ice plant. To the golfer whose ball has landed in the dreadful stuff, it is the most miserable foliage on earth. Try to hit it out and you just drive it deeper into the thicket, enlivening the phrase "going from bad to worse."

Peter used a similar expression: "A dog returns to his own vomit" (2 Peter 2:22). It's not a pretty idea. But Peter was watching some around him forsake their knowledge of Christ. They had fallen again into the entanglements of the world. So Peter observed painfully: "The latter end is worse for them than the beginning." As spiritual brothers and sisters, we must take seriously the urge to spur one another on to love and good deeds (Hebrews 10:24). We must stand by one another against all that threatens our faith, protecting one another from becoming entangled again.

TIP

IF YOUR OPPONENT
HITS IT LONGER
THAN YOU, ENJOY
THE ADVANTAGE
OF PUTTING THE
PRESSURE ON
HIM WITH YOUR
APPROACH.

THE LIVING WORD

For this reason we also thank God without ceasing, because when you received the word of God which you heard from us, you welcomed it not as the word of men, but as it is in truth, the word of God, which also effectively works in you who believe.

1 THESSALONIANS 2:13

You would be crazy to think that a lesson given to you by a local pro was really a lesson from one of the game's all-time greats. The reasonable price would tell you that.

And yet, learning more of Jesus Christ often requires that kind of thinking. We must trust that the men and women God raises up as teachers are giving us God's own words of life. Paul praised the Thessalonians for their decision to believe this way. They had trusted that Paul, Silas, and Timothy were not bringing another human message. They were preaching the Word of God. Paul confirmed their faith by pointing to the object of their belief. And this object— the Word of God—had proven itself in their lives. It continued to work in them. In this way, the Word of God teaches us unlike any other. Its lessons stick.

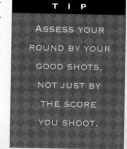

TIP

ASSESS YOUR ROUND BY YOUR GOOD SHOTS, NOT JUST BY THE SCORE YOU SHOOT.

THE VALUE OF OBEDIENCE

"If you love Me, keep My commandments."

JOHN 14:15

Suppose a golfing friend said to you, "Do you know what I value most? I really place a lot of value on being able to get up and down from nearly anywhere."

"I see," you reply. "So you must spend a lot of time practicing your short game."

"Oh, no," your friend tells you. "But I sure value it."

Your friend's thinking sounds much like the person who says in our time, "I still respect the values of the Bible. I just don't live by all those rules anymore."

But what about the value of obedience? Jesus revealed that this was perhaps the value He coveted most from us. Obedience was a certain sign of our love for Him. How we must not miss this basic principle! Our actions reveal our values.

TIP

IN TOURNAMENT PLAY, THOSE WHO AGREE TO WAIVE THE RULES OF THE GAME ARE DISQUALIFIED.

WORK IT OUT

Therefore, my beloved, as you have always obeyed, not as in my presence only, but now much more in my absence, work out your own salvation with fear and trembling.

PHILIPPIANS 2:12

Although the sports psychologists are appalled, here's the way most of us play golf: "Let's see: bunkers in the landing area, water right, and a blind green." In other words, we see the trouble.

Well, here's good news. Seeing the trouble is actually something we should be doing as followers of Christ. We don't march blindly, ducking neatly under every sticky wicket. Rather, we make our decisions carefully—which can be downright tough when Scripture doesn't seem to give a clear-cut instruction.

But Paul reminded us of the great tool that guides us in working through life's trickiest troubles. It is the salvation we have already been given. You see, salvation through Christ is the one great assurance that we cannot goof up. Even our worst decisions are overridden by the great eternal decision to receive Jesus Christ. In Him, our sin is replaced with strength to do the right thing.

> **TIP**
>
> TO CONTROL AN ERRANT DRIVER, CHOKE DOWN ON THE CLUB AND STAND NEARER THE BALL.

GOD'S OWN

But as many as received Him, to
them He gave the right to become children
of God, to those who believe in His name.

What would it take to make your golfing friends think that you are out of your mind? How about if you showed up at the course this afternoon and announced that you would break par today?

Now consider this: What if, sitting around the table after the round, you told your golfing friends that you are a son of God? You had better hope they give you a chance to explain!

And yet, you are a son. You are a daughter. All because of Jesus' willingness to obey God and love you.

What a wonderful truth about our new and true position in life when we follow Christ! Just as when you show up and announce you will make six birdies today, your friends may snicker if you announce that you are God's son. But inside, many of them yearn to be so confident.

TIP

ON TRICKY CHIP SHOTS, PLAY FOR THE WIDE PART OF THE GREEN.

AT PEACE

Not that I speak in regard to need, for I have learned in whatever state I am, to be content.

PHILIPPIANS 4:11

What makes you happiest on the golf course? You may find satisfaction in making a birdie, winning your match, or in something altogether different, like never having to play from the sand. Sometimes, we even find greater joy in one of these odd factors than in how we score.

In life we often pin our contentment on personally selected conditions that have little or nothing to do with the stunning blessings God has given us every day. You remember these blessings. They include the hope of heaven, the assurance of salvation, the strengthening joy of the Lord, abundant life in Christ, the healing hand of the Great Physician, the undeserved mercy of the Great Judge, and the favor of the Great King.

No wonder Paul was content even in jail! A much sadder wonder that we are not content when jailed by the high-rise lip of a greenside bunker.

TIP

IF YOUR PUTT GOES BY THE HOLE, KEEP AN EYE ON IT SO YOU'LL KNOW THE LINE COMING BACK.

LOVE ON THE COURSE

"And the second is like it: 'You shall love your neighbor as yourself.'"

Although golf did not exist, it's easy to imagine that Jesus said, "Love your neighbor" as He recalled incidents on the course with His disciples. How pleased He was when John came across Jesus' ball nestled deep in the rough. And how He had not enjoyed tramping through the knee-high dry grass searching for Peter's wayward tee shot when he had "gripped and ripped it." (Peter was no John Daly.)

We do not always enjoy what we love. Golf is a fine example of this. So are teenagers. (Or parents!) Or even our ministries.

And yet, we love on. We do so because Jesus said to, because Jesus knows best, and following His directions will result in what He called "treasures in heaven" (Matthew 6:20). And in those wonderful cases when we are loved as we love to be loved, we receive treasures here as well.

TIP

A FAIRWAY WOOD IS OFTEN YOUR BEST CHOICE FOR A TEE SHOT ON A TIGHT HOLE.

FULL OF HIM

*And you are complete in Him, who
is the head of all principality and power.*

COLOSSIANS 2:10

As with life's surface questions—"What do you do for a living?" or "Where did you go to school?"— golf has its own questions that allow us to size up one another:

"How did you play?"

"What's your handicap?"

"What did you shoot?"

The danger is not in asking these questions, or even in answering them. It's what we think of our own answers that may matter most.

How much of our identities are tied up in our work, our houses, or our handicaps? Are we full of thoughts about earthly things? These are the questions that really matter, for the "more full" we are of the things of this world, the "less full" we are of Christ. Our souls simply cannot be satisfactorily filled with anything other than Him.

TIP

USE THE
LETTERING
ON YOUR BALL
TO LINE UP
THE BALL
BEFORE PUTTING.

NO PRETENSES

"So he said to him, 'Friend, how did you come in here without a wedding garment?' And he was speechless. Then the king said to the servants, 'Bind him hand and foot, take him away, and cast him into outer darkness; there will be weeping and gnashing of teeth.'"

MATTHEW 22:12–13

Have you ever been made victim of one of those prank golf balls that explodes in a cloud of chalky dust? If you had looked carefully, you would have recognized something wasn't right about that ball.

For all of God's forgiveness, promised and given repeatedly in Scripture, there is one condition of man that God simply does not tolerate: falsehood in our relationship with Him.

In the parable of the wedding banquet, Jesus told of the man tossed from the feast because he was not wearing proper attire. Surely this was not literal, for the poor who were welcomed after the wealthy had spurned their invitations possessed no such clothing. This was a spiritual lesson: Is your heart dressed? You cannot crash the eternal King's party. Your heart must be true before Him.

TIP

PLAY DIFFERENT SETS OF TEES TO WORK ON DIFFERENT PARTS OF YOUR GAME.

MAKING IT REAL

"Therefore whoever hears these sayings of Mine, and does them, I will liken him to a wise man who built his house on the rock."

MATTHEW 7:24

Group lessons are a fascination. The teacher moves up and down the line, individually giving each player something to work on. But you'll notice that each group has at least one golfer who, once the teacher leaves, goes right back to hitting the ball in the same ineffective way as before.

Christ knew His audience would have listeners just like this. Disinterest or distraction or plain pride would keep them from taking what they had heard and putting it to its most excellent use. So He closed His Sermon on the Mount with a simple parable that separated those who only heard from those who heard and then lived out the teaching. The difference, Jesus said, was the difference between wisdom and foolishness.

It's the difference between those who listen and those who listen and learn.

> **TIP**
>
> TAKE SPECIAL CARE ON TEES AND GREENS; GOOD ONES ARE WHAT WE ADMIRE ABOUT A COURSE.

THE MIND OF GOD

"For My thoughts are not your thoughts, nor are your ways My ways," says the LORD. *"For as the heavens are higher than the earth, so are My ways higher than your ways, and My thoughts than your thoughts."*

ISAIAH 55:8–9

"Never start with a birdie." If you've ever started well and gone on to a miserable round, you might draw just such a silly conclusion.

You have friends who reason in similar ways about God. An unfortunate incident occurs in their lives and they think there is no God who loves them. It is hard to know how to respond to this when God has touched us so closely. But God does not reason as we do. For instance, you can argue that a loving God would not allow wars into which we must send our children, possibly to die. But God sent His own Son *surely* to die to win the war against sin and death—a war we started.

God may be hard to understand, but He is no unsolvable mystery. His Son lived and died among us just so that we could know Him—especially in the difficult times.

TIP

HIT A PROVISIONAL BALL IF YOU THINK YOU'VE HIT YOUR FIRST ONE OUT-OF-BOUNDS.

STILL WONDERING

> *A man's steps are of the LORD; how*
> *then can a man understand his own way?*
>
> PROVERBS 20:24

Here are some questions for golf psychologists: What if you have a beautiful mental image of your coming shot, but you produce an ugly result? Was your swing bad? Was your image beyond your capabilities? Was the bad shot preordained by a force outside of you, namely God?

It's okay if you're not comfortable with the thought that God sticks His hand into the middle of your golf game—that may be precisely what He wants. The right to pursue birdies and other forms of happiness is a nice concept, but it doesn't come from Scripture. God is more concerned with our spiritual images. Do they include Him and His glory? Do they remember His grace on the cross and His power in the resurrection?

"Trust Me," He is trying to tell us. "I will lead you where you need to go—even if you cannot see ahead of time where that will be."

TIP

WHILE PRACTICING, WORK TO IMPROVE YOUR MECHANICS AND YOUR CONCENTRATION.

THE TRUE BEST

"Though your sins are like scarlet, they
shall be as white as snow; though they are
red like crimson, they shall be as wool."

ISAIAH 1:18

We've all been taught the ascension to the superlative, Good—Better—Best. But we all know that in golf, the "best ball" can be anything but "good."

No doubt, you and a partner have commiserated after a round, grumbling, "If we could just have that one hole back . . ." It's not a luxury we have in golf. And under normal circumstances, it's not a luxury we have in life either. There, too, our best can look pretty miserable. We cannot rewind the video of our lives and shoot a new scene, erasing our sin.

But this we believe: God is not normal. He is ever present, ever perfect, ever powerful, and ever ready to forgive His loved ones. He offers to take our deadly sins and wash them white as snow. He will not just make what is bad, good—He will make it His best.

TIP

DURING LONG WAITS ON TEE BOXES, PRACTICE CHIPPING FROM NEARBY ROUGH TO TEE MARKERS.

WHAT WOULD YOU TRADE FOR GOLF?

*Husbands, love your wives, just as Christ
also loved the church and gave Himself for her.*

EPHESIANS 5:25

Golf, like sirens on the rocky shore, often calls us away from the things that matter more. After all, the golf course is a wonderful place to spend rich time with friends and a great place to get to know new folks. Fellowship happens there.

But fellowship can become a convenient excuse for avoiding the people in your life who really need your attention.

Paul wrote that men are to show their wives the kind of love that Christ showed the church—when He died for her. Even before the cross, there was no doubt that Christ loved the church. He taught the people and healed them. He joined in their feasts and funerals. But Christ's love (and ours) requires sacrifice. The kind of love that Christ showed when He died for us is not the kind of love that goes to the golf course when the going gets tough.

TIP

EXPECT A GOOD SHOT; ACCEPT A BAD ONE.

MOTIVATED

All a man's ways seem innocent to him, but
motives are weighed by the LORD.

PROVERBS 16:2 NIV

We avid golfers are good at planning our days to include golf. We are even better at making it look as though this is doing everyone around us some good. You know, getting out of the house, into the great outdoors, and all that.

It turns out that most of what we do in life is for our own preservation or participation. Not only would it be strange for us to arrange matters to our disadvantage; most of the time it would seem plain stupid.

But Peter went to the Gentiles and Paul to Jerusalem. They went because God called them to set aside their own agendas and do as He laid out for them. It was hard, but two truths compelled them: First, God knew their true motives. Second, Christ had gone before them, to the cross, in the act of self-sacrifice that made their self-serving motives incidental.

TIP

WHEN CHIPPING FROM A SEVERE UPHILL LIE, BE ESPECIALLY CAREFUL NOT TO DOUBLE-HIT THE BALL, WHICH RESULTS IN A PENALTY.

AN ILL WIND

As a father pities his children, so the
Lord pities those who fear Him. For He
knows our frame; He remembers that we are dust.

PSALM 103:13–14

Some things in life are better viewed from a distance. Rattlesnakes, tornadoes, and bad golf swings top the list. A bad swing makes you quickly turn your head. Like the snake's bite or the tornado's power, this swing just might do your own swing real damage if you imprint it in your brain.

Hopefully, your swing is not that fragile. But your ego—and the egos of those you love—just might be. Indeed, it was mighty King David who wrote these words about our heavenly Father: "He remembers that we are dust." We are not the granite people we pretend to be. Harsh words and thoughtless actions can chunk away at our sensitive selves.

Those we touch in our lives are just like us. They, too, are only dust. Let's show them a life they can look at with respect, not one they will turn from in fear or embarrassment.

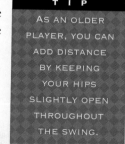

TIP

AS AN OLDER PLAYER, YOU CAN ADD DISTANCE BY KEEPING YOUR HIPS SLIGHTLY OPEN THROUGHOUT THE SWING.

NOBODY'S FOOL

But they could not catch Him in His
words in the presence of the people. And
they marveled at His answer and kept silent.

LUKE 20:26

In a world where it is increasingly difficult to know whom to trust—have you seen the putter with a compass on the shaft?—none of us want to be duped. We're smarter than that!

The Pharisees of Jesus' day thought they were smarter than that too. To show how smart they were, they set out to discredit Jesus and be done with Him once and for all.

In their slyest hour, they tried to get Him to challenge the Roman government. Then they would have force on their side against Him. But He met their question with a remarkable answer they did not expect. Honor the government and honor God, He said. It is not an either-or circumstance. The smart alecks hung their heads like fools.

Jesus could not be out-reasoned. He is the One we can trust absolutely when all others make us wonder.

TIP

WALK NEAR THE LINE OF YOUR PUTT TO "FEEL" ITS BREAK IN YOUR FEET.

BEHAVIORAL SCIENCE

*If anyone speaks, let him speak as the oracles of God.
If anyone ministers, let him do it as with the ability
which God supplies, that in all things God may be
glorified through Jesus Christ, to whom belong the
glory and the dominion forever and ever. Amen.*

1 PETER 4:11

Getting children to understand the intricacies of golf is similar to training the proverbial bull to walk accident-free through the china shop. It's best left in the hands of a professional. And that's what many of us do.

But where can we learn how to behave in the world, especially if we are new to the faith? We must begin, of course, with the Word of God, the Bible.

The Bible was given to us chiefly to introduce us to our Savior, Jesus Christ. When we look to Scripture to find how we are to act as believers in an unbelieving world, we must look to Christ. Peter explained that we should not act in a certain way so much as we should act like a certain One. If you're new in Christ, start reading about Him in Matthew, Mark, Luke, and John. You'll learn how to live!

TIP

A LONG PUTTER MAY MAKE GOOD SENSE IF YOU LACK CONSISTENCY ON SHORT PUTTS.

WANDERING EYES

*For your obedience has become known to all. Therefore
I am glad on your behalf; but I want you to be
wise in what is good, and simple concerning evil.*

ROMANS 16:19

As careful as we are not to let negative mental images plant themselves in our golfing brains, we are not always so wary with the things we allow to influence our day-to-day thought lives.

Paul wrote to the Romans about the need to resist evil in their lives. This involved a conscious choice followed by a definite action. We aren't to just walk around hoping that evil won't cross our paths. Evil is out there. It *will* confront us.

So let us become wise about what is good. Here are some potent ingredients for gaining such wisdom: First, feed yourself regularly on God's wisdom revealed in His Word. Also, like Solomon, ask for wisdom—a gift we know God is eager to give us. Finally, spend time with those you know who have gained a great measure of this godly wisdom.

TIP

MAKE A
GOOD, RHYTHMIC
SWING AND
LET THE BALL
GET IN THE WAY.

NOVEMBER

PRIVILEGED

He who has the Son has life; he who does
not have the Son of God does not have life.

1 JOHN 5:12

Each fall, top amateurs from around the country participate in the Tour Qualifying Tournaments with one hope in mind: a Tour card. For golfers, it is the certificate of ultimate privilege. With it, they can play among the world's most accomplished players and take a shot at proving their talent.

In the bigger world, many people hope for heaven. They suspect that they will get there if they go to church more often than the next person, avoid the "big sins," say their prayers, or simply want to go. All of these appear to be worthy paths to heaven, but not one of them is biblical.

Unlike the Tour, you can't earn your way into heaven. The earning has already been done by Jesus Christ on the cross. Getting to heaven is more like will call. The ticket is waiting and paid for; we simply have to pick it up.

TIP

WHEN THE WEATHER STARTS COOLING DOWN, PREPARE TO REFIGURE YOUR AVERAGE DISTANCES.

BUT FOR THE MERCY

He has not dealt with us according to our sins, nor punished us according to our iniquities.

PSALM 103:10

Surely, you've played many holes where you've clunked three shots, then slammed a putt from off the fringe against the flagstick and watched it fall in the hole. Nice par. A silly hole like this one usually comes a hole or two after you have hit four "perfect" shots and walked off with five.

Golf doesn't always give us what we deserve. God never does.

For that very reason, God's mercy is never mundane. Indeed, it is new every morning (Lamentations 3:22–23). And so we should awake to expect it afresh. Each day, we let our hearts get away from us. We sin. And yet God, holy and perfect, does not batter us as others do when we miss the mark. He does not batter us as some of us batter ourselves. He forgives us. He gives us mercy we do not deserve.

TIP

PAR IS THE GOAL FOR A VERY GOOD PLAYER. SET YOUR OWN REALISTIC GOAL FOR EACH HOLE.

NOVEMBER 2

BETTER JUDGMENT

For I say, through the grace given to me, to everyone
who is among you, not to think of himself more
highly than he ought to think, but to think soberly,
as God has dealt to each one a measure of faith.

ROMANS 12:3

Here's good golfing news: if you are not a scratch golfer, you have errors "built in" to your game. You do not need to be disappointed over every stray shot, be it a wayward drive or a pushed three-footer.

Sometimes it can take a long time to get to the kind of sober judgment that Paul called us to use on ourselves. But to be unduly upset at every missed shot—or every bad decision we make in life—is to think of ourselves more highly than we ought.

Soberly, we must be aware that we will at times miss God's righteous standard. But we don't grieve and grovel. We own up, repent, and seek God's continuing renewal. It is His kindness, not His wrath, that leads to repentance. More than anything, He wants us to live for Him—realistically.

TIP

GOING FOR THE FLAG CAN COST YOU; THE MIDDLE OF THE GREEN RARELY WILL.

RELIGIOUS FAITH

Save me, O God! For the
waters have come up to my neck.

PSALM 69:1

 Now, there's a psalm with a golfer's lament! Or is it too honest for you?

True religion is just that—honest. To be truly religious is to live openly before God, regular and focused in purpose. But above all, true religion does every day what it would do in the church building or in front of the pastor.

Many people practice another kind of religion altogether. It's the kind that is more sentimental and tired than real. In a lot of ways it's like the kind of practice many of us fall into on the driving range—we beat balls brainlessly, with no targets in mind. Our game is unchanged and therefore unhelped.

But you don't want to live life like that. When the waters come up to your neck and you cry out to God, you want Him to be familiar with the sound of your voice.

TIP

IF YOU DRAG YOUR FEET ON THE GREEN, BE SURE TO REPAIR YOUR SPIKE MARKS.

FAR GREATER

For I consider that the sufferings of this
present time are not worthy to be compared
with the glory which shall be revealed in us.

ROMANS 8:18

Struggling with your game? It's the torment of the golfer when what's right goes left— way left. When that happens, it's hard to think of anything else. You look for anyone whose game is better than yours, because if you can tell them your woes, maybe they will have an idea about how to make it better.

Paul knew all about difficulties. Although he saw the repeated joy of men and women entering the kingdom of God, there were also the imprisonments, the beatings, the exposures to death, and the hunger (2 Corinthians 11:23–28). But as numerous and numbing as Paul's troubles were, they were nothing, he said, compared to the glory that was coming.

Why do we bother to recount our hardships? These mean nothing. It is time to talk of heaven, of the new people we will be when we come into His kingdom.

TIP

DON'T ALWAYS
PRACTICE FROM
THE PERFECT LIE;
YOU'RE LIKELY
NOT PLAYING A
PERFECT COURSE.

A HIGH PRICE

*[We] endure all things lest
we hinder the gospel of Christ.*

1 CORINTHIANS 9:12

Golfers put up with inconvenience several times a year. Overseeding shuts down the course. Greens punched and sanded make for a week or two of absurd putting. And any major overhaul sets up one of the greatest inconveniences of all: temporary greens.

Actually, it would be a delight if all our inconveniences came on the golf course. At home, at the office, on the road, in the store, inconveniences take our patience and squeeze it tight. We fuss and fume, sometimes rudely, but by tomorrow, it all means very little.

The damage of an inconvenience usually comes through our response to it. Each time we allow our characters to lapse because of frustration about inconvenience, we hide the good news within us. We send a message to the Lord: my troubles right now are bigger than Your presence in my life. That's a message we never want to send.

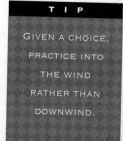

TIP

GIVEN A CHOICE,
PRACTICE INTO
THE WIND
RATHER THAN
DOWNWIND.

POINTED PRAYER

Therefore I exhort first of all that supplications, prayers, intercessions, and giving of thanks be made for all men, for kings and all who are in authority, that we may lead a quiet and peaceable life in all godliness and reverence.

1 TIMOTHY 2:1-2

Now, here's a golfer's prayer! A request for peace and quiet!

In recent times, we have found ourselves in the midst of the wars and rumors of wars that might mark the end of days. But God has provided us an opportunity to seek from Him an intervention. How foolish we would be not to seize this chance.

We are to ask that God prevent a disruption of the peace and freedom that allow us to quietly worship Him. We are to intercede (pray on behalf of those who do not or cannot) for our political and military leaders, as well as those who lead our enemies—all make decisions that could turn the climate of our days. And we are to offer thanksgiving to God for those He has already used to maintain the peace and defend our freedoms.

TIP

LARGE HANDS AND SKINNY GRIPS DON'T GO TOGETHER. IF YOU HAVE LARGE HANDS, HAVE YOUR GRIPS BUILT UP.

OUT OF MY WAY

*Therefore we also, since we are surrounded by
so great a cloud of witnesses, let us lay aside every
weight, and the sin which so easily ensnares us, and let
us run with endurance the race that is set before us.*

HEBREWS 12:1

One glaring difference among golfers is that some wear watches, never remove their bulging wallets, even dangle large towels from their belt loops, whereas others avoid every possible disturbance from extraneous objects. In golf, this difference does not matter much; in life, it may matter greatly.

Scripture teaches that we are to recognize the many things that keep us from running the race that is marked for us. This is the race for eternity.

Knowing Christ was completely righteous, we can be assured that He did not carry with Him the weight of sin or the distraction of fruitless pastimes. And as men and women of God, we must stick to our purpose: to become like Christ, running an unhindered path to our heavenly Father. To those other things we say, "Out of my way!"

> **TIP**
> JUNIORS WANT TO PLAY? A SET OF JUNIOR CLUBS FAR OUTSHINES CUT-DOWN ADULT CLUBS.

FAITH FIRST

For in it the righteousness of God is revealed from faith to faith; as it is written, "The just shall live by faith."

ROMANS 1:17

Any good professional will tell you that the foundations of the golf swing are stance and grip. Without these twin pre-shot necessities rightly set, disaster awaits. But put these two features at the top of your priority list, and much that happens as you swing will fall into place.

This may be one of the simplest analogies for our relationship with the heavenly Father. Get your heart set first; then your religion will matter.

The beginning of our saving relationship with Jesus Christ is faith. We are reminded throughout the New Testament of the weakness of our own works. Thus, we cannot "prove" our way into heaven by the goodness of the things we do. Our works are secondary to our faith, built on the good that has been done for us.

Faithfully follow Christ. Then rightfully live by the Spirit. This way, you'll eternally look to the Father.

> **TIP**
> TO HIT A BALL FROM OUT OF A DIVOT, PLAY IT BACK IN YOUR STANCE AND SWING DOWN STEEPLY.

Then after some days Paul said to Barnabas, "Let us now go back and visit our brethren in every city where we have preached the word of the Lord, and see how they are doing."

ACTS 15:36

Let's see. Professional golfers, those who make their living at the game, spend their vacations traveling and playing golf. No wonder they call it the Silly Season! After all, we would never keep so busy in our work, would we?

Actually, busyness has grown to epidemic proportions. Although our culture tells us that it doesn't really matter what we do, it does send this message loud and clear: you must be doing something.

But the opposite of activity is reflection. As Jesus did, we must take time to stop and reflect on our lives and ministries. Off-seasons and year-ends are good for that. Like Paul and Barnabas returning to the places they had preached, we would be well served to revisit what we have done and those we have seen. In this way, not only will we be better disciples, but we also will become those who disciple others over time.

TIP

MOST COURSES LIKE YOU TO PLAY IN FOUR HOURS OR LESS—SO DO MOST OTHER GOLFERS!

SPEAK UP

And since we have the same spirit of faith, according to what is written, "I believed and therefore I spoke," we also believe and therefore speak.

Faith in God cannot be lived in a vacuum. Separating faith from the real world makes faith worthless, like a hole in one made without witnesses.

When you vote, your understanding of God's Law and His love of human life should guide your selection process.

When you invest or donate, your understanding of God's love for all people should guide the release of your money into the hands of those who will use it.

When you teach or learn, you should look to place all knowledge in the context of God's priorities. Learning for earning is not enough; we must learn so that we live the life God has called us to live.

No, try as you might, you cannot leave an ever-present God behind.

TIP

A LEGAL DROP IS MADE FROM SHOULDER HEIGHT AT ARM'S LENGTH.

NO QUESTION

And if Christ is not risen, then our preaching is empty and your faith is also empty.

1 CORINTHIANS 15:14

When we go to our professional with the too-late cry of "Help!" we hope for something technical and sophisticated to cure our ills. But our pro almost always begins with the grip and stance, checking our basest fundamentals.

Writing to the Corinthians, Paul had many issues to address. Sin and dissension had found their way into the local church, and Paul confronted and addressed these issues. But in the end, Paul rebuilt the foundations of faith and godly living for the Corinthians: the Holy Spirit, love, and community.

Then Paul got even more basic. He returned to the resurrection, that glorious event that brought the hope of eternal life to us all. This resurrection is where we must go when our faith wavers and feels weak. Its glory must not fade. It is the essential of all essentials. It puts our power in Christ's hands.

TIP

IF YOU'RE JUST BEGINNING, FINDING A PARTNER IS AS IMPORTANT AS FINDING A SWING.

NEAR TO GOD

Let us draw near with a true heart
in full assurance of faith.

HEBREWS 10:22

It is common gimmick during recreational tournaments to plant a forest of flagsticks on the green of an easy par-3. Certainly, having a nearby cup no matter where you hit your tee shot gives you a better chance at birdie or par. But it sure feels like cheating!

Interestingly, the contemporary approach to religion is similar to those flag-filled greens. It goes like this: when you are ready to get serious, just look up, and the best choice for you will present itself rather nearby.

Biblical faith is easy enough, but it was never meant to be that easy. As was written to the Hebrews, sincerity is a key ingredient of approaching God in faith. But more important than sincerity is faith's object. Draw near to the gods of this age and you've gained nothing. But draw near to the God of All Ages and your faith hits the mark.

TIP

TO IMPROVE YOUR BALANCE, PRACTICE IN TENNIS SHOES.

ESCAPED!

For you, brethren, have been called to liberty;
only do not use liberty as an opportunity for the
flesh, but through love serve one another.

GALATIANS 5:13

For many golfers, the worst thing they can imagine is swinging "free and easy." Such an approach conjures up images of wayward shots of all kinds—especially the kinds that find water and white stakes and rooftops along the fairway. The truth is, they don't know how to swing free and easy. They feel more comfortable with tight and restricted.

Paul taught strongly against life's tight and restricted approach. He called it religion. Its expectations upon appearance, social behavior, speech, or training send a strong message: you have a ways to go before you are as good as we are.

Christ had no such requirements. He came to forgive and to remove the burden of sin. From us, He asks only that we do not return to that sin. Replace it, Paul said, with something wonderful in God's sight. Use your freedom to serve others freely. Give them what you've got—with no obligation!

TIP

WATCHING THE TOUR PROS PRACTICE CAN BE MORE VALUABLE THAN YOUR OWN PRACTICE SESSION.

BETTER THAN THIS

And as it is appointed for men to die once, but after this the judgment, so Christ was offered once to bear the sins of many. To those who eagerly wait for Him He will appear a second time, apart from sin, for salvation.

To avid golfers, the dreaded words come from the last player in a group that has just hit four awful shots off the first tee. He turns his head and announces, "Don't worry. It can't get any worse than this." Previous experience has taught him otherwise.

Many people steel themselves against the tragedies of life with the same type of unfounded platitudes. "It can only get better from here," they say, trying to pump themselves up. This may help them accept troubled times, but the world offers no soul-satisfying answer for sorrow or death.

Only our gracious and compassionate God offers heaven. On earth, we can never say with certainty that tomorrow will be better. In earthly terms, tomorrow may never even come. But because Christ was sacrificed to remove our sins, and because He will return to take us to heaven, that better day is promised to those who follow Him.

TIP.

IF YOU PLAY FOR THE WIND TO AFFECT THE BALL, MAKE SURE YOU HIT THE BALL UP INTO THE WIND.

BALANCED

All Scripture is God-breathed and is useful for teaching, rebuking, correcting and training in righteousness, so that the man of God may be thoroughly equipped for every good work.

2 TIMOTHY 3:16–17 NIV

Here's a silly golf question: Which part of your game are you going to let fall to pieces first? We would never intentionally let any one part of our game go before another! Rather, through lack of interest or time, our whole game drifts away from us when we do not play.

The game of life is also too complicated to focus on just one of its several critical parts. We cannot live with blinded attention to just one thing. Our lives are too big for that. And so is our God. Just look at His Word.

When Paul wrote to Timothy of Scripture's value to us, he did not settle on one verb alone. The Bible teaches us, rebukes us, corrects us, and trains us. It does all this because we need it. We are meant to be fully equipped, not partially prepared. God wants us ready for "every good work."

TIP

IF YOUR PUTTS AREN'T FALLING, TRY MINOR ADJUSTMENTS TO GET THE FEEL BACK.

SURROUNDED

He who walks with the wise grows wise, but a companion of fools suffers harm.

PROVERBS 13:20 NIV

How much of your golfing pleasure comes from your golfing partners? For many golfers, the ability to choose one's own foursome is a significant piece of their golfing enjoyment.

The Bible teaches that we are influenced by the companions we choose. If we surround ourselves with wise people who consistently choose right over wrong, we will learn wisdom. But if we surround ourselves with foolish people whose decisions are impulsive or temporal, we will swap foolishness between ourselves.

Let this be your guide: at the times when you know you are most vulnerable—the end of your week, as each day gets started, or when you're relaxing (perhaps even on the golf course)—surround yourself with wisdom. When your own strength is most prone to failure, walk in the strength of a wise group—a group committed to abundant life in Christ.

TIP

WHEN ADDRESSING A DRIVER, SET THE SHOULDER NEAREST THE TARGET HIGHER THAN THE BACK SHOULDER.

ALL WORDS

O Timothy! Guard what was committed to your trust, avoiding the profane and idle babblings and contradictions of what is falsely called knowledge.

1 TIMOTHY 6:20

Extraneous matters—free agency, drug testing, violent fans—often turn modern sport into controversy, fueling the talk shows and inviting every would-be expert to pipe in on games they otherwise care nothing about. Golf has had its arguments too: Should women be members? Does the driver go too far? Is it Hogan or Nicklaus or Woods?

As people of the world, we are so easily pulled away from what is most important, frequently focusing on issues that have little to do with the heart of the matter. Paul's first epistle to a young pastor, Timothy, closed with a warning against such pointless chatter. He wanted to make it clear that not everyone who talks of God is staying on the subject. We would all rather play golf than talk about the "issues" that surround it. Likewise, we should desire exclusively to know and serve God—not babble our way around Him.

TIP

WATCH YOUR PARTNERS PUTT FIRST TO GET A SENSE OF SPEED AND BREAK.

HIS WAY

Oh, that you had heeded My commandments!
Then your peace would have been like a river,
and your righteousness like the waves of the sea.

ISAIAH 48:18

God is wholly convinced of His authority. He is certain of His instruction and positive about its reward. And so, He gives us a picture that we can understand, likening His promised peace and righteousness to forces that outlived our ancestors, outlive us, and will outlive our descendants.

No one else can make such a promise. Your parents may offer earthly rewards and familial relationship in exchange for adhering to their direction. Your boss offers you monetary compensation for your committed labor. Your golf pro helps you produce a few more good shots per round if you diligently practice what he or she has laid out for you.

But it is God alone who says, I teach you "what is best for you," I direct you "in the way you should go" (Isaiah 48:17 NIV). We can depend completely on Him.

> **TIP**
>
> ELIMINATE LEAN.
> TURN YOUR
> SHOULDERS AND
> HIPS AROUND
> A CONSISTENTLY
> HELD SPINE
> ANGLE.

IN RESPONSE

In this is love, not that we loved God, but that He loved us and sent His Son to be the propitiation for our sins.

1 JOHN 4:10

Independent minded as they are, both professional golfers and successful businesspeople will confess that there are events over which they have no control. But then they will say that even these challenges are only hurdles to be cleared. A stop sign is only a temporary command.

When it comes to our relationship with God, many of us act like star athletes or Fortune 500 CEOs. We assume that we are in control, that we are the ones who love God—whether we feel as though He is loving us or not. Our faith is built on our will.

But Scripture teaches that love comes from God. If God had not first loved us, we would not know how to love. Through His own Old Testament hand, His New Testament incarnation as Christ, and His presence as the Holy Spirit, God has taught us how to love. All we can do is copy Him.

TIP

TAKE DEEP, LONG BREATHS AND WALK "IN SLOW MOTION" IF YOU'RE NERVOUS ON THE COURSE.

DESIRE

One thing I have desired of the LORD, that will
I seek: that I may dwell in the house of the
LORD all the days of my life, to behold the beauty
of the LORD, and to inquire in His temple.

PSALM 27:4

You don't have to be a golfer to understand the yearning to become a better golfer. We all harbor desires for things that we know will not last beyond our time on earth.

King David certainly desired earthly things. At least one of these, infamously, caused him great trouble. But he also experienced many noble, fulfilled desires, such as the able defense of God's people and the establishment of Jerusalem. Above all these, however, David wrote of the one thing he desired more than anything else: David longed for the presence of the Lord. Our world, with its barrage of myriad messages, is a confusing place. But we are in a position to keep it all in perspective if we do as David did—submit all desires to the primary objective of knowing and loving God.

TIP

A SIDE VIEW OF YOUR PUTT CAN GIVE YOU AS MUCH INFORMATION AS READING IT FROM BEHIND THE BALL.

For I delivered to you first of all that which I also received: that Christ died for our sins according to the Scriptures, and that He was buried, and that He rose again the third day according to the Scriptures.

1 CORINTHIANS 15:3-4

Golfers know how to count their blessings. In fact, if they have recently had a good round, they can start on the first tee and work their way right through a particular number of them! But when a day like Thanksgiving rolls around and a friend asks, "So, what are you thankful for?" golf seems like a pretty meager answer. You know you must search your heart for something deeper.

Well, here's some help. All the earthly blessings that God gives us still fail to match up to the One Great Gift. And it is for this reason that Thanksgiving is such a beautiful precursor to the Christmas season. If we make our meditation of Thanksgiving the real saving work that Christ has done through His death and resurrection, we can be thankful right past today and right through the most hectic of all seasons.

TIP

REMEMBER, IT'S THE PLAYER'S RESPONSIBILITY TO KNOW THE RULES AND APPLY THEM TO HIMSELF.

EVER WATCHING

He who keeps you will not slumber.

PSALM 121:3

From the look of the weather map, the golf season is pretty much over for many who will not travel south this winter.

Right about now we can identify with what the pros call the Silly Season. Do you see holidays that signal anything but rest? Worse yet, the days surrounding these holidays are marked with a bustle unlike any other time of the year.

Still, reflection often settles in about this time. Just when we are winding down, just when our calendars have conspired against us in a cascade of commitments, just when we have to find another gift, God is gearing up—in the middle of the night, in the crush of draining activities, even on Thanksgiving afternoon after far too much dinner. God is always there, right through the Silly Season.

TIP

THINK A SHOT AHEAD TO MAKE THE APPROPRIATE PLAY WITH THE SHOT AT HAND.

ALL TOGETHER NOW

*Keep your heart with all diligence, for out of
it spring the issues of life. Put away from you a
deceitful mouth, and put perverse lips far from you.
Let your eyes look straight ahead, and your eyelids
look right before you. Ponder the path of your feet,
and let all your ways be established. Do not turn to the
right or the left; remove your foot from evil.*

PROVERBS 4:23–27

If you take regular golf lessons, you may
become frustrated that you can only get help a
half hour or so at a time. If only your professional
had written a book that you could read at your own
pace, gaining more and more golf wisdom.

To help us in life, God and His chosen authors
did write the book that can teach us everything we
need for living. It can help us become wise.

In Proverbs, Solomon gave us some very certain
steps for wise living, showing us a picture of the body
doing wise things: a diligent
heart, clean lips, focused eyes,
sure feet. These are individual
notions but as a whole they say
this: give everything you've got
to God.

TIP

A GOOD PARTNER
DOESN'T POINT
OUT ALL HIS
PARTNER'S
TROUBLES.

BALANCED

Now concerning spiritual gifts, brethren,
I do not want you to be ignorant.

1 CORINTHIANS 12:1

The great courses all prove the adage "One skill won't do it." A good score will require you to hit it long when necessary and control your approach shots. You will have to recover well and make putts. Balanced play is critical.

Balance matters as well in the gifts that God gives to each of us.

We must guard against giving greater value to a spiritual gift that we prize. And we must not develop only the principal gift that God has given us, ignoring other opportunities for Him to work through us. Simply because we are gifted with faith, for example, we cannot spurn those who are financially troubled when we have income to spare. For above all, we are called to love. If we don't show love in all that we do, our gifts are exercises in vanity, amounting to "nothing" (1 Corinthians 13:1–3). Love brings balance to the believer.

TIP

PRACTICE CAN GROOVE BAD HABITS TOO. KEEP RECHECKING YOUR GRIP AND STANCE.

FOR GOD'S SAKE

> *. . . having your conduct honorable among the Gentiles, that when they speak against you as evildoers, they may, by your good works which they observe, glorify God in the day of visitation.*
>
> 1 PETER 2:12

Know a practice-range junkie? Sure you do. But although there are a handful of players out there who practice simply because they love it, the rest of us practice for one reason: to improve our game. We do it for us.

One of the lies of the enemy is that you can be a goodness junkie. That is, you can be good for goodness' sake. Or, the enemy whispers, you can be good for your own gain. But goodness for selfish reasons is not really goodness at all. Who ever heard of righteous conniving?

Goodness—true, God-inspired goodness—brings two chief results. It ignites nonbelievers and it glorifies God. When the sinful world sees true goodness, it sees the broad gap between righteousness and evil. And it looks across that gap and yearns for the other side. This way the kingdom is built. This way goodness is done for God's sake.

TIP

CONSIDER GRAPHITE SHAFTS IF YOU EXPERIENCE REGULAR ELBOW OR WRIST PAIN.

WHAT WE DO

Even a child is known by his deeds, whether what he does is pure and right.

PROVERBS 20:11

Are you infamous for your slice? Away from the golf course, we are also known, from early in our lives, by our actions. How we act—righteously or unrighteously—is what causes others to approach us either with confidence or with reservation.

If you don't want to be known for your slice, you take a lesson and get to work on slice-curing drills. If you want to be known for righteousness, you dig into Scripture, listen with purpose to Bible-based teaching, and make changes in your life.

Don't expect to rush this process. Trust takes time to establish. But keep doing what you know is right. In the meantime, remember that God has a purpose for our weaknesses as well. Simply, they keep us from pride. As men await our righteousness before they lift us up, God awaits our humility (James 4:10).

TIP

PLAY EACH ROUND ACCORDING TO YOUR GOALS, NOT YOUR OPPONENT'S ACCOMPLISHMENTS.

SHARING THE WEALTH

"Go therefore and make disciples of all the nations."

MATTHEW 28:19

Perhaps you have never felt confident in your ability to disciple another. You are nervous that your own sin will hold you back.

But consider your relationship with your golf professional. Teaching pros are not the world's best players. If they were, they would be on Tour. But they are committed to studying the game and improving its play among us millions of amateurs. In doing so, they often point to the examples of the pros we watch on TV, giving us a higher pattern for our game.

So it works in our discipling. Sure, we strive to be dedicated examples of our Savior, but we inevitably will fall short. In making disciples of others, however, we are not making them disciples of ourselves. Rather, we are pointing them to Jesus.

You can disciple others. Know Jesus and teach others how to live for Him.

> **TIP**
>
> THE PENALTY FOR OUT-OF-BOUNDS IS STROKE AND DISTANCE; YOU MUST REPLAY FROM WHERE YOU HIT THE ORIGINAL BALL.

THAT CLOSE

*A friend loves at all times, and a
brother is born for adversity.*

PROVERBS 17:17

Birdies are easy to love. So are shirtsleeve afternoons that show up surprisingly in the wrong season. Putts that go in from forty feet and longer—no matter what you're putting for—are easy to love.

How about you? Are you easy to love? Well, even when you're complaining, arguing, bossing, and lying, your true friends will be there for you. They know you well, and they are willing to stand by you when that patience of yours, that smile, that ready word of encouragement, are displaced by circumstances.

And there is your Fairest Friend, He who is the Closest Brother. His name is Jesus. Are you at the end of your rope, or just the end of a long day? Tell Him that you're hurting. That you're hungry. That you need Him. He will come, likely bringing those earthly friends and brothers, too, ready to carry you when you're hardest to love.

SUNSHINE

"But I say to you, love your enemies, bless those who curse you, do good to those who hate you, and pray for those who spitefully use you and persecute you, that you may be sons of your Father in heaven; for He makes His sun rise on the evil and on the good, and sends rain on the just and on the unjust."

MATTHEW 5:44–45

Perhaps you have felt cheated in your golf game lately. You, who have put your trust in Christ, stumble at critical moments on the course. Your opponent, who forsakes religion, rolls in birdie putts from the edge of the green and always hits the fairway.

You might think this odd. After all, if God clearly favored believers over nonbelievers, wouldn't the nonbelievers see the difference and run for spiritual cover? But God is not about preference. He is about love. And no matter how wicked a worldly person may be, God will always look to love that one. Jesus instructs us to do the same. We must love those who have positioned themselves against us. We must love them and we must pray for them—we must love them face-to-face and we must love them before the Father.

> **TIP**
>
> HAVING A "FAVORITE" CLUB IS FINE AS LONG AS YOU STILL PRACTICE WITH THE OTHERS.

370 | GO FOR THE GREEN

DECEMBER

NOT FOR NOTHING

"Why do you spend money for what is not bread, and your wages for what does not satisfy? Listen carefully to Me, and eat what is good, and let your soul delight itself in abundance. Incline your ear, and come to Me. Hear, and your soul shall live."

ISAIAH 55:2-3

Golfers take a lot of criticism. One criticism we likely do deserve has to do with our attention to the game. In fact, we often practice just to maintain our game, with little hope of really improving.

In building our relationship with God, however, we should not be content with maintenance. We should desire growth. No wonder God used His oracle, Isaiah, to juxtapose His gifts for us against the empty promises of earthly toil. Although work can help build us as God's people, the stuff that draws our gaze and an undue portion of our paychecks cannot. We cannot buy health, time, or companionship. Even these are fleeting until they are purchased from Him. A sound soul, hours with Him, and the open lines of friendship with our Lord and Savior—these riches last forever.

> **TIP**
>
> MOST GOLF CARTS DON'T HAVE SEAT BELTS; DRIVE CAREFULLY TO PREVENT ACCIDENTS.

THE GOOD NEWS

And they were preaching the gospel there.

ACTS 14:7

Like golf professionals tirelessly reiterating the need for a sound grip and setup, it is important to return frequently to basic themes in our walk with Christ.

One key theme is the extensive scope of the good news of Jesus Christ. It is news so good that it applies not only to a singular "salvation experience" but also throughout our lives.

Yet what exactly made this news good in the beginning? For the first-century Jew, oppression by Roman rule was nasty enough. But the common Jew was oppressed more greatly from within, as the religious leaders taught a law so strict and penal that no man or woman could exist in either obedience or joy.

The good news of Jesus was utterly different. For Jews and non-Jews, God had provided the perfect Intercessor. What man could not do, Christ did, restoring us to God. That remains the best news for us today.

TIP

HABITS COME THROUGH PRACTICE; COMMIT YOURSELF TO IMPROVING.

ANOTHER POWER

*"This is the word of the LORD to
Zerubbabel: 'Not by might nor by power,
but by My Spirit,' says the LORD of hosts."*

ZECHARIAH 4:6

In golf, pros and amateurs share one common realization: no matter how much you practice, some days no ball will land on the green and no putt will go in the hole. Discipline has its purpose, and applied rightly, it produces consistent results. But always in golf, something "mysterious" can come between a good round and a bad one.

In the frenetic holiday season, we will grow frustrated if we keep trying to take things into our own hands. But unlike golfers, we do not need to hope the whims of some mystery component turn our way. Instead, we depend on God's ever-present, ever-mindful Spirit to sustain us. We cannot break from our reliance on Him simply because we are busy. Indeed, now is the time to rely on Him as never before. Then we'll look back and say, "That was a holiday season like none other! It was wonderful!"

TIP

DON'T MILL AROUND AFTER YOU'RE DONE PUTTING; CLEAR THE GREEN SO THOSE BEHIND MAY HIT THEIR APPROACHES.

GOLF GODS

"You shall have no other gods before Me."

EXODUS 20:3

There are no golfing gods. Okay, we've said it. And in the presence of the superstitious, we may be told that now we've done it: we've incited "them."

Sounds ridiculous, doesn't it? Yet even those of us who follow Christ sometimes let slip deferential allusions to magical outside forces that decide whether our approach bounces into the bunker or our ball takes that last half roll into the cup for par.

But any credit given to a "force" is credit taken away from God. Of course, we would never say that those forces are gods "before" God. They are, however, gods "besides" Him—and "besides" is the word that some translators use in this first of the Ten Commandments: "You shall have no other gods besides me."

You see, the imaginary is very real when it causes us to turn our heads away from the One who really does shape our lives.

TIP

TO ALIGN YOUR SHOT, TRY SELECTING A VISUAL TARGET JUST A FEW FEET IN FRONT OF YOU.

MAKING CONNECTIONS

*"For I also am a man placed under authority,
having soldiers under me. And I say to one, 'Go,'
and he goes; and to another, 'Come,' and he comes;
and to my servant, 'Do this,' and he does it."*

LUKE 7:8

Golfers—believe it or not—sometimes know their golf games better than their Bibles.

The people Jesus taught were much the same way. They knew fishing and farming. So He taught them with pictures from the sea and the earth. Paul's readers, more cosmopolitan, knew soldiering and athletics. He used those analogies to increase their understanding. Peter's proteges were most often Jewish, respecting tradition and the temple, so he likened them to living stones being built into a spiritual house (1 Peter 2:5). And Jesus "marveled" at the Roman centurion who acknowledged Jesus' authority with an analogy to his own authority (Luke 7:9).

God speaks our language. Do you know golfers? Give them the good news in terms they can understand. Do you know sales reps or state reps, patriots or expatriates, guards or gardeners? Give them Jesus in their language.

> **TIP**
>
> ON YOUR BACKSWING, YOUR WEIGHT SHOULD TRANSFER TO THE INSIDE OF YOUR BACK FOOT.

THE TRUTH TEST

*Demetrius has a good testimony from all,
and from the truth itself. And we also bear
witness, and you know that our testimony is true.*

3 JOHN 12

One objective statement ends all questions about a golfer's true ability: "He plays to a scratch handicap." In his third letter, John suggested there is a similar standard for us as God's people. That standard is the truth.

As trusting as we may be, we have learned through experience that the words of others may prove wrong—even when one is "well spoken of by everyone." But John wrote that a person (in this case a man named Demetrius) can be commended by something more objective than the words of others. The truth itself can attest to our character.

What truth is this? It is God's truth, found in Scripture. It is the standard by which, as followers of Christ, we *want* to be measured, for above all else it points to the One we follow.

TIP

WHEN PUTTING,
CHOOSE A LINE
AND COMMIT TO
IT. MOST PUTTS
ARE MADE WITH
CONFIDENCE.

I AM THIRD

"I have set you an example that
you should do as I have done for you."

JOHN 13:15 NIV

It has long been a common phrase among Christ's followers: "I am third." Its intent is to cement in us the hierarchy of the kingdom of heaven. God first. Others second. Ourselves third. Oh, if we could get that right!

In a lot of ways it is similar to the golf swing. Stance first. Grip second. Takeaway third. Get those elements out of whack and your best shots are not good—they are lucky.

Jesus gave the disciples a powerful lesson in "I am third" when He humbled Himself and washed their feet. When He was finished, Jesus said, "I have given you an example." In these few words, Jesus set the focus of His followers. First, watch Jesus. Second, emulate Him by serving others. Begin with these two priorities, and you'll be blessed to see how wonderful the results are for you!

TIP

FOR LONG BUNKER SHOTS, IF THE LIP IS NOT IN YOUR WAY, CONSIDER RUNNING A CHIP TO THE HOLE.

TELL ALL

And this is the testimony: that God has given us eternal life, and this life is in His Son.

1 JOHN 5:11

Even as amateurs, and even as not-so-good ones, we are able to join the fun as golf storytellers anytime we hit one flush or play someplace enviable.

Now, here are some thoughts about improving your storytelling ability when it comes to sharing Christ with others.

First, remember that it is not your testimony but the testimony of what God has done in your life. Focus on Him, emphasizing the difference He has made in your life.

Next, talk comfortably. You don't have to be a theologian to give your testimony. Start with golf; start with family; start with business. These things represent you, and you will naturally find connections in these things.

Finally, don't be afraid to practice. Think about what you want to say, and let the words play on your lips. And as God continues to work in your life, your testimony will keep improving.

TIP

WHEN TEEING A SHORTER IRON ON A PAR-3, TEE IT LOW TO THE GROUND SO IT SITS LIKE A GOOD LIE.

OPENHEARTED

*"O Jerusalem, Jerusalem, the one who
kills the prophets and stones those who are
sent to her! How often I wanted to gather
your children together, as a hen gathers her
chicks under her wings, but you were not willing!"*

MATTHEW 23:37

Jesus stood overlooking the city He loved in
an emotional exchange of anger and sorrow,
grieved by what had become of the chosen people
for whom this great city had been destined.

But Jesus' heart was not just broken. Jesus' heart
also was open. He had come with the purpose of
saving these people. He sought to gather them under
His loving attention, to care for them, to be each day
their Savior. He was not just weeping over them; He
was willing to work with them. Is your heart this
open to the people at your club, your course, the
other places you live your life? Are you willing to go
beyond merely hurting for them? *Aching* and *aiding*
can be blocks apart. Aching
drops a sympathy card in the
corner mailbox. Aiding gets in
the car, drives across town, and
knocks on the door. Aiding sits
for as long as it takes, loving by
listening. Aiding is doing as Jesus
would do.

TIP

DON'T SPEND
YOUR ENERGY
ON MULTIPLE
PRACTICE SWINGS;
SIMPLIFY YOUR
PRE-SHOT
ROUTINE.

THE SOURCE

*Therefore with joy you will
draw water from the wells of salvation.*

ISAIAH 12:3

When we begin at golf, few things strike fear like water. Eventually, when we consistently hit the ball in the air and gain ability at directing its flight, water isn't so daunting. In fact, it's often forgettable.

But water is important in God's spiritual imagery. Indeed, if God is our air, God's salvation is our water. Without Him, we would not be. Without His salvation, we cannot go on.

We must not attempt to live outside salvation's embrace. If we do not drink water, our cracked lips and parched throats announce our need. In the same way, worry, hopelessness, self-reliance, loneliness, and sin are all signs of a thirsty soul.

If you find yourself spiritually dry, God has revealed what you can do to attain revival—go to the abundant source of strength. Go to the wells of salvation.

> **TIP**
> IN TOURNAMENT PLAY, BE SURE YOUR CADDIE KNOWS THE RULES TOO—YOU CAN BE PENALIZED FOR HIS ILLEGAL ACTIONS!

TRADING IT ALL

*"The kingdom of heaven is like a
merchant seeking beautiful pearls, who,
when he had found one pearl of great price,
went and sold all that he had and bought it."*

One of the funny laws of golf is that for every
one of your own wayward balls that you find,
you come across three or four more lost by others.
But if one of those you discover is better than your
own, such a ball is like the pearl of great price.

You know this pearl. Jesus spoke of a merchant
who was always looking for fine pearls. One day he
found a pearl unlike any he had ever seen. From
that moment, he had to have that pearl. Indeed, he
sold his entire inventory of lesser pearls to make that
one great purchase.

Jesus said that this is how God's kingdom is. We
recognize it to be like nothing we have known before.
We are willing to surrender
everything that has gone before
to acquire it. What fullness there
is in such dedication! What a
holy possession!

TIP

CARRYING
BAND-AIDS AND
TYLENOL IN YOUR
BAG CAN HELP
YOU GET PAST
LATE-ROUND PAIN.

A WORD OF WARNING

From that time Jesus began to preach and to say,
"Repent, for the kingdom of heaven is at hand."

MATTHEW 4:17

It is a cry issued too flippantly at times, not seriously enough at others. But it is a cry that can save you from a great deal of pain: "Fore!"

The Bible contains such a word. It is *repent*. And if ever there is a word that makes the spiritual hairs stand up on the back of your neck, it is this one: *repent*. Most believers are about as reluctant to use the word as golfers are averse to wearing checkered slacks.

But if the word was good enough for Jesus, then it remains appropriate for us. It can be a life-saving word of warning. Say the word *repent* and you may grab some ears. Then talk about what the word means and what is promised to those who turn to Christ and you may grab some hearts. It's okay, the Holy Spirit will be right there with you.

TIP

IF YOU'RE STARTING OUT WITH AN OLDER SET OF CLUBS, PAY TO HAVE THEM REGRIPPED— THEY'LL FEEL LIKE NEW.

SEEKING MORE

Repent therefore and be converted, that
your sins may be blotted out, so that times of
refreshing may come from the presence of the Lord.

ACTS 3:19

Walking away from God and heading back out on your own is a lot like thinking you're ready for the back tees once you have hit two good drives on the practice range. We all know it takes a lot more than that to groove a swing. In fact, professional Tour players never let themselves get too far from the range. It's where a life on Tour is maintained.

Disciplined men and women of God never let themselves out of sight of the Father. Without Him, we fall back into a life where the only meaning is survival, and that isn't much of a meaning at all.

Our purpose is found in Christ—living for Him and leading others to Him. To pursue this purpose as the whole of what we do, we can't go to God only when we *think* we need Him. We must go to Him when we truly need Him—which is all the time.

TIP

TAKE SOME WAIST-HIGH BASEBALL SWINGS TO FEEL THE CLUBHEAD AND REDUCE TENSION.

"UP FROM THE PIT"

Then I said, "I have been cast out of Your sight; yet I will look again toward Your holy temple."

JONAH 2:4

God gave a simple direction to the prophet Jonah: go to Nineveh. But like many of us faced with our most feared golf hazard, Jonah saw only the negatives surrounding his assignment. So Jonah ignored Nineveh and headed to Tarshish.

Before he knew it, Jonah found himself in trouble so deep that he called it "the pit" (2:6). In fact, it was the belly of a great fish. Yet there was something truly good about Jonah's experience. He learned his lesson.

Inside the fish, Jonah prayed. "You did this to me, Lord," were essentially his words. "But I am still alive. You must have something in store for me."

Jonah would go to Nineveh. But he no longer saw this as a bad thing. He recognized the discipline he had received for his disobedience. Likewise, he knew what the reward for obedience would be. Jonah would look again on God's temple.

TIP

VOICES TRAVEL WELL ACROSS OPEN SPACES; KEEP THE NOISE DOWN EVEN FOR PLAYERS ON ADJACENT HOLES.

PURE

To the pure all things are pure, but to
those who are defiled and unbelieving nothing is
pure; but even their mind and conscience are defiled.

TITUS 1:15

No other sport uses the expression like golfers. A baseball slugger "belts it," but a golfer hits it "pure." In fact, we often forgive the fact that we have sailed a shot over the green by fifteen yards because we have hit the ball so "pure."

There is a very distinct feel to a "pure" golf shot. Likewise, Paul wrote to Titus that there is an absolute distinction between people who are pure and people who are not. Those who truly belong to God know that in the same way He has created and forgiven them, He has touched each man and woman. All, then, deserve the kind of love that God has given to us. They deserve to be treated with integrity, seriousness, and soundness of speech. This is true religion, lived out in every quarter of our lives, with purity of intention and execution.

TIP

COURSE ARCHITECTS ALWAYS LEAVE A SAFE PLACE TO FIT YOUR BALL. LOOK FOR THAT INSTEAD OF THE TROUBLE.

BLIND SHOTS

The prophet is a fool, the spiritual man is insane, because of the greatness of your iniquity and great enmity.

HOSEA 9:7

Living unrighteously is like playing a golf course blind. The more we give our thoughts and our actions to activities that are not of God, the more our eyes cannot see trouble as trouble or reward as reward. Discernment vanishes.

What greater reason, then, is there for us to know God and obey Him? Life is forever full of confusing circumstances and difficult decisions. Daily we need to recognize wisdom and choose it.

Spiritually, we have two choices: Live according to our own desires, however godless they are, and suffer the inability to think clearly in times of trouble. Or live according to God's plan for us, collect the rewards for this obedient surrender, and be strengthened yet again by the joy of the Lord. Put like that, the choice is pretty obvious.

TIP

A GOOD, BALANCED FINISH WILL HELP EVERYTHING THAT PRECEDES IT.

STRENGTH CONDITIONING

Thus says the LORD: "Cursed is the man who
trusts in man and makes flesh his strength,
whose heart departs from the LORD."

JEREMIAH 17:5

In the twenty-first century, there appears to be only one standard for a good golfer anymore: power. With the younger players making themselves bigger and stronger, even on our local courses we talk most of all about how far a player hits it.

It is a curse of our time that we so quickly assess others by surface traits. We actually trust a person's outward appearance to give us a reliable first impression of his or her overall character. And by elevating the value of people's bodies in our evaluation of them, we raise the bar in our own lives, placing pressure on ourselves to build ourselves a certain way.

TIP

YOU'LL PUTT
BETTER IF YOU
LEAVE YOUR
APPROACH SHOTS
BELOW THE HOLE.

True strength, godly strength, comes from the heart of a person. With a pure heart we can make right choices. With a heart that is charged by God, we can do things that even our bodies might suggest we cannot do.

THINKING GAME

But his delight is in the law of the LORD,
and in His law he meditates day and night.

PSALM 1:2

Oh, the number of thoughts that can go through your head in that brief series of instants known as the golf swing—many more than is good for you! Simple concentration brings much better results on the golf course.

Simple concentration can work wonders in our spiritual lives as well.

In the first psalm, we are given the picture of two men: the righteous man and the unrighteous man. The righteous man delights in God's law. He meditates on it day and night.

Meditation isn't heavy-duty brainwork. It is simple concentration, and the Bible encourages us to do it. Get yourself to an undistracted place and quiet the disruptive machinations of your mind. Then turn your mind to a single attribute of God—perhaps mercy, joy, or justice—or a brief passage of Scripture. In this way, His thoughts will replace yours.

TIP

FOR BURIED LIES IN THE BUNKERS, SQUARE YOUR WEDGE TO ELIMINATE BOUNCING THE CLUB.

SECOND DEATH

I have been crucified with Christ; it is no longer
I who live, but Christ lives in me; and the life
which I now live in the flesh I live by faith in the
Son of God, who loved me and gave Himself for me.

GALATIANS 2:20

Psychologists who write about youth sports warn parents not to live vicariously through their athletic children. Parents who do are often called "Little League Dads," although they exist in all sports, including golf.

When it comes to Christ, however, a vicarious life is precisely what we need. We must let Him live in us so that we may live through Him. But first we must dare to die with Him. We die to the desires of our old selves: the lust of the eyes, the lust of the flesh, and the pride of life (1 John 2:16). We exchange what has defeated us for what will allow us to live.

Many people receive Christ for the sake of their future. That's okay. In Him, our future is assured. But if we offer Him all that we are, we can have much more now. We can have all that He is, locked within us.

TIP

TO HELP CURE A SLICE, PRACTICE BY RELEASING YOUR TRAILING HAND FROM THE CLUB AT IMPACT.

NO MIDDLE GROUND

*Likewise you also, reckon yourselves to be
dead indeed to sin, but alive to God in Christ
Jesus our Lord. . . . And . . . present yourselves
to God as being alive from the dead, and your
members as instruments of righteousness to God.*

ROMANS 6:11, 13

Golf has no middle ground. Sure, we've
established the "gimme" to speed up play and
save a bit of face, but when played right, the ball is
either out of the hole or in it. And until it is in the
hole, there is work to be done.

The line between heaven and hell is likewise
sharply defined. You cannot, as evangelist William
Fay says, be "almost there" when it comes to heaven.
We are to carry this stark truth to our friends. Hell
is real. But so is heaven, and to go there we must
finish in Christ. God, through the sacrifice of His
Son, has made it possible for us to hand Him not
just the putter but every club in
life's bag. Every care, every habit,
every cry, every call, every today,
and every tomorrow, we can give
to Him. No—each of these we
must give to Him. Otherwise, we
will just keep missing and missing
and missing.

> **TIP**
>
> IF YOU CAN'T
> WIGGLE YOUR
> TOES, YOU'RE
> LEANING TOO
> FAR FORWARD AT
> ADDRESS.

TURNED FROM DEATH

Let him know that he who turns a
sinner from the error of his way will save
a soul from death and cover a multitude of sins.

JAMES 5:20

What is the measure of a good golf lesson? That's a pretty simple question with a pretty obvious answer. A good golf lesson works. It fixes our swing, lowers our scores, and—oh, yes—makes us a herald for a certain teaching professional who worked wonders with a wreck. We have been rescued from the error of our ways, and we are eager to tell others just who did this for us, who worked this mighty miracle.

Simple as this sounds, most followers of Christ are not so good at recommending the One who has performed the biggest miracle in their lives: Jesus. You know, it's funny we're so flimsy in this regard. Because the burden isn't really ours. We are not the ones who have to fix our friends' error-filled ways. We only must point them to the One who can.

RIGHT FROM WRONG

> *. . . who show the work of the law*
> *written in their hearts, their conscience also*
> *bearing witness, and between themselves their*
> *thoughts accusing or else excusing them.*
>
> ROMANS 2:15

When an athlete's physical prowess is so smooth that it must have been inborn rather than ingrained, we call that athlete a natural. Such athletes are rare. The rest of us must be trained.

But as spiritual beings, we all are naturals.

For one, we have a sin nature. When Adam sinned, he introduced a dark legacy of separation from a holy God.

But when Adam sinned, he also became aware of good and evil, things he did not need to know before. And that knowledge has been written on our hearts ever since. There were no Ten Commandments when Joseph resisted Potiphar's wife. He knew adultery was wrong. And in the same way, we know within us right from wrong. Let's pray for the courage to always choose the way of the Lord over the way of the world.

TIP

GROUP LESSONS HELP YOU LEARN THE GAME AND FIND PARTNERS TO ENJOY IT WITH!

ALONE PREEMINENT

*Then to Him was given dominion and glory
and a kingdom, that all peoples, nations, and
languages should serve Him. His dominion is an
everlasting dominion, which shall not pass away,
and His kingdom the one which shall not be destroyed.*

DANIEL 7:14

People who "kind of" like golf are an unusual bunch. In a crowd of addicts, they seem so, well, uncommitted.

Far more people, however, approach God in the same way. They "kind of" need Him. When big trouble comes, they recognize that no human solution will do. But in their hearts, they know that the One who came as a human can help. Perhaps Jesus is very different from that wishy-washy God that pop culture says is the same no matter what you call Him.

In no other faith is Jesus Christ granted the deity that the Bible ascribes Him. He was not just a special man to whom great talent or wonder were uniquely awarded. Jesus Christ alone came as Emmanuel—God with us— alone came to save us from sin, and alone will be given dominion over every people and nation.

TIP

DON'T RUSH YOUR EQUIPMENT PURCHASES; YOU'LL BE PLAYING YOUR NEW CLUBS FOR A LONG WHILE.

THAT TIME OF YEAR

"Glory to God in the highest, and
on earth peace, goodwill toward men!"

LUKE 2:14

Are you about ready to "peace" together your life again? Have the many demands of holidays running into year's end just about laid you flat? Then take heart! You are in the perfect position!

On the night of Christ's birth, shepherds watched over their flocks around Bethlehem. Likely, only a portion of these shepherds kept active eyes against encroaching enemies. The others, although ready to wake at a moment's notice, were catching their rest. They were laid out flat.

But they were about to receive history's most overwhelming awakening! In the middle of the shepherds' night, an angelic announcement woke them with frightful start. They watched and listened in awe, until the host sang, "Glory to God in the highest, and on earth peace, goodwill toward men!"

Oh, that we would be those favored people! Oh, that we would know that peace!

TIP

PLAY TO YOUR STRENGTHS; PRACTICE TO YOUR WEAKNESSES.

THE GIFT GIVER

So it was, that while they were there, the days were completed for her to be delivered. And she brought forth her firstborn Son, and wrapped Him in swaddling cloths, and laid Him in a manger, because there was no room for them in the inn.

LUKE 2:6–7

On the night Jesus was born, you can bet that Joseph had better ideas for this arriving Savior. Like any good father, he would have been proud to provide an "appropriate place" for Mary to give birth. Now all these visitors were showing up and seeing just what kind of a provider Joseph really was.

Jesus came into Joseph's life that night just as He comes into ours. He asks us to set aside ourselves and make way for Him. For one who lived so selflessly, it can seem like a selfish request—unless we remember all that He gives to us when we have given our lives to Him.

With Jesus, every day is like Christmas Day. He offers unfathomable peace, unhindered joy, and undying love. That beats a dozen premium golf balls anytime!

TIP

IF YOU HAVE THE HONOR BUT AREN'T READY, ENCOURAGE YOUR PARTNERS TO GO AHEAD.

HAND-ME-DOWNS

We will not hide them from their children, telling to the generation to come the praises of the LORD, and His strength and His wonderful works that He has done.

PSALM 78:4

In the past, every kid started playing golf this way: take an old club, cut it down, regrip it, and let the child swing away. And it has always been a delight to pass on your golf knowledge and experience to eager children.

The Bible sets forth consistently the role of adults in educating children in the character and laws of God too. Psalm 78 encourages us to pass on the deeds, power, and wonders of our heavenly Father. In the classic sense, we must testify before our children, explaining to them how completely God can care for them, as He has cared for us.

In Deuteronomy Moses also directed the people to pass on their history, especially the stories of God's intervention in their lives. Children love stories. Tell them yours, with God as the hero.

TIP

IN A FAIRWAY BUNKER? KEEP YOUR LOWER BODY QUIET AND TAKE ONE EXTRA CLUB.

MATURE DECISIONS

But solid food belongs to those who are of
full age, that is, those who by reason of use have
their senses exercised to discern both good and evil.

HEBREWS 5:14

Reading greens is the golfer's discernment, the ability to consider the whole of a situation and choose the wisest course. In life, discernment also comes through experience and—for the believer—the knowledge of Scripture.

When you began to follow Christ and read God's Word, you probably noticed that God was adamant about things you had approached loosely in the past. You had learned that guilt was God's way of saying, "You've done something wrong here. You need to confess." And you were encouraged to repent and receive His continuing forgiveness.

In other words, you were maturing in Christ. Your spiritual self was being trained to discern good and evil. This is a lifelong process, and we should thank God for it. The discernment that comes from Him protects us from a world of hurt.

TIP

KEEP A SMALL NOTEPAD IN YOUR BAG, AND RECORD HELPFUL SWING THOUGHTS TO USE AGAIN.

UNDER GOD'S CONTROL

Teach the older men to be . . . self-controlled. . . .
Similarly, encourage the young men to be self-controlled.

TITUS 2:2, 6 NIV

Paul was a purveyor in the nature of God—
and how that nature would change men's lives.
And it is men, specifically, to our shame, who seem
to struggle most with the enemies of self-control:
anger, excess, and rashness.

On the golf course anger sounds profane, looks
fierce, and behaves without regard for others. Off
the golf course anger appears much the same.
In excess, we pursue More and Better, as if these
alone are worthy goals. And rashly, we make hasty
decisions, attempting to control the outcomes of
our lives.

So, Paul wrote, let men be self-controlled. Of
course, self-control does not come from one's
"self" at all. It comes from the Holy Spirit. When
the Spirit rules us, our very
appearance changes. We act
wisely, submitting to the greater
good. We look as though we have
it all together—God rebuilds us
just so.

TIP

TAKE THE
PUTTER BACK
AND FOLLOW
THROUGH
EQUIVALENT
DISTANCES.

FREE TO WORK

*For this is the love of God, that we keep
His commandments. And His commandments
are not burdensome. For whatever is born of
God overcomes the world. And this is the
victory that has overcome the world—our faith.*

1 JOHN 5:3–4

All work either makes us better or wears us down. A task that is drudgery to one person can be fulfilling to another. Some golfers can stand on the range till dark, content to beat balls right up to closing. Others can think of no assignment more mundane. In the end, however, all the world's work will beat us up. For some, the task itself drives them away. For the rest, it is the eventual realization that each goal reached is still not fulfilling—tomorrow's milestones become yesterday's tombstones.

Not so with the work of the Lord. If we will take the first steps—latching on to that one biblical instruction that we have always pushed aside and honestly do it for a day, a week, a month—we will realize two stunning truths of Scripture: God's commands are easy and God's commands satisfy. They set us free to love God.

CHOOSE THIS DAY

"And if it seems evil to you to serve the LORD, choose for yourselves this day whom you will serve. . . . But as for me and my house, we will serve the LORD."

JOSHUA 24:15

Ever played with a golfer who was sure he was king of the foursome? He walked where he wished, talked when he wished, and played at his own fits-and-spurts pace.

Such a fellow is like many people today. They are convinced that, despite the rules established for the common good, the world is theirs to play in as they wish. They make up life as they go along. And whatever way they make it is the way they consider right.

The sinful desire to serve only yourself, writing and rewriting the rules so that they fit your present quest, is no new thing. Joshua was confronted by this approach among God's people. But like the golfer who knows rules and etiquette, Joshua knew one truth alone: the almighty God. Joshua was taking no chances with any other truth. "Choose whom you will serve," he told the people. "I'm serving God."

> **TIP**
>
> KEEP MISSING TARGETS? HAVE A PARTNER CHECK YOUR AIM FROM BEHIND BEFORE YOU SWING.

CREATIVE AND RESOLUTE

"For the sons of this world are more shrewd in their generation than the sons of light."

LUKE 16:8

Many golf shots require two qualities that we lack: creativity and resolve. We must think of a way to get out of trouble, perhaps in a way we've never done before. Then we must trust our intuition and confidently put the shot in play.

Creativity and resolve are great traits when entering any new phase of our lives, be it expected, like a new year, or unexpected, like the loss of a job. And according to Jesus, they are godly traits as well. In Luke 16, Jesus' parable of the shrewd manager highlighted the man's creativity and resolve in order to spark similar qualities in His own followers.

When waiting for the next "move of God," we must remember that God has already moved us to where we are right now! While we are here, we should be advancing as kingdom people—using invention, wisdom, and diligence to prepare for what comes next.

TIP

TO SMOOTH YOUR TEMPO, HUM EVENLY THROUGHOUT YOUR SWING.

LINKS PLAYERS
INTERNATIONAL

The daily thoughts in *Go for the Green* first appeared as part of the *Links Daily Devotional*, sent each Monday through Friday via e-mail by Links Players International. Since 2000, each day's devotion has been freshly written, with connections to current golf events and everyday golf occurrences.

Links Players is a Christ-pointed ministry committed to speaking the language of golf to communicate the good news of Jesus. In addition to the *Links Daily Devotional*, Links Players prepares Bible studies, articles, and outreach materials for use by individuals and the more than 100 Links Fellowships at clubs and courses around the country.

For more information about the ministry of Links Players, visit www.linksplayers.com, or call 1-800-90-LINKS.

To receive the *Links Daily Devotional*, send your e-mail address to linksplayers@linksplayers.com. Write "Subscribe" in the subject line.